THE MIRROR OF ANTIQUITY

The Mirror of Antiquity

AMERICAN WOMEN AND THE CLASSICAL TRADITION, 1750–1900

CAROLINE WINTERER

CORNELL UNIVERSITY PRESS

ITHACA AND LONDON

Cornell University Press gratefully acknowledges a grant from
Stanford University that has aided in the publication of this book.

First published 2007 by Cornell University Press

Printed in the United States of America

Library of Congress Cataloging-in-Publication Data

Winterer, Caroline.
   The Mirror of antiquity : American women and the classical tradition, 1750–1900 /
Caroline Winterer.
       p. cm.
   Includes bibliographical references and index.
   ISBN 978-0-8014-4163-9 (cloth : alk. paper)
   1. Upper class women—United States—Intellectual life—18th century.   2. Upper class
women—United States—Intellectual life—19th century.   3. Classicism—United States—
History—18th century.   4. Classicism—United States—History—19th century.   5. Classical
education—United States—History—18th century.   6. Classical education—United States—
History—19th century.   7. Women classicists—United States—History—18th century.
8. Women classicists—United States—History—19th century.   9. United States—
Civilization—Classical influences.   I. Title.
   HQ1418.W56 2007
   305.48'9621097309033—dc22
2006102923

Cornell University Press strives to use environmentally responsible
suppliers and materials to the fullest extent possible in the publishing
of its books. Such materials include vegetable-based, low-VOC
inks and acid-free papers that are recycled, totally chlorine-free, or
partly composed of nonwood fibers. For further information, visit
our website at www.cornellpress.cornell.edu.

Cloth printing 10 9 8 7 6 5 4 3 2 1

For Julia and Nicholas

haec ornamenta sunt mea

CONTENTS

ACKNOWLEDGMENTS

A book about the rich networks supporting intellectual life in the past has made me especially grateful for those that sustain my own. I benefited greatly from the reader reports solicited by Cornell University Press from Mary Kelley and Catherine Kelly, both of whom have been supporters of the project from the beginning. Their comments on the manuscript were thorough and judicious, but I also appreciated their enthusiasm for the idea of writing a book about the totality of women's lives, both the world of ideas and the world of things. Paula Findlen, Estelle Freedman, and James Turner read a first draft of the manuscript and offered extensive comments that went far beyond the call of scholarly duty. Each brought their own areas of special expertise, and I owe all three an enormous debt of gratitude.

I have been fortunate to share my work in several seminars and workshops. At Stanford, a number of groups read chapters and offered constructive comments: thanks to the members of the Gender Workshop, the Ancients and Moderns Workshop at the Stanford Humanities Center, and the indefatigable Junior Faculty Reading Group. I also presented work at a number of other institutions, and I thank the colleagues in various departments who organized these forums: Theda Perdue, Barbara J. Harris, and Phiroze Vasunia at the University of North Carolina at Chapel Hill; Barbara Beatty at Wellesley College; Mark Antliff, Patricia Leighten, and Grant Parker at Duke University; Beth Schweiger for the Southern Intellectual History Circle; and the Triangle Intellectual History Seminar at the National Humanities Center, especially Anthony La Vopa and Malachi

Hacohen. I have also benefited from chapter readings by and conversations about various points with John Carson, Christopher Celenza, Jay Fliegelman, Edith Gelles, and Philip Hicks. Finally, I have appreciated the warmly collegial environment in the Department of History at Stanford.

I cherished my year of uninterrupted research and writing time at the National Humanities Center in Research Triangle Park, North Carolina, a sabbatical year also supported by a generous Howard Foundation Fellowship from Brown University. The Spencer Foundation supported the project in its earliest stages through its Small Grant program. Finally, I am grateful for research funds made possible as the William H. and Frances Green Faculty Fellow at Stanford in 2005–6.

Archivists and librarians at a number of institutions were helpful in tracking down sources. In addition to the museums, libraries, and foundations that gave permission to use images from their collections in this book, I owe special thanks to the helpful staff at the Museum of Early Southern Decorative Arts in Winston-Salem, North Carolina, the Connecticut Historical Society, the Library Company of Philadelphia, the Rauner Special Collections Library at Dartmouth College (especially Jay Satterfield), the Southern Historical Collections at the University of North Carolina at Chapel Hill, the Boston Athenaeum, and John Mustain and Benjamin Stone at the Stanford University Library. I benefited also from the wisdom, encouragement, and advice of Alison Kalett, my editor at Cornell University Press.

An early version of what became chapters 3 and 4 appeared as "Venus on the Sofa: American Women, Neoclassicism, and the Early American Republic," *Modern Intellectual History* 2 (April 2005): 29–60. I thank one of the editors, Charles Capper, for soliciting useful reader reports and for providing his expert input on some major intellectual problems of the early republic. Part of chapter 7 appeared as "Victorian Antigone: Classicism and Women's Education in America, 1840–1900," *American Quarterly* 53 (March 2001): 70–93, and I thank the journal for allowing me partially to reprint it here.

My parents, Edward L. Winterer and Jacqueline Mammerickx Winterer, have been the cheerleading section all along, and for that I am very lucky. Kurt has always been willing to listen to half-baked ideas (about this book and a lot of other matters), but more importantly has been my best friend for half a lifetime now. Julia and Nicholas tell their friends that their mother writes books. I do indeed, and this one is just for them, with love.

ILLUSTRATIONS

THE MIRROR OF ANTIQUITY

The history of Greece should be to our countrymen, what is called in many families on the continent a boudoir; an octagonal apartment in a house, with a full-length mirror on every side, and another in the ceiling. The use of it is, when any of the young ladies, or young gentlemen, if you will, are at any time a little out of humour, they may retire to a place, where, in whatever direction they turn their eyes, they see their own faces and figures multiplied without end. By thus beholding their own beautiful persons, and seeing at the same time the deformity brought upon them by their anger, they may recover their tempers and their charms together.

JOHN ADAMS
*A Defence of the Constitutions of Government
of the United States of America* (1787)

INTRODUCTION

If we could spend a day with an elite American woman of the early republic, it might go something like this. A busy mother of many children, she would be up with the birds and would quickly rake the embers in a fireplace adorned with cornucopias and garlands. In front of her Sheraton mirror—a looking glass encased in classical columns—she would lace her corset and then slip over it a Grecian gown made of frothy white muslin. Sitting on a soft sofa, one built by American craftsmen from neoclassical furniture-making manuals imported from England, and holding a Wedgwood tea cup emblazoned with a Cupid or an acanthus leaf, she could open a magazine and read a short story about the Sabine women of ancient Rome or find an ode to Columbia, illustrated with a flowing-haired goddess. Later in the morning, she might read to her children from an Englished Plutarch or Homer, a book she would have saved from her teenaged years in a female academy. Afternoon would bring a walk to the market. Her purse jangling with coins emblazoned with the goddess Liberty, she would walk in the shadow of the massive public buildings whose fluted columns and imposing pediments affirmed to all the world that this new nation was a Rome reborn, a new order of the ages, a *novus ordo seclorum*, as the Great Seal of the United States had declared since 1782. In these buildings she was not so welcome. The bank, the courthouse, and the Senate still remained the world of men. But her world, this Rome of her own, was equally classical, equally rich, and equally revolutionary, and it is the subject of this book.

Ancient Greece and Rome were places in time, but we can only retrieve them through the modern project of classicism, a concern with the ancient

Mediterranean that is put into the service of modern needs. For many people today, classical antiquity seems musty and obsolete, but well into the nineteenth century the Greco-Roman past represented the dazzling avant-garde in science, art, and literature. New discoveries in classical archaeology, such as the exhumation of the Roman cities of Herculaneum and Pompeii, made conversations about the Greco-Roman world seem thoroughly new and exciting, even as they appealed to a venerated past. In the era of the American Revolution and nation formation, a time of great political, social, and ideological turbulence, Americans appealed to the republics of classical antiquity not just for instruction and inspiration but also to cloak political and social novelties in the ennobling veil of the classical past. The appeal to Greco-Roman antiquity papered over parochial, regional, and party differences, supplying the young republic with a shared collection of conversations and images and tying provincial Americans to a cosmopolitan, transatlantic world of taste and refinement. All these things—its ubiquity, its authority, its simultaneous timeliness and timelessness—made classicism a commanding and enduring enterprise in America before the twentieth century.

Although American national mythology centers on George Washington and other founders as heroic Romans reborn, women, no less than men, were responsible for America's spectacular resurrection of classical antiquity during the period of nation formation. Long viewed by historians as a citadel of masculine knowledge about statecraft and erudition, classicism was equally meaningful to women: it was the wallpaper of their world, a world of reading and writing, getting and spending, aesthetics and experience. But the project of building a modern nation in the image of ancient republics had to proceed differently for women than for men. The ideals of citizenship in ancient Rome and Greece were warrior, masculine, and public. In the new American republic, men had a "useful" outlet for their classicism. They attended colleges steeped in Greek and Latin, which were springboards for entry into politics, the military, the ministry, and the bar, careers where Greco-Roman ideals of civic virtue and oratory took tangible form. American women had no such options. They were legally disabled by coverture laws, denied the right to vote, to hold elective office, to serve in apprenticeships, and to bear arms in defense of the nation. In an age of Enlightenment, they were believed deficient in the capacity for reason and originality. What could ancient Greece and Rome offer to the women of the new republic?

As it turns out, very much. Following four generations of women, from the middle of the eighteenth century to the late nineteenth, this book shows how each generation found in classicism's many literary and material

forms a way to imagine and to articulate new roles for themselves. Beginning in the largely extra-institutional female intellectual world of the mid-
eighteenth century, the book shows how rising female literacy rates and
new venues of sociability like the salon encouraged a vernacular classicism
in women, one built on French and British versions of Greco-Roman favorites. From this informal classical world emerged three novelties in the
following decades. First, in the 1770s women made the first attempts to
politicize their classicism, that is, to add women to the classically steeped
revolutionary rhetoric that shaped colonial opposition to Britain. They
summoned ancient female exemplars like Portia who could match the republican virtue and patriotism of male favorites like Cicero and Cato. Second, by the 1790s women began to publish the first classicized polemics
about women's place in the new republic, invoking ancient figures like the
women of Sparta and Venus to ask key questions about topics like female
patriotism and the place of passion in a republic built on the reasoned
consent of the governed. Third, they also began in the 1790s to found
some of the first female academies and seminaries, a good number of
which by the 1820s had established classical curricula quite similar to what
college boys followed. Through these three revolutions in women's
classicism—a sense of its political voice in the new republic, printed venues in which to articulate that political voice, and improvements in classical education—American women by the third decade of the nineteenth
century had forged a new platform for women's classicized, public action.

We know this group of women who sprang onto the national scene in
the 1830s as the first generation of female moral reformers, supporting
movements such as abolitionism and feminism. It is important to see that
their public sense was built in part on the classical foundations laid down
by their predecessors. Educated in new, classically steeped female academies and reading circles, and accustomed to a print culture imbued with
classical female exempla, they now reached into their quivers of classical
history to attack such social injustices as chattel slavery and female subservience. Some of these women were elite; others were self-consciously
middle-class; a few were black. Imbued with the idea of self-perfection and
social reform engendered by the Second Great Awakening, and schooled
to a sense of civic duty by years in female academies, they were the first
American women to use the motifs of classicism for the moral reform of
the individual and the social reform of the nation.

The most vocal member of this new group was the classically learned
Lydia Maria Child, who turned the blazing light of historical inquiry onto
the persistence of female slavery over the long haul, from Greece to Rome
to the Turkish seraglio to the Virginia plantation. Free black abolitionists

joined her cause, asking whether female slaves who died escaping to freedom qualified for Roman heroism, the most noble death immortalized by
a Roman in Joseph Addison's play *Cato* and again (apocryphally) by the
American patriot Patrick Henry in the famous phrase, "give me liberty, or
give me death." This reformist strain of classicism naturally invited a
counter-reformation. In the years before the Civil War, the classically erudite South Carolina slaveowner Louisa McCord styled herself a Roman
matron to write one of the most unyielding defenses of slavery and patriarchy ever published by an American woman.

To write about women and classicism is necessarily to look at social
elites. The etymology of the words *classic* and *classical* demonstrates the
long connections between high status and the infatuation with Greco-
Roman antiquity. The words, which emerged around the sixteenth century in modern English, can refer either to the art or literature of a certain
period in Greece or Rome or in general to anything that represents the
peak of quality or perfection. The words derive from a first-century Roman grammarian's use of the word *classicus* (literally, belonging to the
most elite rank of citizens) to refer to ancient writers who are authoritative
enough to be imitated. *Classic* and *classical* rapidly become synonymous in
English with the study of the Greco-Roman past, an education bestowed
upon social elites. The trappings of high social class, in other words, were
cultivated in part through classicism.[1]

Many of the women in this book were the wives, daughters, and mothers
of wealthy merchants, politicians, lawyers, planters, and even presidents and
Constitution makers. In an age of feeble medical care and few legal rights,
these women knew the despair shared by all women who buried baby after
baby or silently suffered philandering or abusive husbands. But unlike most
other women in their time and place, these women could call upon servants
and slaves to relieve much of the toil and drudgery of daily life. Swathed in
silken gowns, their heads festooned with ostrich feathers and pearls, they
nestled their feet in soft kid slippers. Their houses gleamed with the latest
and most luxurious classical furnishings and art. They clustered in wealthy
urban and rural familial enclaves so distinctive, entrenched, and intermar-
ried that at various points they acquired their own names: the Brahmins
of Boston, the River Gods of the Connecticut River Valley, and so on. Like
beads on a necklace, these women linked themselves to the elites of other
places through visits and correspondence. They also traveled abroad, accompanying their husbands to the centers of cultural and diplomatic power
in London, Paris, Rome, Russia, and Egypt.

It is easy to dismiss these women as idle butterflies preoccupied with the
vapid frivolities of fashion and reputation. But they too have much to tell

us, especially if seen as a sequence of generations passing on a distinctive tradition of female culture and erudition. A generation of remarkable social and even microhistory of America's less privileged women has resulted in a curious inattention to the scrupulous totality of the lives of women at the top of the social spectrum. Denied so much political, legal, and economic power, these women had something else: they had cultural power. Through the many motifs of classicism, they fashioned themselves as women of taste and learning, as important arbiters of the meaning and uses of classicism at a time when it was the central political, artistic, and intellectual conversation of the nation.

Early on, in the middle of the eighteenth century, the very privilege of these women located them at the front lines of revolutions in female literacy. They were not just literate but superliterate, reading the most refined literature of the age—very often classical in form, like Alexander Pope's best-selling translations of the *Iliad* and the *Odyssey*—and in some cases writing it, too. Their visual fields were equally filled with classicism. To bedeck their houses with classically themed embroideries, drawings, and paintings that announced their feminine "accomplishment" or "ornamentation" (as these skills were then called), these women pored over the stacks of illustrated books and journals that crossed the Atlantic, finding inspiration in lavish copperplate engravings of scenes from classical mythology or fingering soft fabric swatches for Grecian gowns. Infused with a new language of taste, they patronized artists and cabinetmakers in the classical style; some even went to Europe to visit classical ruins or to buy Wedgwood china and Sèvres porcelain. In an age when women's learning was largely informal and noninstitutional, these women forged a fragile community linked not just by such tangible things as marriage and money but also by the more ephemeral ties of knowledge, taste, and style. In letters and books, in houses and galleries, through social skill and artistic patronage, they played a major role in making the new nation a congenial home for the many varieties of classicism that came and went.

This book shows how classicism also gave women a language with which to confront some of the central questions raised by the transition to republicanism. Especially durable was the republican nightmare of "luxury and effeminacy," a conjunction made with precisely the same words by John Adams in 1783 as by writers well into the nineteenth century. Luxury and effeminacy were the twin sins of a new republic modeled on the austerity and masculine virtues exemplified by stock ancient Roman figures such as the general Cincinnatus, who relinquished his sword to retire to the bucolic serenity of his farm. Because he left behind the Continental

Army and retired to his plantation at Mount Vernon in the lush farmlands of northern Virginia, George Washington also became known as Cincinnatus. Routinely contrasted to cherished republican traits like manly virtue and agrarian simplicity, luxury and effeminacy implied citizens' servile dependence on pretty and comfortable things, one that mirrored women's dependence on men. The dangers of luxury and effeminacy were often mapped onto the bodies of women, especially women in monarchical and Oriental societies. Luxury and effeminacy were envisioned as the machinations of the corrupted courts of European princes and Oriental pashas, those splendid palaces where bejeweled beauties used their personal "influence" to sway the men who governed rather than using the virtuous republican mechanisms of voting and representation. Not just classical in source, the preoccupation with female luxury also had biblical roots, with women's ornaments frequently marshaled as metaphors for virtue. "Who can find a Virtuous Woman? For her price is above rubies," women read in Proverbs, a phrase repeated in the female conduct manuals of the eighteenth century.[2]

Sitting at the apex of American society, so many of these wealthy, classically educated women embodied "luxury and effeminacy," the problems of personal influence in a republic based on law, of material desire in an agrarian nation, and of female adornment in a Christian republic. These problems became all the more urgent as Americans wallowed in a sea of consumer goods that made daily life more pleasant and promised upward social mobility but that gave headaches to republicans besotted with the ideal of Roman and Spartan self-abnegation and thrift. The disjuncture has preoccupied historians. Were early national Americans liberal getters and spenders preoccupied with fulfilling individual desires, or were they austere republicans deeply troubled by ascending consumerism and its distractions from the common good?[3]

The answer, as these elite women show, is that the malleable forms of classicism helped American women marry the two impulses into a manageable whole, to be both consumers and republicans at the same time. It was not just *that* there were more things to want and to buy in the eighteenth and early nineteenth centuries, a development in and of itself with important political and social ramifications,[4] but that those things were so often "classical" in shape. Classical aesthetics was not a thin veneer on these new consumer goods: it was their very essence, a way industrialists cloaked the novelties of technological progress and factory production in forms appealing to the upper and middle classes.

Neoclassicism, the style that dominated American consumer culture in the period from roughly 1800 to 1840, was, in fact, the first international aesthetic movement that was fueled on the one end by the productive capacities of the industrial revolution and bolstered on the other by the rising purchasing abilities of consumers around the Atlantic. It was classicism that made these dresses and sofas and wallpapers and tea sets not just palatable but alluring. The classical form communicated both the austerity and simplicity that new Romans desired and the luxurious cosmopolitanism that elites craved. This book shows how a few important classical objects, especially the so-called Grecian robes and sofas, became lightning rods not just for anxieties about buying and wanting but also about women's buying and wanting.

The project of reconciling republican political rhetoric with consumer culture was aided by another feature of classicism at this time—its Orientalism. Today, Orientalism (popularized in Edward Said's influential 1978 work of the same name), evokes the tendency among Europeans and Americans to view the East as a place that is very different from, and even opposed to, the West. Europeans had long identified the vast and mysterious realm of the Orient with the luxury trade in cloth and spices and with the gilded decadence of the harem. In the eighteenth and nineteenth centuries, American political rhetoric frequently pitted masculine Roman simplicity—the bulwark of the republic—against effeminate Oriental luxury, which corroded the state by causing people to seek private riches and personal comforts at the expense of the common good. But the women in this book show that classicism and Orientalism often mingled in literature, art, and material culture, those realms of knowledge more accessible to women than political discourse. Women deeply interested in classical antiquity were often also infatuated with the Orient. They read Oriental travel narratives and "Oriental tales," and snapped up furniture and clothing with Oriental elements. But they cared little whether this Orient was modern or ancient. Like many Europeans at this time, they thought of the Orient as a timeless place, the same now as thousands of years ago, when ancient Persians and Egyptians had rubbed elbows with Greeks and Romans. Eastern peoples, made lazy by their sultry climate, were thought to be incapable of Western change and progress and so lived in a timeless stasis. According to the French *philosophe* Montesquieu in his influential *Spirit of Laws* (1748), the dress, manners, and laws of Oriental people were "the same to this very day . . . as they were a thousand years ago." To fully understand the range and power of American women's classicism, it is important to see that it often embraced Orientalism rather than rejecting it. Classicism and Orientalism were points on a continuum of infatuation with the remote antiquity of the Mediterranean basin, mingling in different ways at different times.[5]

Greece was the pivotal player in this fluidity because it was situated at the crossroads of East and West. American women summoned ancient Greece at different times for either classicism (which implied virtue, simplicity, beauty, and democracy) or Orientalism (which implied debauchery, luxury, aristocracy, and exoticism). Indeed, ancient Greece could often suggest both at once, creating a mélange classical enough to satisfy republican aspirations to austere virtue but exotic and luxurious enough to slake the thirst of consumers craving the beautiful trappings of an aristocracy whose legitimacy had vanished with the revolution. Lacking a natural elite of birth, the nation would now have an aristocracy of beauty.

The idea of the Orient as a place of feminine exoticism also gave women some maneuvering room within republicanism's stifling injunctions to female domesticity, sexual propriety, and modesty of dress and carriage. In books and pictures freely available to them, women sympathetic to Roman ideals of civic virtue also saw other social, sexual, and sartorial possibilities which they invoked in different ways at different times. Underneath American women's fascination with the Orient, however, lay pressing political and economic questions. In what way was sexual liberty tied to political liberty? What did personal pleasure, achieved in part through access to beautiful, luxurious, things, have to do with the commercial prosperity celebrated in such texts as Adam Smith's *Wealth of Nations* (1776)?

Classicism was a way to talk about a new world of beautiful things; it was also a way for women to talk about themselves, especially through the popular ideal of the "Roman matron." While men crafted a national ideology based on the reverence for the Greco-Roman soldier/farmer/hero, women created the complementary but different ideal of the Roman matron, a pillar of female virtue, the woman who was a married mother, learned, chaste, sober, and dignified. Rising in popularity during the imperial crisis of the 1770s, the Roman matron is everywhere in the visual and verbal toolkit of these women from the revolutionary period to the Civil War era. The "Roman matron" was a term used by Americans until roughly the late nineteenth century, and it showed women's aspirations for themselves and other women within a frame of reference they would have recognized.[6]

The idea of the Roman matron was complex and nuanced. First, it was nationalistic, allowing American women to enter the wide-ranging conversation about how to create a new republic and what rights and duties women had in it. Second, the idea of the Roman matron was cosmopolitan, situating American women in an ongoing transatlantic conversation among the English, Scots, and French about femininity, literature, politics, and aesthetics. Last, because it was already in place before the revolutionary decades, the transatlantic conversation about the Roman matron clearly reveals the timing and effects of republican revolution for American women, showing both continuities and novelties in women's self-perceptions.

The secret of the popularity and longevity of the idea of the Roman matron was its flexibility. Part of a shared set of classical symbols that allowed women and men to discuss difficult or subversive topics under the cover of indirection and respectability, the Roman matron could assume a bewildering variety of forms. For some women, she formed part of a domestic language, a learned idiom for women to use when they spoke with male relatives more educated than they. This was the case with Abigail Adams, who wrote as "Portia" to engage her classically erudite husband, John Adams, in conversations that were not just about national politics but also about the difficulties of being left alone to care for a farm and children. To others, the Roman matron gave a nascent political voice through the public language of classical pseudonyms and classical history. By using classical tropes, a woman such as Judith Sargent Murray (who under the pseudonym "Constantia" published essays about female equality) could enter public debates dominated by men. Still other women silently summoned the Roman matron through the language of art by dressing for a portrait in antique garb or embroidering favorite Roman matron parables onto silk panels.

What do the classically learned women in this book have to do with the international popularity of female classical icons like Liberty, Columbia, and Minerva during the late eighteenth and nineteenth centuries? These icons seem to thumb their noses at us as reminders of the paradox of how the classicized female form could represent the republican body politic even as flesh-and-blood women continued to be denied the right to vote or hold office.[7] Yet, as this book makes clear, the heyday of the classical female icon was also the heyday of women's engagement with classicism. The popularity of female classical iconography had much more to do with women's growing access to education and cosmopolitan culture than with their political disenfranchisement. Classical female icons were successful in part because women could now participate in their generation and circulation in a public culture constituted by print. This is not to say that women were not excluded in many ways from exercising full rights of citizenship in the republic during the time period covered by this book. But classical female icons, far from being barricades of exclusion, in fact became women's portals of entry into public life. Women grabbed onto classical tropes and symbolism once dominated by men to make claims for political rights in a public discourse still saturated with classicism.

What is more, symbols like Liberty that appeared so often in print and public statuary were just the tip of the iceberg of women's classicism, a world of texts, art, commerce, and ideas that also circulated in the private sphere of home and family. Icons like Columbia and Liberty are most fully understood not as symbols of women's exclusion from politics but as part of the total world of women's classicism that could be both public and private. A few elite women in the United States posed as classical female icons, examples of how the channels of women's private artistic patronage occasionally fed the stream of public iconography. In an artistic tradition stretching back to the Renaissance—when queens and other aristocrats posed as classical goddesses—American women tapped their patronage networks to fuse female classicism with republican symbolism.[8] The handsome Liberty on the 1795 silver coin is modeled on the wealthy Philadelphian Anne Willing Bingham, the brilliant sun around which Federalist high society orbited, and it was adapted from a portrait made by her friend Gilbert Stuart. The classically steeped sonnet that frames our reception of the Statue of Liberty ("Give me your tired, your poor") is the work of the classically educated New Yorker Emma Lazarus, daughter of a prosperous sugar refiner. She published the sonnet in 1883 to raise money for the new statue's pedestal, but her words marked the beginning of the end of this female world of classicism because she used them to redirect attention away from the statue as a classical icon. The Statue of Liberty was, in the words of the title of the sonnet, a "new colossus," a beacon for new immigrants. It was not an old symbol of vanishing Greco-Roman authority, of storied pomp that moderns no longer needed.

The middle decades of the nineteenth century marked the high tide of American women's distinctive engagement with classicism. Both women and men in the late nineteenth century gradually turned away from classicism when the language of the natural and social sciences gained more predictive and explanatory power in the political and social realms. The declining popularity of female classical icons like Liberty in the early twentieth century had less to do with women's achievement of such political landmarks as the franchise than with women's (and men's) abandonment of classicism as a rich, total culture. Classicism, of course, has never gone away, but for women it moved from a public language to a largely private one. They discovered by the early twentieth century that while they had gotten hold of classicism as a language of high culture and personal cultivation, it was rapidly fading as an effective political language in comparison to the attractions of scientific discourses. Even though women had achieved many institutional parities with men—university degrees, even the first PhD's in classics—that before had been denied to them, the rhetoric of political and social authority was now infused with a different voice. Greece and Rome no longer beckoned as compelling political models for the nation or for individual citizens. As a result, educated women who lobbied for political, economic, and social reforms in the early twentieth century would not turn in large numbers to the women of classical antiquity to frame their arguments.

There was a great irony in this grand arc of women's classicism because women gained full access to the language of classicism just when this age-old discourse had lost its political muscle. But in the pages that follow is the lost world that came before, when the full richness of the classical past—as politics, as art, and as learning—was alive to the women of the new Rome.

ONE

THE FEMALE WORLD OF CLASSICISM
IN EIGHTEENTH-CENTURY AMERICA

Death by classics? For twenty-year-old Eliza Lucas (c. 1722–1793), who presided over a prosperous indigo plantation in colonial South Carolina, the idea seemed ludicrous. An avid reader of Plutarch's *Lives*, she scoffed at the warnings of an older woman from the neighborhood, who advised her that rising at 5 a.m. to read Plutarch would send her to an early grave—or worse, wrinkle her skin and "spoil" her marriage. After narrowly preventing the older woman from hurling the toxic text into the fireplace, Lucas cheerfully polished it off, and then begged a friend to send her some Virgil. An extreme instance of devotion to classical reading, perhaps, but Eliza Lucas (later Pinckney) was not atypical among elite, white American women in the mid-eighteenth century who began in growing numbers to immerse themselves in the wondrous literary and material vestiges of classical antiquity.[1]

It was a project of striking novelty. Few intellectual enterprises have been wrapped in paranoid rhetoric for as long as classical study, a branch of learning that seemed to possess infinite capacities to illuminate, refine, and ennoble men, and an equally dependable ability to corrupt women. Since the Renaissance, classical learning had been as much an academic subject for boys as it was a male puberty rite. Boys learned Latin and Greek in school not just to master the judicious statecraft and heroic deeds of the ancients, but also as a combative initiation rite into the mysteries and privileges of languages, exemplars, and sayings that gentlemen knew and ladies did not. In this world, the gold standard of erudition was

Greek and the silver standard was Latin: to know and to use these languages with grace and agility was to sit among the gods of Olympus itself, dispensing wisdom both philosophical and political. Both languages were so difficult to acquire that they remained the realm of privileged boys and men who had the time and tutoring to learn them. The occasional, highly privileged girl might be taught Greek and Latin and encouraged to emulate classical female worthies, but this was often done in the spirit of virtue-building busywork, a kind of lexical embroidery. Advanced study of the classical languages was discouraged for women lest they "appear threateningly insane and requiring restraint," as the fifteenth-century Italian humanist Leonardo Bruni had put it. A woman, he observed, should leave "all public severity to men." The classically learned woman also became dangerously unfeminine, a *virilis femina* or an *homasse* (man-woman). The Renaissance humanist conversation about classical civic virtue was both the language of politics and the idiom of exclusion.[2]

In colonial America, the intellectual life of adult women reflected this traditional bifurcation between the classicism given to boys as part of their training for public life and the rudimentary literacy offered to women. The public, political role of classicism is clear in this pedagogical rift: excluded from existing learned institutions such as colleges, philosophical and scientific societies, and fraternal organizations, women had no professional or public roles like the law, the ministry, or politics in which their classicism would be useful. Nonetheless, they found other means by which to avail themselves of classical learning, and other ends to which to put that knowledge.

Born several decades before the American Revolution, some of these women would become involved ideologically with that struggle, and they would help to mobilize a new kind of classicism in the revolt against Britain. But this chapter will capture them before the revolution, when classicism connoted neither American republicanism nor American nationalism, associations that had to be deliberately crafted during and after the 1770s. Before that time, the Greco-Roman past, whether apprehended through texts or images, served to tie women in the colonies to British and transatlantic trends in taste, religion, and learning. As Americans remade their classicism in the republican idiom, they did not entirely displace the earlier style; they plundered it, drew elements freely from it, and then enlisted the elements for new purposes. Underneath the spectacular proliferation of new revolutionary icons like Columbia lay a deeply rooted cultural familiarity among male and female American elites with older textual and visual conventions.

THE FEMALE WORLD OF CLASSICISM

Elite women in mid-eighteenth-century America lived at a moment of great intellectual ferment, of expanding prospects for female erudition. With some exceptions, such as the Quakers and German Pietists who founded secondary schools for girls, the majority of colonial girls had been taught only the rudiments of reading, writing, and ciphering by their families, or in privately funded schools that admitted and educated girls only as an afterthought. But for elite women, a few other options were available, such as the "adventure" schools, which offered Latin as part of their curriculum.[3]

Opportunities for female classical reading expanded rapidly as British polite culture permeated the colonies in the middle decades of the eighteenth century through a swelling tide of newspapers, magazines, and books. At salons and tea tables, groups of upwardly mobile men and women gathered for conversation, reading, society games, and the like. Modeled on British precedents—which were themselves modeled on French versions—this new colonial "polite" society created a whole new arena for sociability between the sexes. But what to say there? And how to say it? Being polite required a whole new social register of gentility and accomplishment. In feats of steely self-control, polite people strove to appear languid and easy, restrained and learned.[4]

For this dazzling project, classical learning became imperative. Long associated with the pinnacles of masculine erudition, judgment, and statecraft, classical learning now also became a conversation, like the weather, to which all could contribute, each in his or her own measure. The shift in the function of classical learning was not easy; it tried both men and women in different ways. From men, it required restraint: a polite man had to resist the urge to trumpet his classical learning pedantically. Pedantry was a minor offense in the scholarly republic of letters but a mortal sin in the mixed company of the salon, where a man would be written off both as an eye-rolling bore and as a scholar, two attributes believed to be incompatible with the ideal of the gentleman.

For women the effort bordered on the impossible. Politeness demanded that elite women contribute elegant conversation appropriate for the ears and minds of both sexes. Women now had to acquire, without formal schooling, a grasp, however tenuous, of the civilizations of peoples who had lived two thousand years before. But they had to do it within narrow boundaries. Ancient history was acceptable for women, but the classical languages (especially Greek) were not; admiring the heroism of Cicero or Scipio was acceptable, but tying the heroism to prescriptions for modern statecraft was not; reading about ancient orators was acceptable, while declaiming aloud less so. A woman's conversation should be ornamental but not instructive in its own right; she should have enough learning to take an interest in her male companion's conversation, but not be so learned as to surpass his grasp of the subject.

The precarious balance between feminine frivolity and petticoat pedantry was so difficult to achieve that magazines and books rushed in to fill the void with advice. Published mostly in Britain and then imported to or reprinted in the colonies, these texts conjured a vision of what many of them called a "female world" of conversation in which the proper deportment of women was essential. The idea of a female world had first formed in the French court to describe the salon culture governed by women. Taking root in England, it spawned such publications as the anonymous *Wonders of the Female World* (1683), which discussed exemplary historical and mythological female figures from classical antiquity. The title page envisioned this female world as a classical one. Clio, Athena, and Lucretia cluster around the bubbling "font of Helicon" as the "Hill Parnassus" squats in the distance (see figure 1).[5]

One early help for navigating this female world of classicism was the *American Magazine*, published in Boston between 1743 and 1746 and filled with reprints of articles originally published in London. Its pages were crowded with articles that discussed how women might acquire some classical learning—but not too much. One author in June 1745 encouraged women to emulate the learned women of Greece and Rome, such as Cornelia, mother of the Gracchi (who had "contributed much to the Eloquence of her Sons"), the daughter of Loelius (who "express'd in her Conversation the Eloquence of her Father"), and the daughter of Hortensius (who delivered an oration before the Triumvirs). Such a woman was "the Honour of her Sex." Nearly pharmaceutical in its powers, reading about the noble women of antiquity would inoculate the modern woman against the "too prevailing Custom of Cards, Visitings, and other Ways of killing the Time." But while a woman's classicized conversation with men could let her sparkle and shine, it easily crossed the line into unattractive pedantry. "Shun learned Clacks, and Females talking Greek," admonished another article in 1744 that gave advice to a young woman just after her marriage.[6]

Advice books were another source of information for young women on how to navigate the treacherous terrain of classical conversation in mixed company. Hester Chapone addressed this question head-on in her popular *Letters on the Improvement of the Mind, Addressed to a Young Lady*, which was first published in 1773 in London and reprinted in the United States

1. The female world of reading and writing is envisioned as a classical paradise in this engraving. Anon., *Wonders of the Female World* (1683). Special Collections Research Center, University of Chicago Library.

beginning in 1782. Citing Rollin and Plutarch as the best vehicles, Chapone recommended ancient history as the most profitable kind of classical learning for young women, a pursuit that would find them both interested and entertained. "It is thought a shameful degree of ignorance, even in our sex, to be unacquainted with the nature and revolutions of their governments, and with the characters and stories of their most illustrious heroes," she observed. Like others, Chapone cautioned women against undertaking the ancient languages themselves. Greek and Latin were useless for women and the essentials of knowledge they imparted were equally available in English, French, or Italian translation. Sticking with English and French also averted the greatest danger of all: female pedantry. "The danger of pedantry and presumption in a woman—of her exciting envy in one sex and jealousy in the other—of her exchanging the graces of imagination for the severity and preciseness of a scholar, would be, I own, sufficient to frighten me from the ambition of seeing my girl remarkable for learning."[7]

Another book showing mid-century women how to use classical eloquence to their own advantage was Madeleine de Scudéry's *The Female Orators* (1714), an English translation of a French work reprinted a number of times in the eighteenth century. In the author's introductory note to the "Fair Sex," she points out that eloquence is a "bright *Ornament* to All," and then presents a series of short set pieces in which classical women deliver inspired words that show them to be pivotal actors in the great events of antiquity. Here were noble exemplars indeed, women who later fired the imaginations of erudite women of the revolutionary period: Portia (wife of Brutus), Sophonisba (queen of Numidia), Lucretia (wife of Collatinus), Volumnia (mother of Coriolanus), Livia (wife of Augustus), Octavia (wife of Mark Antony), and Agrippina (wife of Germanicus). In some editions, each woman's speech was illustrated with an engraved portrait bust, forming a gallery of Roman-style nobility (see figure 2). In Northampton, Massachusetts, Esther Edwards Burr (1732–1758), the daughter of the minister Jonathan Edwards and the mother of Aaron Burr, Jr., wrote to a friend in 1757 that she found this book admirable and its characters exemplary. "The Female Orator I admire excedingly. The Carracter and conduct of Emilla is truly Amiable and to be patterned after by all her sex."[8]

Prescriptive literature declaring what women *should* know about classical antiquity exposes the public side of the "female world." Equally important was the private female world of classicism revealed in diaries, letters, commonplace books, manuscripts, and embroidered samplers. These show what women in fact *did* know about the classical world, which books they read, which images they saw, and how they gained access to them. These

2. A portrait of Portia, wife of Brutus, from Madeleine de Scudéry, *The Female Orators* (1728). The Library Company of Philadelphia.

sources also reveal why women living in a British colony found the doings of the Greeks and Romans of two thousand years earlier relevant to their daily lives of caring for children, overseeing the laborious work of a farm, and worshipping a god these ancient pagans could never had prophesied. Such sources show how women—cut off from formal institutions of learning and professional life—created and sustained networks of female classical erudition and accomplishment.

Eliza Lucas, who risked life and limb to rescue Plutarch from the flames, showed how one woman could acquire a love of classical reading and apply it to her particular situation as a struggling and lonely young planter. Born in the West Indies around 1722, she was the eldest daughter of the sugar planter George Lucas and his wife, Ann. Like many of the children of the British colonial elite, she was sent to London for her education, probably when she was nine or ten, for a total of about five years. She traveled from Antigua to London, accompanied by a merchant family from Antigua, and once in London, lived with the family of Richard Boddicott, a sugar merchant and insurer. There she attended a boarding school and learned accomplishments like fine sewing, in addition to bookkeeping, English literature, history, "the globes," and some botany.

It is unclear where and how Lucas was exposed to classical reading, but she seems to have learned Latin somewhere along the way. It may have been at the boarding school, but also simply in the course of her life with the colonial mercantile community, whose sons and fathers trafficked in such books, and whose bookshelves would have housed them. She made sure her only daughter, Harriott, learned French and Latin. She considered this kind of learning essential to a woman of social standing. "To be greatly deficient in this matter [of learning] is almost inexcusable in one of our Sex, who have had an Education above that of a chamber maid, unpardonable then it must be in a scholar, as it must proceed entirely from Idleness and inattention." A letter from 1743, when she was just twenty one, suggests that she did not know how to read ancient Greek: "How came it into your head to ask me to write a poem on Virtue for you; into mind to give you any hopes that I would attempt it. I am sure I could as well read Homer in the Original as write a piece of good poetry on any subject whatever."[9]

By the time she was seventeen, she found herself in the colony of South Carolina managing her father's plantations while he remained permanently in absentia. For this difficult task, Eliza Lucas discovered that her classical reading was both an instruction and a balm. She was surprised that Virgil (she does not say which work, but likely the *Georgics*) was not just about battles, but also about farming the Roman campagna two millennia before, a situation that reminded her of her own.

> I have got not further than the first volume of Virgil but was most agreeably disapointed to find my self instructed in agriculture as well as entertained by his charming penn; for I am persuaded tho' he wrote in and for Italy, it will in many instances suit Carolina. I had never perused those books before and imagined I should imediately enter upon battles, storms and tempests that puts onc in a maze and makes one shudder while one reads. But the calm and pleasing diction of pastoral and gardening agreeably presented themselves, not unsuitably to this charming season of the year, with which I am so much delighted that had I but the fine soft language of our poet to paint it properly, I should give you but little respite till you came into the country and attended to the beauties of pure nature unassisted by art.[10]

The *Georgics* and other favorites of the pastoral tradition, associated by Thomas Jefferson, James Madison, and others with the sturdy agrarianism of freeholding yeomen that nurtured civic virtue, would become staples of the republican revolutionary tradition in eighteenth-century America. Eliza Lucas's reading of Virgil suggests one origin for republican men's commitment to agrarian ideals—their mothers. When she was twenty-two, Eliza Lucas married Charles Pinckney. Her children learned the classics—most likely including Virgil's *Georgics*—at her knee, and two of the children went on to become staunch patriots. Charles Cotesworth

Pinckney (1746–1825) was a brigadier general in the revolutionary war and a signer of the Constitution, and Thomas Pinckney (1750–1828) served in the revolutionary war and was later governor of South Carolina.[11]

Eliza Lucas shows how deeply relevant ancient texts could be to the lives of eighteenth-century women. At the other end of the colonies, the Adams family of Massachusetts was a cross-section of linguistic expectations in the eighteenth century, with each member learning Greek or Latin, both languages, or neither, depending on age and sex. John Adams (1735–1826) knew Latin and Greek but little French (the last an embarrassment so palpable he described it as a physical "Pain"). Abigail Adams (1744–1818) knew French but neither Latin nor Greek. Their eldest child and only surviving daughter, Abigail (1765–1813), called Nabby, was taught Latin and French but not Greek. Their eldest son, John Quincy Adams (1767–1848), called Johnny, who was being educated for a life in public service, was taught French, Latin and Greek.

Because of his frequent absences, the senior John had engaged a tutor, Abigail's nephew John Thaxter, to school the children. But he also relied on Abigail to carry out this complicated classical pedagogy. In his letters to Abigail and to the children, he encouraged translations of classical history for her, Latin for Nabby, and both Greek and Latin for John Quincy. Abigail, that is, had to pass Greek and Latin on to her children without knowing the languages herself. "I answer in the Words of Horace," John wrote to Abigail along with a Latin transcription of multiple stanzas from the *Satires*, "which I desire your Son and mine to translate for you and study well for himself." The fact that Nabby was learning Latin showed her parents' sensitivity to new educational ideals of politeness that encouraged a deeper classicism in women. "I smiled at your couplet of Lattin," Abigail wrote to her husband when Nabby was eleven. "Your daughter may be able in time to conster it as she has already made some considerable proficiency in her accidents; but her Mamma was obliged to get it translated." Only John Quincy was taught ancient Greek, but it took time, and, in the meantime, translations would have to do. "You will find in your Fathers Library," John Adams wrote to his ten-year-old son, "the Works of Mr. Hobbes, in which among a great deal of mischievous Philosophy, you will find a learned and exact Translation of Thucidides, which will be usefull to you."[12]

These linguistic gymnastics took their toll on Abigail Adams. Later in life, she supported Benjamin Rush's (1745–1813) proposals to eliminate Greek and Latin from boys' education. John Adams explained in a letter to Rush in 1810: "Mrs. Adams says she is willing you should discredit Greek and Latin because it will destroy the foundation of all the pretensions of the gentlemen to superiority over the ladies and restore liberty, equality, and fraternity between the sexes."[13]

In this female world of classicism, a library housing classical books loomed like Parnassus itself, a fantastic place of wonders. In a number of well-stocked private colonial libraries, classical texts ranked in numbers close to the ever-popular Christian devotional works, and circulating libraries appear to have admitted women and allowed them to borrow books of classical literature and antiquities. It was not an entirely free-market economy for women, however. Letters and diaries indicate that private libraries were considered men's property, and that traffic in books and library access was part of a ritual of power negotiation between women and their male relatives. Eliza Lucas, trusted by her father to preside over his plantations in South Carolina, nonetheless declared the books in the library to be his. "I have a little library well furnishd for my papa has left me most of his books in wch I spend part of my time," she wrote in 1740, when she was eighteen.[14]

The Virginia planter William Byrd II (1674–1744) of Westover shows the classical library in action. He used his library as a kind of reward system for the women in his life. As a man lunging relentlessly at genteel propriety through his own acquisition of Greek and Latin, he sought compatible erudition in a mate and encouraged a pleasant measure of female classical erudition. He told his second wife, Maria Taylor, that he had fallen in love with her in part because she knew Greek. "When indeed I learned that you also spoke Greek, the tongue of the Muses, I went completely crazy about you," he wrote her in a letter. "In beauty you surpassed Helen, in culture of mind and ready wit Sappho." His first wife, Lucy Byrd, put her name in a classical book in the vast Westover library, among the largest in the colonies; it was an English translation of the Greek-language meditations of the Roman emperor Marcus Aurelius entitled *The Emperor Marcus Antoninus: His Conversation with Himself* (1701). Yet such privileges could be revoked on a whim. On 30 December 1711, Byrd noted in his diary that he quarreled with Lucy "because I was not willing to let her have a book out of the library."[15]

Other men encouraged the classical learning of their female relatives by translating classical books themselves. The prosperous Quaker merchant James Logan (1674–1751) like William Byrd had an impressive private library numbering in the thousands of volumes. Logan himself was among the most accomplished humanists in America during the colonial period. Like most of his male contemporaries, he did not believe girls should be taught to read Latin or Greek, but thought highly enough of the sterling morals imparted by (some) classical authors that he believed girls might profitably read them in English. With his daughters in mind, he produced an English translation of Cato's moral sayings that was published as *Cato's Moral Distichs* (1735). The book may not have been as appealing to young women as Logan had hoped, since it exactly translated advice intended primarily for boys. "Regard not Woman's Passions, nor her Smiles/With *Passion* she ensnares, with Tears beguiles," reads one saying.[16]

As the availability of books increased during the eighteenth century and attitudes toward female classicism liberalized, women's access to libraries and books improved. The case of Julia Stockton Rush (1759–1858) is revealing. In 1775 Benjamin Rush became engaged to Julia Stockton, who had been raised in an exceptionally cultivated New Jersey family. Her mother was the classically learned poet Annis Boudinot Stockton, and her father was the politician Richard Stockton. Benjamin Rush was fourteen years her senior and vastly more educated, with a medical degree from the University of Edinburgh, in addition to a college education at Princeton. He encouraged his future wife to read widely. In his letters to her from Philadelphia, he described what he called "your library," a collection of one hundred volumes that he was assembling for her. "You are anxious to cultivate your mind, & to rise above that drudgery to which our sex have consigned yours, and those follies to which too many of your sex have consigned themselves." It was an eclectic assemblage that included the Bible, classical and modern history, poetry, and "Several treatises on cookery."[17]

For all its focus on Greco-Roman antiquity, the female world of classicism in eighteenth-century America also included an interest in the Orient. In their reading, it seems that women saw no conflict between classical and Oriental histories. Indeed, the two could be mutually reinforcing. In the ancient Mediterranean, cultural contact and fusion had been the order of the day. The sea-faring, plundering, and trading ancient Greeks and Romans had built their civilizations on cultural borrowing and melding with other Mediterranean societies, even though—like Herodotus describing the Egyptians—they thought those cultures did many things upside-down. In reading and looking at both modern and ancient texts, American women grasped two Orients, an ancient and a modern one, and they fused a chronologically vague Orient with their classicism. Though the Orient connoted the several-centuries-old European trade in luxury goods and the exoticism of the harem, in some sense these activities were believed to be timeless features that existed not just in the present but also in the classical Mediterranean. The whole project, that is, was characterized by an acute temporal flabbiness.

The intertwining of Orientalism and classicism would always be especially pronounced for Greece because it was situated in the eastern Mediterranean at the crossroads of classical and Eastern cultures. Historians of

Greece writing in the early eighteenth century found it difficult to organize the Greek past into a coherent narrative along the lines of Roman history, which was easily describable as a linear progression of swelling imperium. Temple Stanyan's popular *Grecian History* (1707, 1739), a book found in numerous colonial libraries and consulted by American women, bemoaned this problem with the Greek past. In Greek history, explained Stanyan, "it is no easy Task to marshal so many Events in due Order of Time, and Place, and out of them to collect an intire unbroken Body of History." The Greek past lacked chronological specificity, a clear beginning or end, or even a clear geographical boundary of what was Greek and non-Greek. Stanyan's work relates the numerous Greek encounters with the Persians, and it included a category he calls "the Asiatic Grecians."[18] Far from being traditions of hermetic character, classicism and Orientalism were chronologically and culturally porous.

This eclectic, Oriental-classical mélange is revealed in the books American women read at this time. Julia Rush owned Andrew Michael Ramsay's *Travels of Cyrus* (1727), which followed the travels of ancient Greeks into Persian territories. From the Library Company of Philadelphia, which admitted Sarah Wistar as its first female member in 1769, women of the time could borrow *Almoran and Hamet: An Oriental Tale* (1761). The plot of this book centered in "Persia" and unfolded at a time specified only as "the one hundred and second year of the Hegyra," a moment certainly meaningless to the average reader. In 1766 Margaret Rees of Hatboro, Pennsylvania, is known to have borrowed Lady Mary Wortley Montagu's famous *Letters*, published in America in 1766 and 1768, from the Hatboro Union Library. A British aristocrat who had traveled to the Ottoman Empire before 1720, Montagu returned smitten by Turkish manners and dress. Montagu's *Letters* ruminated freely not just on the modern "Orient" (such as Constantinople), but also on the frequent "footsteps of antiquity" she saw there in the ruins of ancient Egyptian, Greek, and Roman monuments.[19]

The willingness to merge classicism with the Orient helped to attract some elite women in the colonies to a startlingly erotic and exotic style of portraiture: *turquerie*, in which respectable, elite women appear in portraits wearing costumes and striking poses that hinted at the mysterious and vaguely decadent Orient. The classical tradition, then, appears to have ushered in, through its back door, another visual and literary world of expansive sensual possibilities. As she was in literature, Lady Mary Wortley Montagu was a major instigator for American colonial portraits *à la turque*. When she returned from the Orient, she posed in Turkish garb in a portrait, and generally shocked polite society by appearing in the streets wearing her startling Oriental ensembles. Influenced by painters exposed to British aesthetic trends and by the American publication of Lady Montague's *Letters*, a few elite American women in the mid-eighteenth century chose to be depicted *à la turque*, an aesthetic choice that catapulted them to the top of the visual register of the luxurious. In the late 1760s and early 1770s, the painter John Singleton Copley (1738–1815) painted a number of elite women in various modes that are Orientalizing in style of dress (Turkish), corset (absent), pose (recumbent), headwear (turban, sometimes loosened or unfurled entirely), or prop (camelback damask sofa). The depictions were widely renowned, and were displayed in the semi-public halls and parlors of the stately homes of women who knew and visited one other. Rural enclaves of refinement received and refracted a paler version of this brilliant metropolitan *turquerie*. Families in central Connecticut, for example, tapped less skilled painters such as Ralph Earl (1751–1801) to execute stiffer but nonetheless recognizably opulent sultanas.[20]

The *turquerie* was not something entirely distinct from classicism, but was part of a larger cultural infatuation with the temporally or geographically exotic. It also formed part of women's growing interest in the humanist project of artful self-fashioning, which their classical reading also encouraged. In his *Essay on the Theory of Painting* (1715), the English aesthetic theorist Jonathan Richardson urged painters to portray women in "Historical" drapery rather than the "Dress of the Time," so that the portrait would not show the inevitable, rapid "Change in Fashion." Loose robing—whether biblical, classical, or Oriental—was really just a matter of emphasis rather than stark differentiation. The idea behind women's "portrait dress" was to place them in historical costumes that suggested refinement and dignity because such garb was much more sumptuous and outlandish than everyday clothing. Portrait dress required a willingness by colonial American women to engage in an imaginative kind of artful self-presentation, that is, to be both themselves and an idealized version of themselves. It was a project encouraged as part and parcel of the humanist legacy of the Renaissance.[21]

Copley's portrait of Margaret Kemble Gage (1734–1824), the American-born wife of the commander in chief of British forces in America, Thomas Gage, not only epitomizes the spectacular possibilities of *turquerie* in colonial America, but also shows how in one case it helped to evoke a real connection to Greece (see figure 3). As one of the most socially prominent women in New York (some called her "the Duchess"), she was widely renowned for her beauty and intelligence. She was the daughter of the fantastically wealthy Peter Kemble, whose own mother, in fact, was Greek and born in Smyrna. It is very likely that Margaret Gage joined with Copley in

3. Margaret Kemble Gage posing *à la turque.* John Singleton Copley, *Mrs. Thomas Gage* (1771). The Putnam Foundation, Timken Museum of Art, San Diego, CA.

choosing the clothing and pose. Her square-necked red gown, cinched slightly above the waist with a gold-embroidered blue sash (thought to be Greek and called a "zone"), is draped loosely around a torso so undefined that a corset is improbable. Strands of pearls trickle from her sleeve, her neck, and the slightly unfurled turban on her head. Leaning back doe-eyed on an indigo camelback sofa, Margaret Gage is as languid as her clothes are luxurious. Copley rejoiced at this sublime creation, pronouncing it "the best Lady's portrait I ever Drew," and—always eager for approval from the metropole—sent it to London for exhibition. It was his artistic calling card and her social entrée. The portrait would bring painter and subject to the attention of the British elite, whose approval each—for different reasons—energetically courted.[22]

VERNACULAR CLASSICISM: ROLLIN, POPE, AND FÉNELON

In the female world of classicism, four books stand out as favorites: Charles Rollin's *Ancient History* (13 vols., 1730–1738), Alexander Pope's *Iliad* (1715–1720) and *Odyssey* (1725–1726), and Fénelon's *The Adventures of Telemachus* (first published in French in 1699). Men loved their Rollin, Pope, and Fénelon, but these authors, mentioned frequently in women's diaries, letters, and magazines, attracted an equally devoted following of American women.

Several things make these books stand out. First, although they were about the Greco-Roman past and therefore "classical" in the broadest sense of the term, they were all written in a modern vernacular language. They were part of what might be called a "vernacular classical" tradition, a category that was rapidly encroaching on the cultural reverence for ancient texts in Greek and Latin. Two of the texts in this vernacular classical group (by Rollin and Fénelon) were originally published in France and were immediately translated into English in Britain. Both French and English editions were imported to America. There seems to have been a linguistic hierarchy within this vernacular classical world. Some American women took pains to point out that they read Rollin or Fénelon in French, a sign of their doubly Olympian accomplishment.

Second, women linked these books to the expanding eighteenth-century Atlantic trade in goods. They did not just read the books, but surrounded themselves with a veritable gallery of related artifacts that they either bought ready-made or created. Women moved easily between the bookish culture of letters and the material culture of accomplishment, and did not see the cultures as opposed but as parallel paths to the formation of sensibility and taste. They made embroideries and watercolors based on the books' engravings, covered hatboxes with bought or hand-made drawings, and bought fans with classical themes. Some women covered rooms in their homes in pricey theme wallpapers. Such activities meshed with eighteenth-century views of female intellectual and artistic capacities, which were thought to be imitative rather than original. While men produced and imagined, the thinking went, women merely copied by using drawing manuals or prints to help them. And unlike men, who produced art to sell on the market, women's "accomplishments" were explicitly intended to adorn the domestic interior rather than to be exchanged for money in the vulgar marketplace.[23]

Last, all three texts were not only eminently compatible with the project of cultivating female godliness, but in some cases were explicitly promoted as conducive to forming Christian piety. Even the wives and daughters of ministers snapped up classical texts in the eighteenth century, and some took up Latin for the explicit purpose of reading "pagan" literature. When Esther Edwards, the daughter of the minister Jonathan Edwards, married the Revered Aaron Burr, she left behind neither piety nor classicism. "My husband, Mr. Burr," she observed, "has persuaded me to take up Latin with him. I had learned it a little in our home at Northampton, where there was much teaching of the classics." It was possibly an intimidating pedagogy because Aaron Burr was not just the author of a Latin grammar but the president of Princeton.[24]

We can begin with Charles Rollin's *Ancient History*. This staple of American men's reading in the eighteenth century was prized by women in part because he seamlessly melded classical themes with Christian ends. It was an especially important achievement in this age of novels, with their mesmerizing plot lines about female dissipation and godlessness. By contrast, the works of Rollin "inspired the love of virtue, and respect for religion," according to an anonymous contributor to the *American Magazine* in 1745. In the long-winded preface to his *Ancient History*, Rollin argued that there was no conflict between sacred and profane history. The entire human past was simply God's object lesson in showing his sovereignty; it proved "that he alone determines the fate of kings, and the duration of empires; and that he, for reasons inscrutable to all but himself, transfers the government of kingdoms from one nation to another." But why did God allow Greco-Roman pagans to wander for thousands of years in a state of "ignorance and dissoluteness"? First, to show the necessity of God, for by walking in error these nations clearly brought about their own doom. Second, by anticipating the Gospel with their admittedly compelling philosophy, men like Socrates prepared the world to receive Christianity. By uniting the

Mediterranean with the universal languages of Greek and Latin, pagan philosophers prepared all to hear the Word at the birth of the Messiah. Still, there were limits to the propriety of introducing pagans into a Christian education. Do not "enter too far into the spirit of them," Rollin cautioned. The reader had to remain vigilant, or else risk imbibing "unperceived their sentiments, by lavishing too great applause on their heroes."[25]

Abigail Adams is an unusually well-documented reader of Rollin who shows how the book navigated between the female and male worlds of classicism. Though comfortable, her family was not of the colonial aristocracy, and she received a limited education at home. "My early education," she recalled in 1817, "did not partake of the abundant opportunities which the present days offer, and which even our common country schools now afford. *I never was sent to any school.* . . . Female education, in the best families, went no further than writing and arithmetic; in some few and rare instances, music and dancing." Yet she was introduced to enough in the way of classical history and literature that she made a lifelong practice of using classical exemplars in her letters. She and the young women in her circle obviously knew enough of the eighteenth-century practice of classical phrases and pseudonyms that they deployed these in letters to each other as a way to show off their learned intimacy, to articulate an ideal version of themselves. To Abigail's "Diana"—the young forest goddess— her friends answered as Calliope, Silvia, Myra, and Aspasia. Rollin's *Ancient History* was just the kind of book that cultivated this easy familiarity with antiquity. In her courtship letters to John Adams she calls him Lysander, a figure praised in Rollin as one of the brave Spartans who "distinguished themselves in a most extraordinary manner."[26] As their relationship matured, she and John continued to use this flexible language of classical cognomens and phrases to communicate about private, marital matters, and to manage the increasingly onerous demands of his public service.

In her letters during the 1770s, Abigail mentions reading Rollin. Abigail reported to John in 1774 that she found "great pleasure and entertainment" in its pages. It was also the kind of reading that was appropriate for her son, John Quincy, who was just seven years old when Abigail told John that she "perswaided Johnny to read me a page or two every day." She might also have shown young John Quincy—the future president, trained early on for a life of public service—an inspiring illustration from the 1768 edition of Rollin: "Hannibal at Nine Years of Age Swearing Enmity to the Romans."[27] Though he was leader of Rome's archenemy, Carthage, Hannibal was greatly admired in eighteenth-century Europe and America as a brave and shrewd general.

Rollin can also expose the status dimensions of American women's classicism, how his *Ancient History* could be used to out-Rollin someone else, to form an elite within an elite. The Charleston plantation mistress Alice Delancey Izard (1746/47–1832) was just two years younger than Abigail Adams, but her upbringing in rural Westchester, New York, in a wealthy family, exposed her to a level of cosmopolitan Francophilia unknown to Adams, and she read French fluently. In 1767 she married the wealthy Charlestonian Ralph Izard (1742–1804), and she began a life of transatlantic travel and exposure to elite European society in England and on the Continent. Abigail Adams might teach her son from an Englished Rollin, but it was to Alice Delancey Izard to school her young son in Rollin *en français*. Hearing that he had lost his books on a visit to Mt. Vernon in 1803 (a setting that already tells us something about the kind of society the Izards kept), she recommended replacements:

> I am sorry to hear that you have lost your books, and hope you are able to get such as are proper for you to read at Washington. I wish you to have a good general knowledge of ancient, as well as modern history. Mr. Rollin's Ancient & Roman history is the best I know, & it would give me great pleasure to send it to you. Borrow it, if you can, & read it with attention. The French edition is much superior to the translation, & I believe you sufficiently Master of that language to understand a book so well written.[28]

Second in the group of prized female classical texts were Alexander Pope's rhyming English verse translations of Homer's *Iliad* and *Odyssey*. The most popular translations of Homer in the colonies, Pope's *Iliad* and *Odyssey* sold nearly twenty thousand copies in the year 1774 and were steady sellers before and after.[29] They were cherished by Americans in the eighteenth and early nineteenth centuries as bookends of timeless ideals, as relevant to subjects of a monarch as to citizens of a republic. The *Iliad* exalted masculine, warrior virtues, while the *Odyssey* ruminated on the pleasures and sorrows of homecoming. The heroines of these epics—Helen, Andromache, Penelope—were as memorable as the heroes, and in Pope's quotable heroic couplets, they leapt from the page into the imaginations of American women. Pope had worked hard to cultivate a wide audience (the sale of the two translations made him a wealthy man), and he secured patronage for lavish copper plate engravings that made the plot line accessible even to those with marginal reading skills. The result of these factors—accessibility, visual appeal, readability, and relevance—made Pope's *Iliad* and *Odyssey* exceptionally popular among American women, who helped sustain the vogue for Pope's translations well into the nineteenth century.

4. *The Parting of Hector and Andromache.* Needlework by Maria Bissell. CHSM #1934.6.1. The Connecticut Historical Society Museum, Hartford, Connecticut.

The evidence of women's love for Pope is in the quiet ephemera of their lives. They lifted snippets of his verses into their diaries, letters, and commonplace books, and they worked his words and images into their needlepoint. Julia Rush, the daughter of the classically erudite Benjamin and Julia Rush, filled a commonplace book in 1810 with extracts from Pope's *Iliad.* Lavishly illustrated, Pope's volumes also inspired a parallel visual culture for women. In 1810 Maria Bissell, who attended a Connecticut academy, made a silk embroidery of the frontispiece of an 1808 Boston edition of Pope's *Iliad*, which depicted the teary parting of Hector and his wife, Andromache (see figure 4). As late as 1829, ten-year-old Pesta Gates of New

England was working on a sampler festooned with the letters of the alphabet and these lines from Pope's *Iliad*:

> "Like leaves on trees the race of man is found,—
> Now green in youth, now withering on the ground;
> Another race the following spring supplies:
> They fall successive, and successive rise,
> So generations in their course decay
> So flourish these, when those are past away."[30]

Like Rollin, Pope also captivated women because his poetry was a way for elites to reconcile Christianity with classicism. By offering a moral world that largely antedated the biblical past known to Americans through the New Testament, Greco-Roman antiquity always posed something of a threat to Christianity. But among elite women, Pope's heroic couplets—so quotable, so universalizing—seemed a way to merge the pagan and Christian traditions. They read and quoted Pope (they also called him "Homer"), finding this reading compatible with, and even conducive to, the formation of Christian morals. "Homer has a deal of morality in his works, which is worthy of imitation; his Odyssey abounds with it," wrote Eliza Wilkinson (1757–1813) of South Carolina confidently about her reading of Pope. The diaries of two Quaker women of mid-century Pennsylvania show how easily this religious and pagan amalgamation occurred. In 1778 seventeen-year-old Sally Wister of Germantown, Pennsylvania, noted to her diary that her suitor picked up "Homer's Iliad, and read to us." Wister did not mention that this *Iliad* was Pope's (perhaps it did not need mentioning?), but she knew the text well enough that she could recall in her diary the precise lines read to her. She quoted just as easily from a different book by Alexander Pope when she needed an apposite phrase about mercy or sympathy. Wister quotes a few stanzas from Pope's *Universal Prayer* ("That mercy I to others show, That mercy shew to me") in her diary for 3 June 1778. Similarly, the twenty-four-year-old Quaker Elizabeth Drinker (1735–1807) noted in her diary that she had "begun to read Pope's Homer; the Iliad" after a crowded morning in church. Her easy slip from Christian worship into pagan reading implies that she saw no conflict between attending church and classicism.[31]

One of the most sustained engagements with Alexander Pope in eighteenth-century America came from an unlikely place—Phillis Wheatley (1753–1784), a black slave living in Massachusetts. Wheatley had been brought from Africa to Boston in 1761 at about age eight, and she was purchased by the prominent Boston merchant John Wheatley. His daughter,

Mary, tutored Phillis Wheatley so diligently that the slave's education surpassed that available to most white men and certainly to white women of the period. Wheatley was taught the Bible, Horace, Virgil, Ovid, and Terence, as well as some Latin. It was a literary education that found expression in her poetry, which set deeply felt Christian piety into a neoclassical literary style. For the last, her model was Alexander Pope, and especially her favorite reading of all, his translations of the *Iliad* and the *Odyssey*. She imitated his poetry in her *Poems on Various Subjects, Religious and Moral* (1773), the first book published by an African American. Since no colonial press would touch it, the book was published in London with the assistance of her English patroness, the Countess of Huntington. Others of the London elite knew of her love for Pope. The second earl of Dartmouth, whom she thanks in one of her poems for his role in repealing the Stamp Act, gave the twenty-year-old in return a five-volume set of Pope's *Iliad*, each volume carefully inscribed with his dedication to her, "Lord Dartmouth to Phillis Wheatley London July—1773."[32] In an age when classically educated women were invariably white, Phillis Wheatley was known to her admirers as the "sable Muse," and the frontispiece of her published poems shows her at her desk, holding a quill.

Wheatley's poems shed light on how deeply threatening black knowledge of classical antiquity could be to white slaveholders. As slavery became ever more entrenched in the south, classicism, as a kind of learning that marked blacks as social and intellectual inferiors, became one of the many cultural manifestations of white racial superiority. The best-known form of this racial use of classicism is the practice among some planters of giving their slaves classical names like Scipio and Venus. Bestowing the noblest of names on the lowliest workers, planters knitted the slaves into their fanciful self-conception as bucolic Romans reborn, who benignly superintended the peaceable kingdom of the tobacco farm. The classical architecture of plantation houses like Mount Vernon and Monticello also obliquely reminded planters that Greece and Rome had been slave societies that sustained an elite of educated, virtuous citizens. Planters relied upon skilled slave labor to create these edifices. "Hector making mortar," reads an entry from the 1801 construction log of the classical Edenton Academy of North Carolina, a phrasing that shows how the most exalted names from classical antiquity—in this case a Trojan hero from Homer's *Iliad*—were routinely bestowed upon the most dispossessed Americans.[33]

American planters' particular use of classicism did not go unnoticed by slaves. Many years after his escape, Frederick Douglass (1818–1895) still remembered how strange it had been, when he was a slave in Maryland, to work near the Greek revival mansion of his childhood. "The great house was a large, white, wooden building, with wings on three sides of it. In front, a large portico, extending the entire length of the building, and supported by a long range of columns, gave to the whole establishment an air of solemn grandeur. It was a treat to my young and gradually opening mind, to behold this elaborate exhibition of wealth, power and vanity."[34]

By writing in a Latinate style, Phillis Wheatley had set a cat among the pigeons. When Robert Carter ("Bob"), the sixteen-year-old son of the Virginia slaveholder Robert Carter III, heard of her poems in 1774, he expressed "astonishment," and he wondered if Wheatley "knew grammar, Latin, etc." Her poems, in fact, inspired one of the first American sociologies of slavery. A rumination on the differences between ancient Roman and modern bondage, Thomas Jefferson's *Notes on the State of Virginia* (1787) singled out Wheatley's poems as illustrations of his conviction that blacks lacked as much "reason" as whites, and that "in imagination they are dull, tasteless, and anomalous." At any one time, Jefferson owned around two hundred slaves, about two-thirds of whom lived at his grandly classical house, Monticello, while the remainder resided at his other, nearby farms. A few had classical names: his meticulous farm book records the presence of slaves named Jupiter (1743–1800), Lucretia (1779–after 1823), Cornelius (1811–after 1827), Caesar, Juno, and Minerva (1771–after 1827). Minerva was a field hand at Monticello who bore nine children with her husband, Bagwell, and she lived in a one-room cabin made of logs and mud far down the mountainside from Monticello; her work usually kept her out of sight of her owner.[35]

By contrast, Wheatley and her poems captured the attention of the bookish, classically erudite Jefferson, whose library at Monticello contained over forty books on the subject of classical architecture alone. According to Jefferson, Wheatley's poems demonstrated that blacks could imitate great literature like Pope's or Homer's, but they could not create it themselves. Wheatley might admire Pope's *Iliad*, but she could never equal or surpass it. Because she lacked imagination, she could feel the base, sensory pleasure of religious feeling, but she could not experience the transcendent imaginative flight of the poet. She would confuse mock epic with real epic. "The heroes of the Dunciad are to her, as Hercules to the author of that poem," wrote Jefferson in reference to Pope's *Dunciad* (1728–1743). In sum, her works were "below the dignity of criticism."[36]

Wheatley's apparent failures to live up to Pope's classical translations helped to fuel Jefferson's extended rumination in the *Notes* on the contrasts between modern black slavery and the "white" slavery that had existed in classical antiquity. Erudite slaves like Phillis Wheatley and field hands like Minerva suggested to Jefferson the possibility that black skin made

Africans more suited to slavery than other peoples. His reading in Roman and Greek history showed him societies rooted in slavery, but not in race-based slavery. In Greece and Rome, "white" slaves could be freed and then transcend their servile condition to ascend into the ranks of the free. The condition of Roman slaves, Jefferson argued, was "much more deplorable than that of the blacks on the continent of America." Roman slaves might be flung into the Tiber when ill, punished by wanton cruelty and murder, or sold when old or diseased. Despite these abuses, some Roman slaves like Epictetus, Diogenes, Phaedon, Terence, and Phaedrus "were often their rarest artists" and "excelled too in science, insomuch as to be usually employed as tutors to their master's children."[37]

How to explain such extraordinary achievement from slaves? They were all "of the race of whites." White, Roman slaves could transcend their servile condition in a way that black slaves in Virginia could not. When freed, a Roman slave "might mix with, without staining the blood of his master." But modern black slaves, when freed, needed "to be removed beyond the reach of mixture." Roman slavery rested on cheap—and chaste—slaves. In Rome "the two sexes were confined in separate apartments, because to raise a child cost the master more than to buy one." By contrast, African-American slaves, naturally more "ardent" than whites, bred "as fast as the free inhabitants," and they were encouraged to share quarters. It is certain that black Minerva bore out Jefferson's hope for modern slave fecundity. "I consider a woman who brings a child every two years as more profitable than the best man of the farm," he stated in 1820. Every day, Minerva brought her hoes to the fields while her mother cared for the children; she would have returned several times during each day to nurse a baby, and was allotted an extra quarter-peck of cornmeal for what Jefferson called her "addition to the capital" of Monticello.[38]

For Jefferson, Phillis Wheatley's erudition—the religion, poetry, and classicism expressed in her published tributes to Pope's *Iliad*—did not suggest black equality with whites but the immutability of black inferiority. He thought that while she could ape genius, her people would never be geniuses.

Last in the category of favorite classical reading for eighteenth-century women was the best-selling book *Les Aventures de Télémaque* (1699) by the French pastor François de Salignac de La Mothe-Fénelon (1651–1715). The book was a publishing sensation in Europe and America: one of the most popular works of political theory of the eighteenth century, by 1830 it had gone through 150 editions and some eighty translations.[39] Read by American women and men both in French and in English translation, the book—like Pope's *Iliad*—also spawned a parallel female world of images and objects which ran from paintings and wallpaper to embroideries and even a shell grotto. Here was a book—and especially a story—that captured the imaginations of American men in one way, but inspired American women in quite another.

Like Rollin, Fénelon had impeccable moral and literary credentials to recommend him to his American audience. He spent ten years as the Superior of the Nouvelles Catholiques, a society for the instruction of young female converts, before writing the *Traité de l'Education des Filles* (1687), which was first translated into English in 1699. In many ways, Fénelon was entirely a traditionalist when it came to the education of girls. These, he reckoned, were corruptible creatures beset by natural character flaws like timidity, false modesty, and a propensity for putting passion over reason. Such failings demanded an education rich in didactic moralism to inspire women to modesty, simplicity, and amiability. Women needed a little Latin and definitely a lot of Greek and Roman history, which were storehouses of exempla such as the mother of the Gracchi, who "contributed very much to the forming of the Eloquence of her Sons, who became afterwards so great Men."[40]

This pleasure principle—robing the didactic lessons of history in fetching tales—resulted in the work for which Fénelon was best known, *Les Aventures de Télémaque*, written while he was tutor to the young dauphin, the grandson of Louis XIV. The tale was directly inspired by the peregrinations related in Homer's *Odyssey*. It follows young Telemachus, son of Ulysses (the Latin version of the Greek name, Odysseus), as he leaves Ithaca and his mother, Penelope, to search for his father, who has not yet returned from the Trojan War. Telemachus is accompanied by his guide, Minerva, who has assumed the shape of a man named Mentor. Along the way Telemachus learns valuable lessons about kingship and self-mastery. The work was popular initially because it was viewed as a satire of the excesses of King Louis XIV (a charge Fénelon denied), and Fénelon was banished to the obscurity of a pastorate in Cambrai. Fénelon's *Telemachus* resonated deeply among revolutionary American men, who found two themes of the story to be particularly relevant to their own struggles against the king of England. They could see in Telemachus's search for his father a parallel to their own search for a new father figure to replace the displaced king, George III. They also followed young Telemachus in his journey of self-discovery, and learned the lessons in self-mastery essential for republican self-government.[41]

But Fénelon's *Telemachus* also found a lasting audience among American women even before the revolutionary war: among only three books inscribed by Sarah Logan of Philadelphia was an edition of Fénelon's *Les Aventures de Télémaque* (Amsterdam, 1719). "Sarah Logan her Book 1723," reads the inscription in the small calf duodecimo.[42] Women seem to have found something different than men in *Telemachus*, something that resonated more deeply in their own lives than the tale of prodigal sons and the cultivation of male self-mastery. We can look at the response of several eighteenth-century American women to *Telemachus* to see what it might have been.

Elizabeth Graeme Fergusson (1737–1801) may have known *The Adventures of Telemachus* better than any other American, man or woman, in the eighteenth century. Born into an elite Philadelphia family, she was raised both in the family's house in the city and in their summer home of Graeme Park, twenty miles north of Philadelphia. Fergusson's mother took great pains with her youngest daughter's education, and, as Fergusson reached her maturity, the house at Graeme Park became a kind of literary salon that attracted Philadelphia luminaries like Benjamin Rush and Benjamin Franklin to soirees of learned conversation that Elizabeth called "Attic Evenings." Calling herself "Sophia" (among other names) and Philadelphia the "Athens of North America," Fergusson hoped to plant what she called the seeds of art and learning in North America, an aspiration she frequently turned into published odes.[43]

Fergusson seems to have been especially captivated by *Telemachus* and viewed aspects of her life through its lens: she called her much older friend, Richard Peters, her "Mentor" in one of her odes, and she worried that a long parting from her husband "exceeds that of the celebrated Ulysses and Penelope." In 1760, at the age of twenty-three, she began an English verse translation of *Télémaque*. She had few female classical translators as models from which to work. There were of course the two European greats: in France, Anne Dacier (1647–1720) translated Homer's *Iliad* from Greek into French, and in England, Elizabeth Carter (1717–1806) translated Epictetus from Greek into English. But for Fergusson, to translate a text from French into English was to chart the newer waters of British America's "vernacular classical" world. It is unclear what motivated Fergusson's translation besides intellectual and literary interest, but a romantic rupture may have given the project some steam. She had been engaged for five years to William Franklin, son of Benjamin Franklin, but in 1759 he jilted her. Fergusson continued to work on the translation over the next several decades, especially after the deaths of her mother and sister, when the work seems to have distracted her from her grief. Throughout the period, she worried that the translating work would make her what she called "a *Classical* pedant, or what is much Worse a *female* one."[44]

The manuscript was complete by the early 1790s, and Fergusson wrote in it that she hoped to "have it printed." Despite encouragement for her

friend Elias Boudinot, Fergusson ultimately declined publication, citing
the "delicacy of [her] Situation" (the fear of a woman having to collect
subscriptions for publication). She may not have seen the decision to
forego publication as a failure. By choosing to keep her translation in
manuscript form, Fergusson stood in a particularly female tradition of
eighteenth-century *belles lettres* in America. Leaders of the female-centered
colonial salons circulated manuscripts unintended for print as a way to
expand literary networks and to distinguish their intellectual pretensions
from the sometimes gossipy and banal conversation of the tea tables.[45]

One particular episode in *Telemachus* seized the imagination of
eighteenth-century American women: the moving story of Telemachus's
stay on the island of Calypso. Calypso was a lovely nymph who lived on an island somewhere in the balmy Mediterranean. The island was truly paradisi-
acal, a place of gentle winds, fragrant forests, and sunny beaches broken by
the shade of mossy grottos. In league with Venus, Calypso had already se-
duced Ulysses, waylaying him for a time on his journey home to Ithaca before he finally escaped her charms. When Telemachus and Mentor arrive
on Calypso's island, she sends some nymphs to detain the young man. Calypso falls in love with Telemachus; Telemachus falls deeply in love with
the nymph Eucharis; jealous complications ensue, and it becomes clear to
the ever-reasonable Mentor that love-struck Telemachus will be ensnared
on the island of Calypso forever. It is only when Mentor actually pushes
Telemachus off a cliff into the churning sea below that Calypso's spell is
broken. Telemachus, released from the slavery of passion, is at liberty to re-
sume his journey. Here was the classic eighteenth-century set-up: Venus
and Calypso, embodiments of passion, conspire unsuccessfully to stymie
Minerva/Mentor, embodiment of masculine reason and sober deeds.

But might not some female readers have been cheering for Calypso?
She seemed to embody the scope and limits of women's possibilities for action. Calypso ruled her balmy island, a "female world" like the one women
were creating through their classical reading, polite conversation, and silk
embroideries. Leading her band of nymphs and commanding men with
her wiles and her beauty, Calypso is a formidable figure in her own right.
But Calypso's plight was heartbreaking, doomed as she was to lose lover after lover, a victim of the competing agendas of Venus and Minerva, stuck
on her little island forever. Her jealousy, rage, and especially her loneliness
are repeatedly and movingly evoked in *Telemachus*: she is a nymph, but her
despair is human. Her little world was defined by men, who suddenly landed
on her beaches and, just as suddenly, sailed away. Calypso's role was akin to
that of the female conversationalist in the salon, who modulated her speech
and silence to meet the needs of her male companion. Comparing Calypso's

role to women's ideal role in pleasant tête-à-tête, one author in the 1806 magazine *Companion and Weekly Miscellany* put it this way: "Yet would she, like Calypso, wish to hear Tellemachus o'er and o'er again." Calypso's beauty never faded but she was ultimately powerless to detain the heroes of Greece on their quest for goals other than eternal love. Her island might be a paradise, but it was a lonely one.[46]

One Philadelphia woman in the 1760s seems to have been especially captivated by the island of Calypso as a kind of female world. She made a small grotto entirely of shells and dedicated it to Calypso, whose name means "the Concealer."[47] Spatially enclosed but imaginatively sprawling, the shell grotto of Calypso may have spoken more meaningfully about the closed lives of American women than did the far-flung adventures of Telemachus and Mentor.

The Philadelphia shell grotto was just one of a number of objects that ruminated in some way on the Calypso of Fénelon. For starters, the subject was a favorite among eighteenth-century painters, and engravings of these canvases made their way to the New World. The virtuoso English painter Angelica Kauffman's *Telemachus and the Nymphs of Calypso* (1788) shows the group, assembled around a table as though for tea, outside a rocky grotto. In England in 1773, Benjamin West (1738–1820) also painted a version of Telemachus's stay on Calypso's island. This painting was known in America and continued to be discussed in magazines read by women in the early 1800s. At least one girl in a female academy in America rendered the scene in silk embroidery. Frances Mecia Campbell, who attended Mrs. Saunders's and Miss Beach's Academy in Dorchester, Massachusetts, created the work from what was probably a book engraving while she attended the academy in 1807. As American women began to decorate with wallpaper, they turned to men like the French paper designer Joseph Dufour, whose most popular product in the American market, titled "Les Paysages de Télémaque dans L'Ile de Calypso," was an enchanting panoramic series of panels that included the episode in which Minerva tosses Telemachus off the cliffs of the island of Calypso. It was expensive paper that only the most elite households could afford, and it required eighty-five colors and a huge swath of wall for full effect. It was the paper chosen in 1836 by President Andrew Jackson (1767–1845) to adorn the walls of the central hall and entryway of his grandly classical Tennessee plantation, the Hermitage (see figure 5).[48]

The female accomplishments of classical reading, drawing, and embroidery were distinctive and new in eighteenth-century America. While resting on the increasing social prestige of a "vernacular classical" tradition, the female world of eighteenth-century classicism partook of the

5. The Hermitage mansion center hall, 1892, showing wallpaper that depicts the adventures of Telemachus on the island of Calypso, familiar to readers from Fénelon's popular book, *The Adventures of Telemachus.* Photograph by Otto Giers. The Hermitage: Home of President Andrew Jackson, Nashville, TN.

same books favored by elite, literate men, while also cultivating a particular number of themes that ruminated more clearly on women's social and intellectual situations. Whatever the stated fears that classical reading would turn women into petticoat pedants, wrinkly spinsters, and dissipated pagans, most women recorded a seamless meshing of classical reading with ideals of female piety, submission, and decorum. In the next chapter we will see how and why this world began to change in the age of revolution.

THE RISE OF THE ROMAN
MATRON, 1770–1790

In May 1776 Oliver Wolcott, Sr., (1726–1797) wrote a letter to his wife, Laura Collins Wolcott (1732–1794). He was in Philadelphia serving as one of Connecticut's delegates to the Continental Congress, and he would be absent often over the next decade, leading militia brigades against the British, signing the Declaration of Independence and the Articles of Confederation, and later supporting ratification of the Constitution. But now British troops were on the move, and amid his gathering anxiety Oliver dashed off a letter to Laura, who had stayed behind in Litchfield, Connecticut, to manage the farm and business, and to tend to their four children. It was perhaps to calm his own fears as much as hers. "Possess your own mind in Peace—Fortitude not only enables us to bear Evils, but prevents oftentimes those which would otherwise befal us—The Roman and Grecian matrons not only bore with magnanimity the Suspensions of Fortune, but Various kinds of adversity, with amazing Constancy, an American Lady instructed in sublimer Principles I hope will never be outdone by any of these illustrious Examples if she should be called to the Exercise of the greatest female Heroism."[1]

Laura Wolcott's reply to her husband's suggestion that she emulate the matrons of Greece and Rome has been lost. But she felt deeply enough connected to the revolutionary cause that she helped to melt down and make 4,250 lead cartridges for the Continental army out of pieces remaining from the equestrian statue of George III, which had been torn down in New York City in July 1776. Her courage and fortitude—Roman matron style—were immortalized by the painter Ralph Earl in his portrait of her completed around 1789, in which he posed her in front of an imaginary fluted classical column, her arm resting on an equally imaginary Roman architectural slab.[2]

Laura Wolcott was not the only American woman to be compared to the heroic matrons of antiquity during the revolutionary period. In the 1770s a few other American women whose husbands were deeply involved in the revolutionary cause began to identify themselves in one way or another as Roman matrons. They did so just as men also changed their classical personae by invoking heroes of ancient Greece and Rome in the service of republican revolution.[3] But women had their own particular genres and strategies. Some signed letters to their husbands using the names of ancient women exceptionally devoted to politically active husbands; some published in magazines or books under pen names of Roman matrons; others published works that connected modern political ideas to the activities of women in ancient Greece or Rome; still others expressed their connection to the women of antiquity visually, by sitting for portraits dressed as Roman matrons.

The Roman matron of the 1770s and 1780s emerged from American women's pressing political, philosophical, and familial concerns. First, the idea of the Roman matron was an embryonic political language that ultimately would help to connect women to a republican polity that found few ways to include them in the rituals of citizenship. Women in the 1770s linked the idea of the Roman matron in new and original ways to the republican revolution against England. In an evolution from moral worthies long known from literature, Roman matrons now became political worthies with immediate, urgent meanings for modern women. Through the Roman matron American women entered into the elite male fiction that the classical past was a shared, historical origin point for the new nation. If the new republic would be a *novus ordo seclorum*, a new order of the ages inspired by the liberty-loving republics of antiquity, America's women needed to be Roman matrons as clearly as its men needed to be Roman senators and soldiers. As with white American men who identified with celebrated Greeks and Romans, the iconic identity of the Roman matron contained the implicit possibility of slaveholding; in an age before sectional rivalries had emerged, both southern and northern women could find Roman matronhood appealing as a source of patriotic unity and shared republican ideology.

Second, women's identification with the Roman matron was not just backward looking but also thoroughly modern, tapping into the latest currents of philosophical historicism sponsored by Scottish and French thinkers. They had proposed that all societies ascended through four stages, from primitive to civilized, an upward progression of minds and morals in which women played a central role. Women benefited from social improvements by being treated better, and, in turn, contributed to the progress of civilizations by softening the brutish passions of men and by refining mores and manners.[4] The only thing better than a real Roman matron, in other words, was a modern Roman matron, a woman who blended the virtues of antiquity with the improvements of Christianity, sensibility, and polite learning.

Last, the Roman matron built a fragile classical bridge across the chasm of the eighteenth-century marriage. Though revolutionary rhetoric was slowly beginning to erode traditional patriarchal family structures, the reality was that elite men's level of education—and so their exposure to classical literature—far outpaced that of their wives. But women from elite families did have some knowledge of the heroic women of the republics of antiquity, and the Roman matron allowed them to join men of their social rank in a commonality of cause through difficult years of separation and deprivation. The strongest tie between men and women remained Christianity, those "sublimer Principles" invoked by Oliver Wolcott. But the Roman matron now became a new voice for elite women, a secular link to political revolution and a domestic code shared with men deeply involved in the patriot cause.

When American women talked about Roman matrons, what did they mean by "Roman" and "matron"? By matron, they seem to have meant a woman who was both married and a mother. The word derived from the Latin word *matrona*, which meant a married woman; in Rome, early on, the word had acquired the accessory idea of a wife's dignity, rank, and moral and sexual virtue. To begin then, women who identified themselves as Roman matrons in revolutionary America were generally not single women, even though single women at any given time formed a significant portion of the adult female population. The women who identified during the revolutionary era with Roman matrons were united by having "partners of Distinguished Zeal, integrity and Virtue," as Mercy Otis Warren wrote to Abigail Adams in early 1775 to describe their two husbands.[5] Roman matrons further enshrined the idealized state of marriage for women in the truth tales of antiquity by papering over the very real legal and social disabilities endured by single women.[6]

What was "Roman" about the Roman matron? The adjective should not be viewed as a historical category of scholarly precision but as a vague compendium energized by imprecision. Americans often clustered the matrons of ancient Greece, Rome, and even Carthage under the umbrella of the "Roman" matron. Roman matrons were extruded through the startling variety of literary genres available: Rollin's *Ancient History*, Pope's epics, Shakespeare's *Coriolanus* (which received a number of modern reinterpretations in England and America in the eighteenth century), daughterly advice literature, and the roll call of exempla that filled magazines and newspapers. If there was one quality that came close to producing consensus, it was that Roman matrons had enjoyed more liberties than any other women in antiquity. The lawyer James Wilson spoke for many when he argued that classical Greek women were degraded by the rigid sex segregation of their society. The "fair sex," he observed in 1790, were "neglected and despised," and condemned to "servitude." By contrast, according to William Alexander's influential *History of Women* (1779), the women of Rome seemed to enjoy more public freedoms. "It was the Romans who first gave to the sex public liberty, who first properly cultivated their minds, and thought it as necessary to do so as to adorn their bodies. Among them were they first fitted for society, and for becoming rational companions; and among them was it first demonstrated to the world, that they were capable of great actions, and deserved a better fate than to be shut up in seraglios."[7]

Radical because she gave women a flexible language for entry into the revolution, the Roman matron was also deeply conservative. Elite women of ancient Rome could not vote or hold public office, and they had restricted access to courts of law. Roman daughters lived under the legal control of the *paterfamilias* until he transferred that power, the *manus*, to the control of the husband. At the time of marriage, women in Rome rescinded control of much of their real and personal property. In ancient Greece, the lives of "respectable" women had been even more restricted. Literary and archaeological evidence suggests that, in addition to being excluded from public life by law and convention, Greek women lived in houses in which sex segregation was built into the very architecture. Women stayed largely in the women's area, the *gynaikonaitis*, and men repaired to the *andronitis* (though of course the realities of daily living would have entailed some contact between the sexes).[8]

Both radical and conservative, the Roman matron helped elite American women support a political revolution that was neither a social nor a domestic revolution. Her conservatism made the Roman matron a form of self-presentation that did not necessarily overturn traditional domestic relationships, as the urgings of Oliver Wolcott to Laura Wolcott suggested. The elite status implicit in the Roman matron likewise secured white women's cultural position. Americans envisioned the matrons of ancient Rome as wives of senators, mothers of emperors, and daughters of generals, that is, as women who wielded significant familial power in a slave society. In the Roman matron, educated women of the revolutionary period could find a voice through which to infuse their activities with politically resonant meaning and to embrace a republican revolution without overtly unsettling their domestic relationships.

THE ROMAN MATRON IN WORDS

One republican in particular seems to have been deeply influential for the rise of the revolutionary Roman matron in America: the English historian Catharine Sawbridge Macaulay (1731–1791). Steeped in deeply republican sympathies and suspicious of the rise of conspiratorial powers in the realm, Macaulay was one of the Whig writers read with interest by restive American colonists in the 1760s, alongside other pet republican manifestos like *Cato's Letters*. One work in particular brought Macaulay to the attention of a growing number of American women. This was her *History of England from the Accession of James I to that of the Brunswick Line* (8 vols., 1763–1783), a highly partisan history of royal absolutism in England that endorsed the execution of Charles I and depicted the years of the English Civil War as a golden age of republican experimentation. The book also propagated the republican idea of the royal court as an effeminate, Oriental-style harem, in which women meddled nefariously behind closed doors. Macaulay held up, by way of contrast, the government of ancient Rome, which, in its most virtuous period, "was never influenced by the low cabals and intrigues of loose vicious women, which is every the consequence of those effeminate manners which prevail in monarchies . . ."[9]

Radical Whigs on both sides of the Atlantic praised Macaulay's *History* for its congenial political message, but they also took note of her sex. In an age when history writing was lauded as the noblest form of writing for men—they could write history because they had been there, in the halls of the legislature and on the fields of battle—Macaulay seemed to have transcended the limits of female erudition and ability.

Here was a new creature on the female classical landscape, a woman whose reading about antiquity taught her the love of liberty and inspired her to the masculine work of history writing. In fact, Macaulay encouraged such a view in her *History*. "From my early youth I have read with delight those histories that exhibit Liberty in its most exalted state, the annals of the Roman and the Greek republics." The lesson she took from this history reading was the need for liberty, and "Liberty became the object of a secondary worship" for Macaulay. Like other girls of her elite status, Macaulay had been tutored at home, but she quickly realized the limits of ornamental female accomplishments and wandered instead into her father's library. Exactly what she read there remains a mystery, but when Elizabeth Carter (the English translator of the Greek Stoic philosopher Epictetus) met Macaulay, she commented that Macaulay's conversation raced around "the Spartan laws, the Roman politics, the philosophy of Epicurus, and the wit of St. Evremond." The result, according to Carter, was "a most extraordinary system."[10]

Catharine Macaulay also promoted improved classical education for girls. Her *Letters on Education* (1790), addressed to a fictional recipient named Hortensia (a name shared by the ancient Roman woman who had dared to address the Forum), included this prescription: Plutarch's *Lives*, Livy, Sallust, Tacitus, Epictetus, Seneca, Virgil, and Terence. She supplemented this with Rollin's *Ancient History* ("in French"), Fénelon's *Telemachus*, and those transatlantic Whig favorites, Joseph Addison's *Cato* and the *Spectator*. Should her listing be interpreted as applying only to boys, she made a careful note at the end: "But I must tell you, Hortensia, lest you should mistake my plan, that though I have been obliged (in order to avoid confusion) to speak commonly in the masculine character, that the same rules of education in all respects are to be observed to the female as well as to the male children."[11]

Macaulay attracted immediate attention among a few Americans deeply committed to the republican cause. She was delighted when a patriotic Boston woman writing under the pseudonym of "Sophronia" initiated a correspondence with her in 1769. (Sophronia was a Roman matron of the early fourth century who killed herself rather than be raped by the tyrant Maxentius.) In an epistolary domino effect, Sophronia put Macaulay in touch with John Adams, who then referred her to Abigail Adams and to Mercy Otis Warren, wife of James Warren, another leading patriot. Macaulay's *History* also appears in the 1775 library of Julia Rush, placed there by her future husband, Benjamin Rush, who had met Macaulay when he lived in London in the late 1760s. Among the most complete responses is from Abigail Adams, who confessed her interest in a letter in 1771. "I have a great desire to be made acquainted with Mrs. Macaulays own history. One of my own Sex so eminent in a tract so uncommon naturally raises my curiosity. . . . I have a curiosity to know her Education, and what first prompted her to engage in a Study never before Exibited to the publick by one of her own Sex and Country, tho now to the honour of both so admirably performed by her."[12]

Mercy Otis Warren took Macaulay as an intellectual model, corresponding with her and eventually using some of Macaulay's ideas in her own *History of the Rise, Progress and Termination of the American Revolution* (3 vols., 1805). It was the first history published by an American woman and was highly laudatory of republicanism. Even John Adams, who told Warren that history was no work for a "lady," praised the remarkable accomplishment of Catharine Macaulay. Macaulay made a deep impression on Mercy Otis Warren when she visited her in 1784. Warren found Macaulay to be a "Lady of the most Extraordinary talent," one "whose elegant writings reflect so much lustre on her sex."[13]

In part because of Macaulay's influence, Abigail Adams became a spectacular example of the epistolary, republican use of the Roman matron. Her commanding eloquence, known to us through the hundreds of letters she exchanged with John Adams and others, concealed a haphazard education: she was educated entirely at home, while John had graduated from Harvard College and read law for three years thereafter. One of Abigail's biographers has observed that the marriage that emerges from the couple's frank and witty correspondence—"Dearest Friend," they so often addressed each other—seems so modern that it is easy to forget that it was an eighteenth-century marriage rooted in patriarchy and the legal convention of stifling coverture laws. But with "Portia," the name of the Roman matron chosen by Abigail in letters to John, she built a bridge of common understanding with a spouse who could match her love of antiquity even if he vaulted over her in legal rights and educational attainment. The long-suffering wife of the Roman senator Brutus (an implacable foe of the tyrannical Caesar), Portia is reputed to have swallowed hot coals after her husband's death. The Roman matron connected Abigail at once to her husband and to her new country. In one of her "Portia" letters to John, written immediately after the signing of the Declaration of Independence, Abigail marveled that "a person so nearly connected with me" had laid the foundation for a future nation. It was the Roman matron that helped to forge and nurture that connection.[14]

For all that John encouraged Abigail's "Portia" identity, however, he never signed letters to her (or anyone else) as Brutus. There may be any number of reasons. Accustomed to identifying with classical orators or lawgivers like Cicero or Solon, he may have been reluctant to implicate himself as an assassin, even a republican one. And unlike Abigail, John did not need to prove or cultivate his own political commitments in the private sphere of letter writing since the large stage of public life was open to him. For Abigail, the circle of epistolary exchange *was* her public, the only written forum in which to develop a classical, political persona.

The arc of the "Portia" letters over time shows why Abigail and John found this persona engaging. It also shows why Abigail eventually abandoned the pseudonym of Portia while continuing to invoke other classical women to describe her personal situation. She first signed her name "Portia" in a letter to John Adams on 4 May 1775, the first letter she had written since he had left their home in Braintree to serve in the Second Continental Congress in Philadelphia. It seems clear that her Portia refers to the Roman one, not the Portia in Shakespeare. A number of her letters from this period make analogies between Britain's imperial crisis and the Ides of March of Caesar, suggesting that Abigail, like other colonists, viewed these political events through a classical lens. Portia helped Abigail to find a personal and spousal identity as a mother left alone in charge of a farm, as a wife of a leading—and absent—patriot, and as a woman groping toward a political voice for classicism akin to Macaulay's through letters rather than a published history. She would be "very insensible and heroick," she told John, embodying the Roman ideals of stoicism and selflessness. The Adamses were smitten by epistolary word play, and had masqueraded under the pen names of classical lovers during their courtship; being Portia, then, was both an old habit because the name was classical, and a novel foray because the name was republican, unlike the Diana of her youth. She also used "Portia" with a small coterie of others. She used the pseudonym for the next nine years; her final signature as "Portia" was 12 April 1784, when the hardest years of the revolution had passed, but John Adams was so delighted with it that he kept using it long after she had dropped it.[15]

It was under the pseudonym of Portia that Abigail could approach John with some of the political problems of the revolutionary period, particularly the matter of women's rights and duties in the new republic. Although the question of women's rights was all but inconceivable during the revolutionary period, a few people began to wonder whether the rhetoric of natural rights applied to women as well as men, and whether women had both rights and duties in the polity. Abigail Adams was one of these early voices, exploring in her private letters to friends and to John the question of women's particular place in the new republic. "Patriotism in the female Sex is the most disinterested of all virtues," she wrote to him in 1782, signing as Portia. "Excluded from honours and from offices, we cannot attach ourselves to the State or Government from having held a place of Eminence. . . . Deprived of a voice in Legislation, obliged to submit to those Laws which are imposed upon us, is it not sufficient to make us indifferent to the publick Welfare? Yet all History and every age exhibit Instances of patriotick virtue in the female Sex; which considering our situation equals the most Heroick of yours." Writing to Abigail Adams in 1776, Mercy Otis Warren told her what it meant for a woman to be "a truly patriotic Lady": she would show the virtues of "Patience, Fortitude, Public Spirit, Magnanimity, and self Denial."[16] These were the building blocks of a Roman matron.

For Abigail, signing as a specific Roman matron did not preclude her invoking other women from antiquity. One of the legacies of Renaissance humanism to which elite colonial Americans were heir was a sense of artful self-fashioning. In her Portia letters, Abigail seems to have exploited the legacy by reveling in the hasty improvisations of taking on one identity and just as rapidly casting it off, or even by piling one exemplar on top of another. During the nine-year period of her Portia letters, Abigail, in letters to John, turned to the particular situations of other Roman and Greek women to claim the mantle of female patriotism while also pleading her cause as a wife.

Both Abigail and John, for example, expressed their sadness about their long separation by invoking the celebrated story of the parting of Hector and Andromache, from the *Iliad*. Amid the relentless carnage of the Trojan War, the scene is a quiet moment of family tenderness, showing that even the bravest heroes long only to return home to their families. The Trojan warrior Hector, resplendent in his bronze armor and plumed helmet, reaches to embrace his little son, Astyanax, but the boy is terrified by his father's helmet and begins to cry. Laughing with his wife, Andromache, Hector lifts his helmet and puts it on the ground: now he is a father, not a warrior. He kisses his son and offers a prayer to Zeus that Astyanax be a great warrior. Turning to Andromache, Hector tries to reassure her that that he will return safely; she should return home to do women's work, to her distaff and her loom. Readers know that the family is saying their last good-bye: Hector will die in battle, little Astyanax will be thrown to his death from the walls of Troy, and Andromache will be captured and enslaved. For both Abigail and John, the story—familiar from Pope's translation of the *Iliad*—became shorthand for familial longing. In France in 1778 John saw a picture of the parting of Hector and Andromache hanging in the Louvre, which made him think of Abigail and the four children. "I had not forgotten Adieus," he wrote, "as tender and affecting as those of any Hector or Andromache that ever existed, with this difference, that there were four Astyanaxes instead of one in the Scene." Seeing the passage a few years later during another extended absence, a teary Abigail told John that "Portia felt its full force."[17]

John's proposal to travel to Europe on diplomatic duties in the 1780s particularly galled Abigail because she had already endured eight long years of separation. In a letter written in April 1782, she invoked Penelope, who patiently awaited the return of Ulysses from the Trojan War, a twenty-year journey that took him to islands inhabited by seductive detainments. "I shall assume the Signature of Penelope, for my dear Ulysses has already been a wanderer from me near half the term of years that, that

Hero was encountering Neptune, Calipso, the Circes and Syrens." After quoting a few lines of poetry in which Penelope pleads with Ulysses to return before her beauty and charms wither, Abigail claimed still to be patriotic (and not just selfishly wifely) because she was trying to protect John's health. His death would imperil the new nation by eliminating one of its most brilliant architects and faithful servants. "You will ask me I suppose what is become of my patriotick virtue? It is that which most ardently calls for your return. I greatly fear that the climate in which you now reside will prove fatal to your Life, whilst your Life and usefullness might be many years of Service to your Country in a more Healthy climate." Piling a selfless Roman wife onto a patiently waiting Greek queen, she signed the letter, "Portia."[18]

The following year she again tinkered with the Roman matron repertoire when she expressed her qualms to John about joining him in France. She had never left Massachusetts. Now she felt provincial, a guileless republican going like a lamb to slaughter into the gaudy courts of Europe. And while she longed to see John "upon the Stage of action," she also felt beleaguered by the continuous call to put aside her own personal desires and projects. The predicament recalled for her the story of the Roman matron Lucretia, chaste and simple, memorialized in a story told by Livy:

> Theory and practise are two very different things; and the object magnifies, as I approach nearer to it. I think if you were abroad in a private Character, and necessitated to continue there; I should not hesitate so much at comeing to you. But a mere American as I am, unacquainted with the Etiquette of courts, taught to say the thing I mean, and to wear my Heart in my countanance, I am sure I should make an awkward figure, and then it would mortify my pride if I should be thought to disgrace you. Yet strip Royalty of its pomp, and power, and what are its votaries more than their fellow worms? I have so little of the Ape about me; that I have refused every publick invitation to figure in the Gay World, and sequestered myself in this Humble cottage, content with rural Life and my domestick employments in the midst of which; I have sometimes Smiled, upon recollecting that I had the Honour of being allied to an Ambassador. Yet I have for an example the chaste Lucretia who was found spinning in the midst of her maidens, when the Brutal Tarquin plotted her distruction.[19]

Here Abigail does not say that she *is* the Roman matron Lucretia, only that her predicament recalls the "example" of Lucretia. Still, she seemed deeply invested enough in her identification with this vulnerable Roman matron that to pile another on top would be one too many: she does not sign this letter as Portia.

Abigail Adams embraced the fortitude and patriotism of the Roman matron Portia during the Revolution, but it remained for her an epistolary pose. Though the letters were in some senses public because in the eighteenth century the contents of such letters were often shared with trusted friends and family, she never made an effort to publish them. The case of her friend Mercy Otis Warren was far different. It shows how the increasing opportunities for female publication in magazines, proliferating by late century, allowed the republican Roman matron to evolve in new directions. Through Mercy Otis Warren the Roman matron moved from the private circle of letter writing to the new horizons of female publication.

Like Abigail Adams, Mercy Otis Warren of Massachusetts was deeply connected by blood and marriage to the revolution. Her husband and father were both involved, and her house was a meeting place for some of the radicals. Warren initiated the use of the pen name, "Marcia," in a letter to her husband, James Warren, in March 1775, and then began using it in letters to Abigail and John Adams. Marcia is probably a reference to the wife of the Roman statesman Cato the Younger, who, like Brutus, was an implacable foe of Caesar and during the eighteenth century lionized as a martyr to the republican cause. She dropped it just five years later, in 1780, after also briefly experimenting with other Roman matrons, like Cornelia, mother of the Gracchi. Warren was always less comfortable than Abigail Adams with her classical pen name, and she used it for less time, with less consistency, and only among a small circle of letter writers. She dropped it when her husband's political fortunes were declining, when they both felt that the republican values of the revolution were faltering, and when she became uncomfortable with the Roman ideal of utter stoicism such a posture required.[20]

Warren's identification with the Roman matron came less through her revolutionary letters than in the dramatic form of the Roman play. She published a series of plays during the revolutionary years, but one in particular, *The Sack of Rome*, brooded at length on the ideal of the Roman matron. Written in 1785 and published in 1790, it was a culmination of her dismal view of the trajectory of American republicanism. Throughout the Revolution, Warren had remained deeply fearful that the republican experiment would flounder without adequate vigilance against those notorious acids of corruption, luxury, and faction. In the 1780s she was already voicing a growing fear that the "giddy multitude" was threatening hard-won American freedoms, and that Federalists would taint republican austerity with wealth and rank. Counting herself among what she called "antiFederals," she saw herself among a small band of holdouts for the Articles of Confederation, or what she called "free principles of the late confederation" among states. Warren poured out her anxieties in a letter to Catharine Macaulay in 1787 by telling her that independence was "almost annihilated by the views of public ambition and a rage for the accumulation of wealth by a kind of public gambling, instead of private industry."[21]

In choosing the medium of the "Roman play" for *The Sack of Rome*, Warren opted for a literary genre that had symbolic significance for her both as a woman and a republican. The so-called Roman play was a five-act tragedy written in the modern period but set in the Greco-Roman past. It had emerged in seventeenth-century Britain as a tool of republican opposition to monarchy. Such plays featured a cast of classical characters who dramatized how ideals of heroic, Roman stoicism might fruitfully interact with modern sentimentality to form a workable form of governance. Imported from England into the colonies, the genre of the Roman play became immensely popular, especially as republican sympathies intensified and colonists identified with favorite Roman heroes. The most popular British "Roman play" in America was Joseph Addison's tragedy *Cato*, first staged in 1713. It was George Washington's favorite play (he had it performed for his cold and hungry troops at Valley Forge), and it went through at least nine editions before 1800 in addition to its frequent public performances.[22]

The Sack of Rome hitched Mercy Otis Warren to a literary tradition thought to be especially republican and patriotic, but it was also her bid for a viable public voice as a woman. It cast her not just as the author of a drama, but as the *published* author of a drama. "I'll take my stand by fam'd Parnassus' side, / And for a moment feel a poet's pride," she declared of the play.[23] Well into middle age (she was now sixty-two), when other women of her generation were becoming grandmothers, Mercy Otis Warren published a play about nothing less than the fate of the new American republic.

What does Warren's Rome look like? In the grand republican tradition, she mapped the vices of nations onto the form of women, seeing the fall of nations as a decline into feminine vices of luxury and effeminacy. Her Rome is fifth-century Rome, a city corrupted from within by luxury and effeminacy and vulnerable on the outside to attacks by Vandal barbarians. Warren describes Rome as a place where virtue "reclined," leaving the city "faint and languid . . . in luxury's lewd lap." Recumbent Rome, contaminated by "soft, effeminate, luxurious sloth," was easy prey for the attack of the Vandal king based in Carthage, a city long identified as Rome's arch-enemy.[24] As in other Roman plays, virtuous women in *The Sack of Rome* are pawns of the political schemes of men but pillars of nobility and virtue nonetheless. Warren's heroines include Ardelia, the wife of a Roman citizen and "the first and fairest matron left in Rome," and Edoxia, wife of the murdered Roman emperor Valentinian, captured and enslaved by the Vandals.[25]

Putting aside the convention of using pseudonyms in published writing, Warren signed the play with her own name, "M. Warren." And though she dedicated the play to George Washington, whom she called a "hero" for leading the Continental army to victory, she also crowned herself with heroic literary laurels akin to Homer's by calling herself a "female bard" in the *Massachusetts Magazine* of 1790. She was, in a way, a Homer, so often viewed at this time as the father of Greek literature: she was the first American to publish a Roman play. Sometimes also set in Greece, the Roman play remained a thriving genre of literature in America well into the middle of the nineteenth century.[26]

THE ROMAN MATRON IN IMAGES

Portraits were also vehicles for alluding to the ideal of Roman matronhood in revolutionary America. As with Roman pseudonyms in letters, women took pieces of an existing classical framework and joined them into something quite new. In his "Discourses on Art," delivered to the Royal Academy in 1776, the English painter Joshua Reynolds had recommended that a "Lady" signal her "dignity" by avoiding what he called "modern dress" and by appearing instead in a style that he called "antique." For some women, as chapter one showed, this meant posing as an Oriental sultana, but in the early 1770s another form of portrait dress emerged that was less Oriental than Roman. It first became fashionable among elite women in England in the 1770s, and then entered the repertoire of formal portraits of elite American women up and down the colonies. The Roman portrait dress appeared in paintings made in New England (by John Singleton Copley), the mid-Atlantic (by Charles Willson Peale), and South Carolina (by Henry Benbridge).[27]

That it appears frequently in the portraits of women married to well-known patriots suggests that "antique" dress was, in part, a self-conscious act of revolutionary self-fashioning by American women, an identification with the austerity of Rome rather than the luxury of the Turk. However, so little evidence remains about women's reasons for sitting for such portraits, that such conclusions must remain somewhat speculative. The contrasts with the earlier *turquerie* are nonetheless suggestive, though both styles inhabit the same loosely Mediterranean world of Reynolds's "general air of the antique." For one, there are no turbans or feathers: the hair, usually upswept, is either left uncovered or is cloaked by a thin, gauzy mantle that recalls the head coverings worn in public by respectable women of ancient Rome. The dress closes loosely at the front and is sometimes cinched by a cloth but not a "zone"-like girdle. The austerity is greater

than in the Oriental dress, but is not total because this is, after all, the idiom of elites. Lustrous pearls dangle from upswept hair and white under-
garments are sometimes trimmed in gold. But on the whole jewelry is
minimal. Vaguely classical artifacts often surround the women in these
portraits: a pedestal, a monument, a statue. These women do not recline
like the invertebrate sultanas of the 1760s and early 1770s, but either sit
or stand bolt upright. The idiom is sober, restrained, and dignified. It is
Roman.

Like the pseudonyms of Roman matrons adopted by some women,
these "antique" portraits clothed women in the garb of a political conversation in which they could not fully participate. Classical portrait dress
appears almost exclusively on women; male patriots usually appeared in
modern military regalia, even when paired with a woman in "antique"
garb. There were other differences, too. Unlike men, elite women robed
in classical gowns did not point to statues of Liberty or stand *ad locutio*, the
pose of the orator; nor did they pose as specific Roman matrons. All these
gestures would have been deemed overtly political and therefore
unbecoming of women.

The power of the Roman matron in portraits is in the vagueness of the
allusion, an ambiguity that kept these portraits within the bounds of female, apolitical propriety, while also infusing them with powerful, contemporary meanings in the social and domestic spheres. They were meant
to be seen by others in the immediate circle of acquaintances, suggesting
the revolutionary allegiance of a patriot's wife but not the political loyalties of the woman herself. Like the legal doctrine of *feme covert*, the garb
of the Roman matron connected women to the revolution through their
husbands. The subtlety and abstraction is what gave these images such
power at a time when women could not participate fully in the political
dramas of the revolution.

The inspiration for the new trend may once again have been that one-
woman Roman matron propaganda machine, Catharine Macaulay. Between 1764 and 1778 Macaulay posed for at least five portraits that cast her
explicitly as a Roman matron. One early image of Macaulay that reached
Americans was the frontispiece to the third volume of her *History* (1767),
which cast her in utter simplicity in classical profile bust, as though she
were on an ancient coin (see figure 6). The subject was as republican as the
artist: it was engraved by Giovanni Battista Cipriani, who, in league with his
English republican patron, Thomas Hollis of Lincoln's Inn, played an important role in forging America's republican iconographic lexicon in the
1760s. Deeply learned and disillusioned by what he thought was Parliament's
bumbling administration of the colonies, Hollis began doing whatever he

6. Catharine Macaulay appears here in a profile bust that evokes the coinage of ancient Rome. Frontispiece to volume 3 of Catharine Macaulay, *The History of England from the Accession of James I to that of the Brunswick Line* (London, 1767). Special Collections Research Center, University of Chicago Library.

could to promote a "Spirit of Liberty" in the colonies by printing and disseminated pro-republican medals, prints, books, and book bindings. The Cipriani image of Macaulay as a republican, Roman matron was a major force in popularizing this aesthetic mode for women.[28]

Other portraits of Catharine Macaulay also established the visual lexicon of republican, Roman matronhood for American women. An engraving labeled "Catharine Macaulay In the Character of a Roman Matron lamenting the lost Liberties of Rome," based on a painting by the English artist Catherine Read, appeared in the *London Magazine* of July 1770 in a review of Macaulay's work (see figure 7). The magazine is known to have been read by colonists in North America. The image showed Macaulay with a flowing gown and hair covered by a cloak—vaguely "antique" but here co-opted into the republican symbolic system of the Roman matron. In Boston, John Singleton Copley made two portraits that may have been influenced by Read's image of Macaulay as a Roman matron. One is the portrait of Sarah Henshaw (1736–1822), completed by Copley around 1770 (see figure 8). The other is the nearly identical portrait of Mrs. Elijah Vose (c. 1770–1772). Both show the modestly covered head evident in Read's engraving of Macaulay as a Roman matron, the uncorseted gown, and the loose cloak draped about the shoulders. Like other American Roman matrons, Sarah Henshaw's connection to the revolutionary movement was through her husband. She was the wife of Joseph Henshaw, a prominent merchant in Boston and member of the radical revolutionary group, the Sons of Liberty, whose members helped to propagandize British soldiers' shooting of five colonists in March 1770 as a Boston "massacre," an egregious British assault on American liberties. The Sons of Liberty regularly met in Sarah Henshaw's home.[29] Copley—fresh from half a decade of painting the Boston elite as Oriental sultanas—seemed to be suggesting in these two portraits a new aesthetic which was equally indebted to the idea of the "antique" but now with an emphasis on classical, perhaps Roman, robing.

Charles Willson Peale (1741–1827), portraitist to the moneyed mid-Atlantic, also turned to this Roman aesthetic in a few of his female portraits. Like Thomas Hollis, Peale was a staunch republican and an early generator of its imagery in the colonies. He freely combined portraits of the colonial elite with explicit, classicized pictorial allusions to his subjects' republican sympathies. In 1768 he painted a portrait of the British Whig statesman William Pitt, who defended the colonial resistance to the 1765 Stamp Act. Pitt is shown standing in Roman garb, gesturing *ad locutio* near a statue of the goddess Liberty. By the early 1770s Peale was painting the colonial elite as resisters of British tyranny. In 1770 he painted a portrait of the Maryland politician John Beale Bordley that recalled the Pitt portrait. Bordley gestures

CATHARINE MACAULAY

In the Character of a Roman Matron lamenting the loft Liberties of Rome from an Original Painting of Mifs Read.

Williams fculp.

7. Catherine Read, "Catharine Macaulay In the Character of a Roman Matron," *London Magazine* (July 1770). Courtesy, American Antiquarian Society.

8. This portrait of Sarah Henshaw may have been based on Catherine Read's engraving of Catharine Macaulay posing as a Roman matron. John Singleton Copley, *Mrs. Joseph Henshaw* (c. 1770). Museum of Fine Arts, Houston; the Bayou Bend Collection, gift of Miss Ima Hogg.

toward a female statue who represents English law, and who holds the pole and pileus (or cap) that represented Liberty. Bordley leans on a book opened to a page that says, "Notamus Legos Anglicae mutari" ("We observe the laws of England to be changed.") Peale also turned to classical, republican motifs in the domestic realm. Famous for naming his sons after great painters of the Renaissance (such as Titian, Rembrandt, and Raphaelle), Peale named one daughter Sophonisba, a princess of Carthage who kills herself rather than submit to Roman slavery. In the eighteenth century, Sophonisba became a byword for admirable opposition in the name of liberty. The character probably became famous from James Thomson's Roman play, *Sophonisba* (1730), a vehicle of Whig political opposition.[30]

In 1773 Peale may have adapted this classicized, republican register in his portrait of the wife of one of the earliest defenders of American liberty, the classically erudite lawyer John Dickinson (1732–1808). Educated at the family's Maryland tobacco farm by a Latin tutor, John Dickinson can be said to have truly lived his classicism throughout his life, and it is likely that he would have sought a modicum of classical compatibility in his wife. As a child he had amused himself by creating miniature models of the bridge over the Rhine that is minutely described in Caesar's *Commentaries*, and in addition to filling his publications with allusions to Greco-Roman antiquity, he published two series of letters under the pseudonym "Fabius" (taken from the Roman soldier and politician Quintus Fabius Maximus, who defeated the more powerful Carthaginian enemy not by pitched battle but through a gradual war of attrition). Synonymous with patience and moderation, the pseudonym "Fabius" was an accurate self-description of Dickinson, who was throughout his long political career the champion of moderation. He advocated this initially in his *Letters from a Farmer in Pennsylvania*, first published in colonial newspapers in late 1767, which defend American liberties against the Stamp Act while aiming for reconciliation with Britain. Dickinson nonetheless counted himself firmly in the ranks of patriots, played a leading role in revolutionary politics, and served under arms during the revolutionary war.

In 1770 he married the Quaker Mary Norris (1740–1803), daughter of Isaac Norris, a wealthy Philadelphia merchant and speaker of the Pennsylvania assembly. Even by the standards of elite Pennsylvania Quakers, who cultivated a relatively high level of humanistic learning in their daughters, Mary Norris enjoyed unusual access to classical texts. Isaac Norris had been an energetic book collector and at his death in 1766 bequeathed not just his estate, Fairhill, but also his extensive library of over 1,500 books to Mary. The library was filled with scientific, medical, and legal texts, and also with classical favorites like Tacitus, Thucydides, and Cicero, a number of them in French translation. Mary Norris had ample access to this library of classical translations, one of the largest in the colonies at the time, although she does not appear to have left her ownership mark on any of the books.[31]

Peale completed Mary Norris Dickinson's portrait in 1773, when the relationship of the colonies to Britain was deteriorating rapidly (see figure 9). The costume and props chosen for Mary (perhaps by Peale, by Mary herself, by John, or some combination) are suggestive of how the Dickinsons' patriotic politics were infused with a rigorous classicism. Mary Dickinson is shown in the loose, flowing, "antique" style that characterizes portraits of the wives of revolutionaries in this period. Her scarlet gown hangs loosely around her body; her sleeves are cinched up at the elbows; her upswept hair is veiled by a gauze of white, and the only jewelry is a strand of tiny pearls at her neck. She smiles and cradles her baby daughter on a classical pedestal, which depicts a veiled classical figure approaching a goddess.[32]

In South Carolina elite women turned to the visual imagery of the Roman matron in their portraits as well. The portrait painter Henry Benbridge (1743–1812), whose canvases form a roll call of the revolutionary Charleston elite, was possibly the most prolific painter of revolutionary women in "antique" poses and garb. Benbridge had studied in Italy in the late 1760s, filling a book there with sketches of draped classical figures he had seen on gems, vases, and in architecture. As did Peale, Benbridge supported the revolution and painted a number of patriots in their modern military regalia. But for their wives he chose the garb of Greco-Roman antiquity: there appear to be at least nine paintings of this kind made in the 1770s and 1780s.[33]

In a few cases, the vague allusion to classical antiquity becomes much more specific and more clearly Roman. Benbridge's portrait of Sarah Middleton (1756–1784) in the garb of an ancient Roman woman is a case in point (see figure 10). Sarah Middleton was the daughter of Henry and Mary Williams Middleton of Middleton Place. The Middletons were among Charleston's wealthiest and most politically influential families; they owned twenty plantations and 800 slaves.[34] Sarah Middleton's eleven siblings included Arthur Middleton, later a member of the Continental Congress and signer of the Declaration of Independence, and Thomas Middleton, who served prominently during the revolutionary war and later in politics. Born to the political elite, she married into it as well: the portrait was made on the occasion of her marriage in September 1773 to Charles Cotesworth Pinckney, son of the classically erudite Eliza Lucas Pinckney.

There is no record of Sarah Middleton's role in crafting this scene: she was just seventeen, and she died eleven years later, after four back-to-back pregnancies on top of tuberculosis. It seems likely that other family members would have influenced the choice of costume and setting for such a youthful sitter, appealing at once to familial and political objectives. (Perhaps even Sarah's formidable mother-in-law was involved in swathing her latest young relative in the noblest garb of an antiquity she herself had cherished as a young woman.) By the year of his marriage, Charles was deeply embroiled in the patriotic cause, and the painting is a pastiche of ancient Roman details and elite southern political and cultural aspirations.

9. Charles Willson Peale, *Mrs. John Dickinson [Mary Norris Dickinson] and Her Daughter Sally* (1773). Courtesy of the Historical Society of Pennsylvania Collection, Atwater Kent Museum of Philadelphia.

10. Just seventeen years old, Sarah Middleton poses here in the garb of a Roman matron in a portrait made around the time of her marriage to the South Carolina patriot Charles Cotesworth Pinckney. *Mrs. Charles Cotesworth Pinckney (Sarah Middleton, 1756–1784)*, by Henry Benbridge (American, 1743–1812). Oil on canvas, Gibbes Museum of Art/Carolina Art Association, 1990.18.

Sarah's unstructured, white Roman-style tunic is simple and noble, with royal blue trimming and gold bodice luminous against her pearly skin. She holds open a book of handwritten script that reveals the elegant, studied penmanship prized by women of her station. The book is in manuscript rather than a published text; this suggests that her literary accomplishment is of the becomingly feminine variety, and that she read and wrote in the female world of unpublished manuscripts rather than in the more masculine world of print. She rests her chin on her hand. It is a pose that recalls the attitude of a Sibyl, a prophetess from antiquity known to Benbridge through paintings of sibyls by Benjamin West (1762), which hung in Philadelphia at this time and that Benbridge may have seen. Benbridge may have known of sibyls also through Anton Raphael Mengs (1760), from whom Benbridge had received advice on painting during the period of his Italian training from 1765 to 1770. By posing her as a sibyl, Benbridge would have simultaneously flattered the sitter and reminded his patrons of his cosmopolitan artistic training.

The background is as significant as the sitter. In the dimly lit distance stands a round Roman temple that was becoming familiar from prints on cloth and paper in the revolutionary period when it appeared labeled as the "Temple of Liberty" or the "Temple of Virtue." It could have these revolutionary associations here, but more likely it is meant to suggest the cosmopolitan classicism of South Carolina's leaders. By the early 1700s elite planters like the Middletons had begun to import English gardening styles as a reminder of aristocratic culture. In the garden of the Middleton plantation was an early colonial example of a round Roman temple, espied approvingly by Eliza Lucas one day in 1743 as she approached the house. The rounded, Roman form was also a reminder of the temple of Tivoli (also known as the temple of Sibyl), a Roman temple in Italy that became a sure-fire stopping ground for European and American aristocrats on the Grand Tour. Charlestonians, in fact, became some of the earliest American promoters of the Grand Tour tradition. Sarah Middleton had not been on the Grand Tour; neither had Elizabeth Allston Gibbes (1766–1806), another of Benbridge's "Roman matrons" pictured in front of this temple. The temple is entirely the creation of the artist, chosen for reasons of culture rather than documentary accuracy. It would have suggested the British aristocratic infatuation with the Grand Tour to the Charleston *bon ton*.[35] Whatever the specific reference, Henry Benbridge's portrait of Sarah Middleton in the garb and landscape setting of a Roman matron is a magnificent window onto the many political and cultural aspirations of South Carolina's elite patriot society on the eve of revolution.

11. In this painting of the Izards in Italy, Alice Delancey Izard shows her husband her sketch of the statue group in the background, known as "Papirius Praetextatus and His Mother." John Singleton Copley, American, 1738–1815. *Mr. and Mrs. Ralph Izard (Alice Delancey)*, 1775. Oil on canvas. 174.6×223.5 cm (68 ¾ ×88 in.) Museum of Fine Arts, Boston. Edward Ingersoll Brown Fund, 03.1033. Photograph © 2007 Museum of Fine Arts, Boston.

The grandest portrait of an elite Southern woman enmeshed in classicized revolutionary politics is John Singleton Copley's double portrait of the Charleston planter Ralph Izard and his wife, Alice Delancey Izard, she who read her Rollin in French (see figure 11). The portrait shows the couple in Rome, where they had gone to collect art and to view antiquities, and where Ralph Izard became Copley's first patron in Europe. The portrait is unusual in showing a woman on the eighteenth-century Grand Tour (at this early date mostly men went), and could be seen as a testament by Ralph Izard to the exceptional education and opportunities enjoyed by his wife. She may have been pleased to accompany him to Rome to view antiquities when so few American women did, but Alice Izard adhered to conventional ideals of female submission. "The rank of a good Woman in Society leaves her little to complain of," she wrote to her daughter. "She frequently guides, where she does not govern, & acts like a guardian angel." For his part, Copley was just now moving beyond the confines of provincial America and was eager to show off his mastery of classical figure drawing. He positioned the couple in front of a menagerie of classical details: an ancient Greek urn, the Coliseum, and a statue group.[36]

The statue group is significant. Although she is not dressed in classical garb, Alice Delancey Izard may be making a claim for ideals of Roman womanhood to her patriotic husband in several overlapping ways. The painting captures her in the act of handing Ralph Izard her sketch of the statue group in the background (though he seems to be looking away). The subject of the group was appropriately demure: it was known as "Papirius Praetextatus and His Mother," and it was based on the parable of a young man who refuses to divulge Senate secrets to his mother, an act for which he is rewarded by the Senate. Alice may have learned to draw from James Ferguson's *Art of Drawing in Perspective* (1755), the 1775 edition of which is listed as one of the books in the Izard family library. Aside from the subject matter, her sketch would have been seen as a badge of her feminine "accomplishment" of classical figure drawing. In the eighteenth-century aesthetic hierarchy, drawing from the antique was considered less exalted than drawing from life. As such it constituted an appropriate outlet for women's allegedly inferior artistic abilities, which were thought to be imitative rather than original. By contrast with Alice Izard's merely imitative drawing of the statue in the background, Copley has shown his masculine mastery of rendering from life, and he literally paints over Alice Izard's drawing.[37] So, on the one hand a woman's classical sketch is at the center of this magnificent painting, a sketch that signals her elite female accomplishment and, perhaps, her ideals of Roman matronly submission; but, on the other, the scene has been captured by the virtuoso hand of Copley actually drawing from life as befitted the superior artistic talents apparently bestowed upon men.

ROMANS BUT NOT MATRONS

Classical learning and marriage to a patriot steered some women toward the quasi-domestic, quasi-political project of identifying with Roman matrons. But what about classically learned women who did not identify as

Roman matrons? Two women from the revolutionary period suggest that women could engage deeply with classicism and revolutionary ideology without taking on the wifely identity of the Roman matron. One was the New Jersey poet Annis Boudinot Stockton (1736–1801), whose husband, Richard Stockton, was an ambivalent patriot, late to join the cause. The other was the Philadelphia poet Hannah Griffitts (1727–1817), who never married. Both show how a woman could find in the language and exemplars of Roman antiquity a way to connect to a political and military revolution without latching on to the marital corollary of the Roman matron.

Annis Boudinot Stockton was particularly well suited to viewing the revolution in classical terms. She learned reading and writing from her brother's tutor and was soon writing neoclassical poems, circulating these as manuscripts among her accomplished literary circle of men and women. In 1757 or 1758, she married Richard Stockton and moved to his family's estate near Princeton. She renamed it Morven after an ancient Scottish ballad and proceeded to model the grounds on the famous English gardens at Twickenham owned by her poetic idol, Alexander Pope. Pope had poured the profits from the sale of his *Iliad* into a lush arcadia dotted with classical statuary, temples, and grottos that recalled those mentioned in Homeric epics. Richard Stockton once returned from England with sprigs of plantings for his wife's revival of Twickenham. Annis Stockton also deeply admired Catharine Macaulay. "The Muse salutes thee as the females pride," she wrote admiringly in a poem composed around the time of Macaulay's trip to the United States.[38]

But unlike Abigail Adams and Mercy Otis Warren, Annis Stockton was married to a man deeply ambivalent about joining the revolutionary cause. Part of this was a function of geography. New Jersey, unlike Massachusetts, was not a hotbed of early radicalism, and Richard Stockton, a favorite of the royal governor and a member of the landowning gentry, held out for moderation and reconciliation. Eventually he threw his hand in with the revolutionaries, and Annis seems to have followed him. During the revolution, Annis Boudinot Stockton's poems praising the military victories of George Washington appeared in a number of magazines under the pseudonym "Emelia." The poems compare Washington's military successes to those of ancient Roman and Greek heroes. "The Vision," published in the *Gazette of the United States* in 1787, helped to establish Washington as the Roman hero Fabius, one of the Roman generals who helped to defeat the Carthaginians in the second Punic War. The pseudonym became a favorite thereafter and was used by admirers of Washington like Alexander Hamilton and Parson Weems.[39] But her pseudonym "Emelia" was not obviously connected to the republican female worthies of the

Greco-Roman past. Her husband's reluctance to join the revolutionary movement is perhaps a reason why she did not latch on to a more resonant Roman pseudonym, as Abigail Adams and Mercy Warren had done. "Emelia" was, that is, a poetic rather than wifely identity. Stockton went public as a classically erudite woman, not as a republican, Roman matron.

And then there was Hannah Griffitts, one of a group of eighteenth-century literary women in the Philadelphia area. The coterie also included Susanna Wright (1697–1784), Elizabeth Graeme Fergusson, and Milcah Martha Hill Moore (1740–1827). Women in this group encouraged one another's literary efforts through the exchange of letters, unpublished prose and poetry, and personal visits. Like many other literary exchanges of this era, it was a conversation imbued with neoclassical literary forms and motifs cultivated through the women's reading of Alexander Pope and other eighteenth-century writers. In contrast to other women in this circle, Griffitts never married. She devoted her life instead to her poetry and to caring for female relatives, some of whom were also unmarried. She was not atypical among Quaker women for whom marriage and motherhood did not loom to ideals of womanhood as centrally as for other groups. In an undated letter to Milcah Martha Moore, Griffitts wrote, "There are many of you wed[d]ed ones who I believe are Placed in your (Proper) Sphere [and] I sincerely wish you encrease of Hap[p]iness in it without envying you one atom . . . everyone is not fitted for the single Life, nor was I ever moulded for the wed[d]ed one."[40]

Elite Quaker culture in the middle of the eighteenth century encouraged female humanism. The sect's emphasis on the spiritual equality of men and women made Quakers in the Philadelphia area more receptive to the idea of female learning.[41] Evidence of the education received by Hannah Griffitts is scanty, but the poetry she wrote during her long life suggests her immersion in the culture of neoclassical literature and reveals a tendency to view her life through classical categories. She frequently used the neoclassical pseudonym "Fidelia" in the poetry she wrote to her friends, and she deployed the customary poetic references to classical antiquity. She deeply admired the English translator of Epictetus, Elizabeth Carter, who like Griffitts never married. Griffitts made copies of Carter's poems and even wrote one extolling Carter's virtues.[42]

Griffitts viewed the events leading up to the revolution through the lens of classical history and literature. As was the case with many other Quakers, her political sympathies lay somewhere between revolutionary radicalism and loyalism. While invoking the nine muses of Greek history to praise the British politician William Pitt for opposing the Stamp Act, she also resented the extremism of Thomas Paine's *Common Sense* (1776). In a poem entitled "The female Patriots" (1768) she urged that the "Daughters of Liberty, nobly arise" so that by their example of wearing homespun cloth women "point out their Duty to Men." She also explicitly compared the colonial advance to Roman history. In a poem entitled, "Beware of the Ides of March," she urged the British Caesar who passed the unpopular Tea Act of 1773 to mind the Marcus Brutus of the colonies who opposed this parliamentary action.[43]

But like Annis Boudinot Stockton, Griffitts did not take on the pseudonym of a Roman matron, though she, on occasion, expressed her feelings about her lifelong spinsterhood in classical terms. She addressed at least two of her poems, which explained her reasons for wishing to remain single, to Sophronia, a Roman woman who was said to "hate men" and "love Greek" so much that she never married. It is clear that the Roman matron suited some women and not others.

Amid the widespread appeal to the republics of classical antiquity that shaped colonial opposition to Britain in the 1770s came a new, nascent political voice for a few elite women. The figure of the Roman matron—dignified, stoic, and selfless—had long been familiar to American women from literature and engravings. The revolutionary crisis caused a few educated American women to transform this literary figure into one with urgent political and familial meanings. Though they were denied direct access to political power, elite women found that the Roman matron could give them a political voice through close, familial connections to patriotic leaders. But ultimately the early use of the Roman matron was confined to a few highly educated women with close connections to the patriot elite. In the decades after the revolution women's classical conversation opened up far more broadly to include a bewildering variety of Greco-Roman women and a whole array of new political concerns, to which we will turn in the next chapter. But the door to these new possibilities had been opened by the Roman matron.

THREE

DAUGHTERS OF COLUMBIA, 1780–1800

"These, ye lovely daughters of Columbia, are amongst *your* patriotic duties!" intoned William Smith at a fourth of July celebration in Charleston, South Carolina, in 1796. "And tho' you are excluded from participation in our political institutions, yet nature has also assigned to you valuable and salutary rights . . . To delight, to civilize, and to ameliorate mankind!" Seldom had one person so clearly enunciated the utterly nebulous character of women's rights and duties in the new republic, the ill-defined revolutionary legacy to a new generation of women born in the 1750s and 1760s, the "daughters of Columbia." The term was coined in the 1780s, accompanied by an exuberant iconography of this invented classical goddess. The daughters of Columbia experienced in the formative stages of young adulthood the wrenching transformations of the American Revolution, but they found that nationhood raised more questions than it answered. As Smith so blandly asserted, they were "excluded from participation in our political institutions"; if so, what indeed were their rights and duties (beyond delighting and civilizing mankind), and did these differ from those of men?[1]

As the Roman matron had given a few women in the revolutionary years a voice for articulating political questions, a new set of classical women gave the daughters of Columbia a framework for discussing women's role in the new republic. In contrast to the revolutionary years, when the discussion had been mostly a private conversation in letters, now an exuberant print world of magazines and books—and a highly literate female population—pushed the classicized conversation about women and republicanism into public view.[2]

Three figures especially stand out in popularity: the women of Sparta, the figure of Roman charity, and Venus. But they were not prim exempla, resurrected intact for modern admiration. They were Trojan horses, familiar classical forms concealing difficult questions. Could women be patriotic, and if so, how—by bearing arms in defense of the nation or supporting the men who did? Here the women of Sparta—seen as warriors or mothers of warriors—set the terms of the debate. With egalitarian rhetoric on the rise, what were women's duties to fathers as opposed to obligation to husbands? For this question, the peculiar figure of Roman charity, a young mother who nursed her own aging father, engaged Americans' attention. Finally, in a republic built on the reasoned consent of the governed, what should be the place of passion, and those people and things that fired it? For this last question, Americans repeatedly invoked the beautiful figure of Venus in words, images, and sculpture.

Before turning to these three major classical conversations, we can look at how two daughters of Columbia—one southern, one northern, and both classically erudite—confronted the changed post-revolutionary political and familial order. Martha Laurens Ramsay (1759–1811) of Charleston, South Carolina, and Judith Sargent Murray (1751–1820) of Gloucester, Massachusetts, were born at opposite ends of the British North American colonies and moved in different political and social circles. They never met. But both were affected by the changes brought by the revolution, and both left behind a rich record of the classically imbued female mind confronting the *novus ordo seclorum.*

As the daughter of Henry Laurens, one of the most prosperous merchant-planters in the colonies, Martha Laurens received an excellent education. She was a quick study, learning to read at the age of three, and her parents indulged her talents. As her husband explained in his edited collection of her papers, "The Latin and Greek classics, she had read in translations at a very early period. By catching from her brother, by studying occasionally his Latin grammar, and books; and by the aid of an accurate knowledge of the French language," she acquired some knowledge of classical history and literature, and appears to have known some Latin and the *koine* ("common") Greek of the New Testament. She combined this erudition with a deep Christian piety. Martha spent the decade between 1775 and 1785 in France and in England, where her father was posted on diplomatic business. In 1787, when she was twenty-eight years old, she married the South Carolina physician David Ramsay, who clearly adored his intelligent wife and eagerly sought her advice and help with his published work. It was the kind of relatively more egalitarian marriage that would be idealized in the late eighteenth century, especially in the wake of republican revolution. Together the couple had eight surviving children, and, Martha once again showed herself to be a woman of her time by nursing them all in keeping with the most up-to-date childrearing literature.[3]

Ramsay deployed her considerable intellect and education in ensuring the classical erudition of those children. Her husband relayed the details of her pedagogy in admiring tones. "She prepared questions, on the most interesting portions of ancient and modern history; particularly Asiatic, Roman, English, and biblical history." So exacting were her lessons that she had to prepare her own aids to study, three packets of "historic questions of this kind, which were her text book, in examining her children, when reading historical work." A fan of the eighteenth-century English translator of Epictetus, Elizabeth Carter (Martha read her biography late in life), she attended to the latest methods in classical education for children. For all of her children she "ran over the Latin and Greek classics, in the short method recommended by Mr. Locke." Only with her sons did she read the New Testament in Greek; with her daughters she read French. This last concession to the social convention of educating boys and girls differently in the classics was a product of her deeply held beliefs about the place of women. According to her husband, "she was well acquainted with the plausible reasonings of modern theorists, who contend for the equality of the sexes, . . . but she yielded all pretensions on this score, in conformity to the positive declarations of holy writ."[4] For Martha Laurens Ramsay, classical learning melded thoroughly and seamlessly with a commitment to wifely subordination and especially to filial piety toward her father, as laid out in the Old Testament.

Eight years older than Martha Ramsay, Judith Sargent Murray had a radically different perspective on the place of women in society, and she became the first American woman to recast age-old classical tropes for an agenda of equality between the sexes. Like Ramsay, she was born into the social elite, the oldest of eight children of a prosperous Massachusetts merchant and ship owner. Aware of her abilities early on, her parents allowed her to be tutored alongside her brother as he was prepared for Harvard. What they learned is unclear, but it is likely that Latin and Greek formed part of this curriculum, since the languages were required for entrance into Harvard. It is certain that Judith Sargent Murray's published writings show evidence of reading in classical literature and history, if only in English translation.[5]

Murray had grand public ambitions to be "*independent as a writer*," and her second husband, John Murray, supported her endeavors. In 1789 she began contributing her work to the *Massachusetts Magazine,* a Boston monthly published between 1789 and 1796. The magazine became a forum for the literary excursions of some of the first published female authors in America, including Mercy Otis Warren and Sarah Wentworth Morton (1759–1846), later known as the American Sappho for her poetic talents. Writing under the common eighteenth-century classicized pseudonym "Constantia," Murray contributed essays that challenged the commonly held notion that intellectual disparities between men and women were rooted in nature, mustering classical and biblical exempla to make her point. In contrast to the traditional piety of Martha Laurens Ramsay, Murray adhered to the tenets of Universalism, introduced into the colonies in the 1770s. Condemning atheism, she saw Christian faith as complementary to human liberty and the separation of church and state. The pseudonym "Constantia" seems to have been a fusion of her classicism and Universalism. In 1791 she gave birth to a daughter, Julia, whose education she hoped would not be confined by traditional prejudices. She took Julia to the theater in Boston, at a time when this still raised eyebrows. Murray jealously guarded her claim to the pseudonym "Constantia." When Sarah Wentworth Morton also began contributing essays to the *Massachusetts Magazine* under the same pseudonym, Murray publicly battled her in the pages of the publication until Morton backed down and used "Philenia" instead.[6]

Rising literacy levels, increasing numbers of magazines and books, and a widespread cultural familiarity with Greco-Roman antiquity opened a new world to the daughters of Columbia after the Revolution. Whether as radicals such as Murray, or traditionalists such as Ramsay, women found ways to explore new questions generated by republican revolution through familiar female classical figures. These conversations took place alongside the proliferation of icons like Liberty and songs about Columbia that seemed often to exclude women while celebrating the brotherly bonds of republican men. The motto of newly founded all-male Union College (1795), its words framing a bust of Minerva, read, "Nous devenons tous frères sous les lois de Minerve."[7] But next to this exclusionary conversation flourished an inclusive one—by women, for women—as women entered the public forum of print to discuss their place in the new Rome.

THE WOMEN OF SPARTA

Could women be patriots? Could they be as attached to the state as their male counterparts, and on what terms? For Americans in the revolutionary and early national periods, it was clear that military service—taking up arms in defense of the nation—was one of the chief determinants of that essential republican trait, patriotism.

It is easy to see why the willingness to bear arms loomed large in the American consciousness in the decades after the revolutionary war. The American Revolution had been more than a political revolt against Britain. The long war, stretching from the first shots fired at Lexington and Concord in 1775 to the Yorktown campaign of 1781, had left over 25,000 soldiers dead. It was second only to the Civil War in military deaths as a proportion of the population. Like the Civil War, the revolutionary war touched a disproportionately high number of American families.[8]

Small wonder, then, that in the decades after the war Americans placed soldiering at the center of ideals of citizenship in the new nation. Renaissance humanists had helped to revive the ancient Roman view that soldiering was an essential act of citizenship, along with its corollary, that citizens made the best soldiers. As historians, Fourth of July orators, and veterans' organizations like the Society of the Cincinnati glorified the revolution, they singled out in particular the battlefield triumphs of the revolutionaries. These encomiums frequently lumped three words together: *patriot, warrior,* and *hero.* The association suggested the mutual importance of these words for describing the ideal attributes of new republicans. George Washington exemplified all these qualities; he was repeatedly termed not just a "patriot" but a "hero" for leading the Continental Army. He deliberately fashioned his image as Cincinnatus, the Roman general who put down the sword and took up the plow.[9]

But where did women fit into this postwar mythologizing of heroes, warriors, and patriots? They had participated in the war as nurses, camp followers, boycotters, farm managers, and in a host of other capacities, but had not (barring a few spectacular exceptions) taken up arms as regular soldiers. Could they be patriots and even heroes, the most virtuous of all citizens in the republic, or would they always qualify for the secondary status of heroines of the helpmeet variety, symbolized by the patient spinning of Penelope as she awaited the return of Ulysses from the Trojan War? The "American Woman" who published a Philadelphia broadside in support of the war effort in 1780 invoked biblical and "Roman Ladies" to argue that only frailty, "opinion and manners" prevented women from joining men on the battlefield. Women's participation in the war effort, though essential to it, was confined to "building new walls, digging trenches with their feeble hands, [and] furnishing arms to their defenders."[10]

The problem of whether female patriotism should be expressed through soldiering peaked in the decades after the war. While Americans were making George Washington into Cincinnatus, the heroic warrior who forsakes the sword for the rural pleasures of the farm, they turned to the women of ancient Sparta to debate the questions of female soldiering and its relation to female patriotism. In the decade and a half immediately following the Revolution, the women of Sparta rose to prominence because they conjured up some essential questions in the new republic. To what degree did women possess the same rights and duties as men to serve in armed combat to defend the nation? Under what circumstances did military service defy their female "nature"?

For eighteenth-century Americans, the ancient Greek city-state of Sparta was a kind of honorary Rome, singled out for admiration because it was not roiled by chaotic democratic politics as ancient Athens was. In the archaic and classical periods, Sparta had been the most powerful city-state in Greece, a position its citizens had achieved through the relentless training of boys and men for the demands of essentially constant warfare. Spartan soldiers were the best trained in antiquity; their ferocity and courage in battle were legendary. Sparta had conquered the vast areas of land around it in Lacedaemon through sheer military might, reducing the people in those territories to the status of slaves, or helots. To secure their conquest and to quell rebellion, Spartans constructed a centrally controlled city-state that placed martial training and martial ideals at its core. Americans in the late eighteenth century deeply admired the selfless patriotism and austere manners of Spartan men. They also thought highly of Sparta's "most excellent political constitutions," as one magazine article in 1797 put it, a form of government that, in high Aristotelian style, balanced the interests of monarchy, aristocracy, and democracy. Glowing reports of Spartan society crop up in numerous published and private writings in America in the late eighteenth century, although these were tempered with the occasional expression of concern for the excessive power of the state in regulating private matters such as education.[11]

But what did American women specifically admire about the Spartans? First we have to ask how they knew about the Spartans. They appear to have gotten much of their information from the Greek historian Plutarch, whose charming and readable *Lives of the Noble Greeks and Romans* formed a staple of eighteenth-century men's reading and gradually became an acceptable part of women's reading. In addition to the snippets that appear in histories like Rollin, a number of English translations of Plutarch's *Lives* were available: Thomas North (1579), John Dryden (1683), and John and William Langhorne (1770). Already in the first half of the eighteenth century some elite American women had been reading Plutarch, and by the late eighteenth century, his *Lives* had joined the ranks of recommended reading specifically for women, aided by the excerpts that began to appear in magazines and books of ancient history for young women. One such recommendation appeared in the 1801 *Philadelphia Repository and Weekly Register*, a magazine aimed at both sexes with a masthead presenting a trumpet-blowing goddess trailed by a banner emblazoned with the words, "Reading Improves the Mind." In one story a man hides intellectual spinach among other literary confections by sneaking a copy of Plutarch's *Lives* into a package of novels and romances he sends to his beloved. Hester Chapone's influential guide for female education, *Letters on the Improvement of the Mind* (1772), also explicitly mentions Plutarch for women's instruction in the great heroes of antiquity, as does the *Flowers of Ancient History* (1804) of the Reverend John Adams, which commends Plutarch's "sound morality."[12] A sign of Plutarch's ascent into the ranks of respectable literature for young women is clear in an otherwise unremarkable portrait of a young girl made by the painter Erastus Salisbury Field in 1840. Titled *A Girl in Blue*, it shows a young girl proudly holding up a copy of *The Juvenile Plutarch*, first published in London in 1801 and in America in 1827. The book carried translations of Plutarch in English, rendering select favorite tales suitable for the interests of young children.[13]

One of Plutarch's lives in particular captured the attention of American women. This was his biography of the great Spartan lawgiver, Lycurgus, which American magazines zestfully reprinted. Here Plutarch relates the frankly astonishing social mores of Spartan men and women. Plutarch tells how Spartan women were essential to the military successes of Sparta. Lycurgus commanded Spartan maidens to prepare for battle as rigorously as boys did. Not only would this physical training help women bear strong sons, it would also help them look beyond feminine frivolity to the field of patriotism, of noble action and glory. Stripped naked, Spartan maidens wrestled, ran, and threw javelins and darts. All of this was done with great modesty. "As for the virgins appearing naked," Langhorne's *Plutarch* assured readers, "there was nothing disgraceful in it, because every thing was conducted with modesty, and without one indecent word or action." Indeed, it produced "simplicity of manners." Spartan women, Plutarch goes on, were encouraged to jeer at the cowardly and to praise the courageous. Because Lycurgus decreed that marriage existed for the sole purpose of producing strong soldiers, couples were allowed to find other spouses if the union proved infertile. The result—several times noted in American magazines and almanacs obsessed with relating the marital improprieties of the ancients—was a society free of adultery.[14]

Plutarch is ambiguous about Lycurgus's reasons for encouraging women to prepare for battle like men. On the one hand, he had a maternalist argument, saying that such exercises made their wombs bear stronger fruit while lessening the pain of childbirth. "*We are the only women that bring forth men*," says Gorgo, the wife of the Spartan king Leonidas. But just a few lines later Plutarch suggests that such martial exercises were also of intrinsic value: they gave women a taste of higher feelings, admitted them to the field of noble action and glory, and made them truly patriotic.[15]

This double potential of the women of Sparta carried over into revolutionary and early national America, where it led to two strands of conversation about the Spartan woman. First was the Spartan woman-as-warrior, who hoisted her shield and sword like any man. The second alternative was the Spartan mother, who bore strong sons so that she could send them into battle. Like so many other keywords in this period, the Spartan woman derived her appeal not in spite of her instability of meaning but because of it; she did not settle debate, but sparked it, channeled it, and gave it palpable shape.

We can begin with the Spartan woman as warrior. As a form of self-identification, the Spartan female warrior allowed women in the eighteenth century to express a kind of righteous belligerence normally unsuitable for women. Abigail Franks, writing to her husband in 1742 about a treasonous politician, tells him that "I am a Spartan, & would have him Suffer." In the revolutionary period, the Spartan woman as warrior might seem especially promising as a form of militant citizenship for American women; yet expressions of this strand of the Spartan woman are vanishingly few. One opponent of women's participation in the French Revolution was Annis Boudinot Stockton, who, in 1793, called upon American women to help George Washington deflect the French threat by taking up arms.

> Columbias *daughters* like the greecian dames
> Would grasp the helmet and enroll their name
> To be his guards and form a phalanx bright
> That soon would put your Sans Culottes to flight.[16]

The frightening category of armed woman was actually rather nebulous; it overlapped in Americans' minds with those other legendary female warriors, the Amazons. Classical scholars have pointed out that the Amazon myth circulated in ancient Greek society as a way to use gender to conceptualize central cultural fears. Amazons were often conflated with defeated foreigners, like the dreaded Persians, and acquired a complete ethnography that cast Amazon culture as an inverted version of ideal Greek culture. In late-eighteenth-century America, Amazons rose in the

American consciousness not just when women's roles in the new republic were under debate, but when it seemed that other places might also breed republics with political females. The remote jungles of South America came under scrutiny now, and some feared that they might hide "female republics," which was a concern reflected in the name of Amazonia itself. But the main fear was that republicanism would unleash a new kind of political, activist woman who would throw off traditional domestic constraints. Thomas Jefferson, stationed in Paris in 1788, dismissed militant women there as Amazons shamed by America's angels:

> Recollect the women of this capital, some on foot, some on horses, and some in carriages hunting pleasure in the streets, in routs and assemblies, and forgetting that they have left it behind them in their nurseries; compare then with our own countrywomen occupied in the tender and tranquil amusements of domestic life, and confess that it is a comparison of Amazons and Angels.[17]

Americans' profound ambivalence about militant Spartan womanhood was expressed in their reception of the French revolutionary assassin, Charlotte Corday, whom they categorized not as a Spartan woman-warrior but as a female Brutus because Brutus implied political rather than military opposition to tyranny. Corday had assassinated the Jacobin leader, Jean-Paul Marat, in 1793, an act that shocked Americans and was widely discussed in the American press. Philip Freneau's *National Gazette*—the highly partisan Republican newspaper of Philadelphia—gave a detailed account of the event in which Corday was described as the "Amazon" who carried Marat's head aloft on a pike. Charlotte Corday might have qualified as a Spartan warrior, but the American response to her was generally favorable because she was condemning what Americans also saw as Jacobin excesses. She might be what one American magazine called "violently patriotic," but this made her not Spartan but "greater than Brutus," an encomium first bestowed upon her by a French admirer and then reprinted in the American press in the first decades of the 1800s.[18]

So much for Spartan women as warriors, hoisting shields and pikes to stave off the enemy. Americans were much more enthusiastic about the second potential reading of the Spartan woman's military obligations to the state, the "Spartan mother." Since the early modern period, the Spartan mother had appeared in print and images as the woman who sends her son off to war with the injunction (again drawn from Plutarch) that he return either carrying his shield or dead upon it. The parable suggested that she valued courage in battle over all else, including the life of her son. In French art of the 1790s, when revolutionary France was often compared to Sparta, the Spartan mother appeared in four paintings at the Paris Salon. That gospel of eighteenth-century American classicism—Rollin's *Ancient History*—vacillates between praising the courage of Sparta's women for sending their sons into battle and wondering if the action contradicts some basic female nature, serving as a sign of the "inhumanity" of the mothers. "Some people admire the courage of the Spartan mothers," wrote Rollin, "who could hear the news of the death of their children slain in battle, not only without tears, but even with a kind of joy and satisfaction. For my part, I should think it much better, that nature should shew herself a little more on such occasions, and that the love of one's country should not utterly extinguish the sentiments of maternal tenderness."[19]

The mythologizing of the Spartan mother became especially prominent after the Revolution, as aging revolutionaries constructed a mythologized version of the events of their youths. David Ramsay, the South Carolina physician and husband of Martha Laurens Ramsay, wrote a history of the Revolution in his state published in 1785. Here he praised the wives of South Carolina soldiers as Spartans. They "conducted themselves with more than Spartan magnanimity" and could be found "cheerfully parting with their sons, husbands and brothers, exhorting them to fortitude and perseverance; and repeatedly entreating them never to suffer family attachments to interfere with the duty they owed to their country." Andrew Beers's almanac of 1811 relates the typical form of the story under the heading, "Spartan Matrons." Here he applies it directly to the American revolutionary era, comparing "Lacedaemonian ladies" to a Connecticut mother who sent five sons and eleven grandsons to battle. When asked if she worried that all sixteen might die, the "noble matron" responded, "I had rather . . . this had been the case, than that *one* had come back a coward." Similarly, the 1812 *Raleigh Register* printed a story about Mary Pruitt of Georgia, who, like her revolutionary forebears, sent eight sons into the military. "The heroic firmness, and public virtue of the Spartan females, is again realized in our day, and country. Let those who think lightly of female patriotism, read this and blush for shame."[20]

Judith Sargent Murray offered the most complete evaluation of the two potential readings of Spartan women in a series of essays on female abilities that appeared in the *Massachusetts Magazine* in the early 1790s. Although no record is left of Murray's precise classical reading, her publications show that she was a reader of Plutarch's *Lives* in English translation. She explicitly mentions Plutarch and even quotes him outright in her essays as a source of timeless wisdom ("The talents and the virtues are modified by the circumstances and the persons, but the foundation is the same"). For Murray, Plutarch's frequent reflections on the warlike women of Sparta appeared especially relevant to her own experiences during the revolutionary war. From her home in coastal Gloucester, Massachusetts, Murray often found the battles perilously close, and she learned of devastating losses nearby, like the sixty-two women in Connecticut who had been widowed in a single hour of fighting. The proximity to battle helps to explain why she began to ponder deeply the particular matter of female patriotism, soldiering, and heroism, three words she knit together in her published writing.[21]

Like Plutarch, Murray saw two possibilities for women's participation in the armed defense of the state, each of which could lead to patriotism and heroism. Murray examined these in a series of essays on the equality of the sexes, published in *The Gleaner* (1798), in which she alludes to Plutarch several times. On the one hand, the "daughters of Columbia" could be archetypal "Spartan mothers" by urging sons (and husbands) to courage in battle. Women's contribution to their state was to act as supporters from the sidelines, sources of moral influence on soldiers rather than belligerents themselves. "With clasped hands, and determined resolution, they have placed themselves in their paths, obstructing their passage, and insisting, with heroic firmness, on their immediate return to death or conquest! They have anxiously examined the dead bodies of their slaughtered sons; and if the fatal wounds were received in front, thus evincing that they have bravely faced the foe, the fond recollection of their valour has become a source of consolation, and they have sung a *requiem* to their sorrows!"[22]

On the other hand, having established women's claim to "heroic" service through Spartan motherhood, Murray immediately establishes another, more direct avenue for women's patriotism and heroism: the battlefield, where women fight enemies, rescue husbands, and save nations. "Women, in the heat of action, have mounted the rampart with undaunted courage, arrested the progress of the foe, and bravely rescued their besieged dwellings! They have successfully opposed themselves to tyranny and the galling yoke of oppressions! Assembling in crowds, they have armed themselves for the combat—they have mingled amid the battling ranks— they have fought heroically—and their well-timed and well-concerted measures have emancipated their country!"[23]

But was soldiering at odds with female nature? Murray was ultimately ambiguous about her answer to the question. She applauded the Spartan female warriors while also suggesting that they were shirking "natural" female roles. Murray's Spartan women saw that duty to the nation— patriotism—overrode private affection. But she also suggested that their essential "nature" was to be maternal, and that to be an arms-bearing patriot was something at odds with being a mother. "At the shrine of patriotism they immolated nature," she wrote of the Spartan women. "The name of Citizen possessed, for them, greater charms than that of Mother."[24] The first American woman to publish an analysis of classical soldiering in the context of modern republican womanhood, Murray nonetheless recoiled from the most radical implications of the Spartan woman, embracing the Spartan mother instead.

ROMAN CHARITY

Of all the real and mythological women of classical antiquity who formed a gallery of female worthies in the eighteenth century, Roman charity was the strangest of all. Her story is simple, and was relayed in Roman writings and even in paintings on the walls of Pompeii.[25] An old man in ancient Rome is condemned to starve to death in prison for defying the Roman emperor. The old man's adult daughter sneaks into the prison and secretly nourishes him from her breast for a year. The emperor, upon discovering this deception, is so moved by the daughter's filial piety that he frees the father from jail and showers the daughter with honors. As peculiar and even disturbing as this story may be, it was popular in the ancient world as an example of heroic filial piety and, in fact, underlay the medieval obsession with the lactating Madonna. Here was the physical embodiment of the milk of human kindness, the breast that nourished not just another person, but, by its exemplum of selfless charity, sustained all of humankind.

Revived in its original pagan form by Renaissance humanists, the story was popular in Europe and America. Among the reasons for its new prominence was that it cloaked in the inestimable authority of classical antiquity a series of imperial and familial relationships that were not only in flux but in crisis. Roman charity first emerged in the early modern Atlantic to describe the hierarchical relationships within new maritime empires, and then she gradually shifted in the American Revolution to become a story about human rather than imperial families. In the aftermath of revolution, she ultimately became a platform for one of the first articulations of women's equality in sensibility and intelligence.

Roman charity first became popular in the seventeenth and eighteenth century as a metaphor of empire, a modern novelty built from ancient sources. Though originally popularized by the first-century Roman moralist Valerius Maximus during the reign of the Emperor Tiberius, there is no evidence that the story was used for explicitly imperial purposes in ancient Rome beyond educating a new nobility in the arts of rhetoric or dutifully praising the imperial father. The imperial metaphor, then, was the invention of the early modern period. There was a long tradition, which stretched into the early days of Atlantic colonialism, of envisioning imperial relationships not only through the metaphor of parent and child, but specifically through the metaphor of the lactating woman. Here was a relationship that was literally about colonial production and consumption. The British politician Edmund Burke showed a typical use of the metaphor of Roman charity in a speech in 1775 favoring conciliation with the American colonies. Burke reminded his countrymen that America was not only a major market for British exports but also propped up the British economy with its own agricultural exports of wheat, corn, tobacco, indigo and rice. "For some time past the Old World has been fed from the New," he said. "The scarcity which you have felt would have been a desolating famine, if this child of your old age, with a true filial piety, with a Roman charity, had not put the full breast of its youthful exuberance to the mouth of its exhausted parent."[26]

Burke was presuming classical knowledge among his listeners, who had doubtless trudged through the likes of Valerius Maximus as boys. But his use of the lactation metaphor went further, making colonial relationships seem natural by clothing them in the language of families and nature. It also invoked the persistent conviction—stemming from the earliest days of English Atlantic ventures in the 1500s—that colonial relationships should be closed, self-sustaining systems. The English word, "system," emerged in the seventeenth century to describe both commercial relations and the physiological processes of living organisms. Empires were hierarchical families of parents and children; milk was the magically nourishing fluid that linked colony and metropole into a benevolent system of production and consumption. The point that center and periphery were linked by ties of kinship was made again—in reverse—in a print from the 1778 *Westminster Magazine* advocating conciliation between mother Britain and baby America (see figure 12). Here Britannia has tossed her shield aside to put her infant American colony to her breast. On the right sits Mentor holding an olive branch and teaching two children the advantages of peace.[27]

Roman charity also classicized the role of African and Indian women in the Atlantic economy. The productive bounty of the British colonies in the West Indies and North America depended heavily on female labor, a dependence cloaked behind rhetoric that insisted on the centrality of men's work and the passivity of females. The parable of Roman charity suggested that female lactation was a physiological process that required no labor whatsoever. Her milk miraculously appears in such quantities

12. This print supports conciliation between mother Britain and baby North America. Minerva/Britannia has tossed her shield aside to put her infant colony to her breast. Mentor sits at right, holding an olive branch and teaching two children the advantages of peace. Frontispiece of *Westminster Magazine* (1778). Library of Congress.

that it nourishes a grown man rather than a tiny baby with no apparent effort on her part. In this sense, Roman charity's imperial role also meshed with the most up-to-date views on the physiology of lactation promoted by philosophers such as Jean-Jacques Rousseau—the frontispiece of his popular work, *Émile* (1762), shows a nursing mother—and physicians like William Cadogan, whose influential *Essay upon Nursing* (1748) cast lactation as a bubbling spring flowing carelessly from the mother's breast: "It is poured forth from an exuberant, overflowing Urn, by a bountiful Hand, that never provides sparingly." The real maker of the milk was Nature herself; the mother was only her willing vessel. Created with no visible labor and dispensed with the eagerness and natural aptitude of a mother suckling her child, the milk of Roman charity was the ideal colonial product, the vital link that sustained and united the empire. It is not surprising that the image of Roman charity appeared in a number of colonial contexts. Indian women of North America were depicted as Roman charity, and in France, Jean-François Marmontel's illustrated book about colonial Peru features an illustration of an Incan woman offering her breast to the ailing Spanish Dominican friar Bartolomé de Las Casas (see figure 13).[28]

For Americans, the parable also resonated more immediately at the level of the family, guiding them on how to manage family relationships transformed by revolutionary ideology. The revolt against monarchical authority did more than displace a king; it gave encouragement to a longer-term trend of upending the familial authority of patriarchs in general. It was not just a question of how fathers should relate to sons, but how they should relate to daughters. Advice manuals jumped in to fill the void: one of the best-selling books of 1775 was John Gregory's *A Father's Legacy to His Daughters*, still so revered in the late 1790s that Mary Willing, daughter of the wealthy merchant Thomas Willing of Philadelphia, chose to be portrayed holding Gregory's book in a portrait by Gilbert Stuart. Guidance in the father-daughter relationship may also have been known through Roman literary and legal sources. Although Americans operated under principles of British common law, they were fascinated by Roman civil law, and well-stocked libraries would have had relevant texts. In a tradition unique among ancient societies, Romans placed a great deal of importance of the father-daughter bond in elite families, seeing daughters as pivotal figures in kinship networks and indulging overt expressions of paternal affection for daughters. The statesman Cicero adored his daughter Tullia, and Cornelia was nearly as celebrated for being the daughter of Scipio as the mother of the Gracchi.[29]

Letters and diaries of elite American women from the late eighteenth century also suggest the influence of their fathers in their lives. On the

13. A model of Roman charity, an Incan woman offers her breast to the ailing Spanish Dominican friar Bartolomé de Las Casas. From Jean-François Marmontel, *Les Incas, ou La Destruction de l'Empire du Pérou* (1777). Bibliothèque Nationale de France.

one hand, fathers could be sources of unyielding authority. But in an age that denied women access to formal higher education, an exceptionally intelligent daughter's main hope for advanced learning was often through her father. There are many examples in this period of educated fathers who nurtured the most intimate emotional and intellectual ties with their daughters. But this filial loyalty also presented a problem at the point of marriage, when a loving daughter—in the act of fulfilling her highest duty by becoming a wife—inevitably suggested that her emotional and fiscal loyalties would shift to her husband. The relationship between Henry Laurens and his daughter Martha showed how a daughter's impending marriage could unsettle an authoritarian father who was intellectually and emotionally attached to her. Henry Laurens's influence on his daughter's life became central when his wife, Eleanor Ball, died in 1770 and left him with five young children. He adored what he called his "dear little Connections," but his was a difficult love, expressed in the manner of an eighteenth-century patriarch. He was deeply involved in Martha's education and sent explicit letters of instruction, from England, for the content of her studies on matters from grammar to handwriting. He was concerned—and frightened for the family fortune—when she told him she wanted to marry a much older man, a person Henry Laurens believed was a fortune hunter. While ruminating on what he knew of fathers and daughters in his social class, Laurens struggled to convince Martha not to marry. "All the Father's whom I have known disappointed in their prospects, by the indiscretion of their Daughters have in their first resentments been outrajeous & violent; I am not disposed to follow the examples." To his daughter's suitor, no fatherly indulgence was forthcoming, and he described his daughter as his property: "You deprive me of my dearest property by craft and subtlety. . . . I have *a right* to gratitude from my daughter, and want no claim on yours." The lovers were clearly cowed by his anger, and the relationship died. How different was this ungloved patriarchy from the marriage Martha Laurens ultimately made at age twenty-eight to the Charleston physician, the gentle widower David Ramsay. The relationship was still far from egalitarian; he was ten years her senior and assumed all the rights of any man upon marriage during the age of coverture laws. But he clearly adored his intelligent and accomplished wife, and they worked together on the histories he wrote.[30]

For all her classical learning, Martha Laurens Ramsay did not use the figure of Roman charity to describe this transition from patriarchal authority to relative marital egalitarianism, but her example illustrates a broader trend, helping to explain the popularity of this classical, mythological figure in American popular culture during the revolutionary period. During the late eighteenth century, Roman charity—recast under a new name, the Grecian daughter—featured in a number of broadsides and plays that have at their center the problem of a married daughter's conflicting duties to husband and father.

The first publication of the Grecian daughter in America was a broadside titled *Worthy Example of a Married Daughter* (1776), which rendered the parable in verse. It was reprinted, with varying illustrations, in broadsides in 1794 and 1798. These broadsides were joined by the first of many American productions of the British playwright Arthur Murphy's five-act tragedy, *The Grecian Daughter*, a play also performed and reprinted in the United States. First performed in London in 1772, it was revived in Annapolis and Baltimore in 1783, and a number of times in Philadelphia into the early 1800s, to repeated acclaim of its "sterling value." Set in ancient and imperialized Sicily and Syracuse, Murphy's tragedy pits the princess Euphrasia, a font of "filial virtue," against the cruel, usurping king Dionysus, who has imprisoned her father, the rightful king. The potentially shocking act of her nursing her father occurs offstage, and is only related to the audience by incredulous guards. Explaining her actions, Euphrasia simply says, "Nature and duty called me." The story concludes with the well-nourished father proclaiming her virtues to all:

> stretch the ray of filial piety to times unborn
> That men may hear her unexampled virtue;
> and learn to emulate THE GRECIAN DAUGHTER!"

Americans became even more familiar with the image of the Grecian daughter as time passed, as it moved from the stiff wood block print of 1776 to the full baroque sensuality of the 1798 version, which is a near replica of Peter Paul Rubens' painting, *Roman Charity* (1612) (see figures 14, 15, 16).[31]

Not just circulating widely in cheap prints and book illustrations, Roman charity also formed part of the gallery in elite homes and some early museums. Rubens' painting of Roman charity was, in fact, in the United States at the time, and was owned and lent out by the wealthy Belgian family, the Stiers, who were descendants of Rubens. The Binghams of Philadelphia displayed a full-length portrait of the actress Sarah Siddons as the Grecian daughter in their opulent home. Rembrandt Peale exhibited his enormous, doorway-sized canvas, *The Roman Daughter* (1811), at his Philadelphia Apollodorian Gallery of Painting (see figure 17).[32]

...thy Example
of
A married Daughter:

Who fed her Father with her own Milk, he being commanded by the
Emperor to be ſtarved to Death, and afterwards pardoned.

To the Tune of *Flying Fame*,

IN Rome, I read, a Nobleman
  the Emperor did offend,
And for that fault he was adjudg'd
  unto a cruel end ;
That he ſhould be in Priſon caſt,
  with irons many a one.
And there be famiſh'd unto death,
  and brought to ſkin and bone.
And more, if any one was known,
  by night, or yet by day,
To bring him any kind of food,
  his hunger to allay,
The Emperor ſwore a mighty oath,
  without remorſe, quoth he,
" They ſhall ſuſtain the cruelleſt death
  that can deviſed be."
This cruel ſentence once pronounc'd,
  the Nobleman was caſt
Into a dungeon dark and deep,
  with irons fetter'd faſt.
Where, when he had with hunger great
  remained ten days ſpace,
And taſted neither meat nor drink,
  in a moſt woful caſe,
The tears along his aged face
  moſt piteouſly did fall,
And grievouſly he did begin
  for to complain withal.
O Lord, quoth he, what ſhall I do,
  ſo hungry, Lord am I,
For want of bread, one bit of bread,
  I periſh, ſtarve and die,
How precious is one grain of wheat,
  unto my hungry ſoul,
One cruſt or crum, or little piece,
  my hunger to controul.
Had I this dungeon heap'd with gold,
  I would forego it all,
To buy and purchaſe one brown loaf,
  yea, were it ne'er ſo ſmall,
O that I had but every day,
  one bit of bread to eat,
Tho' ne'er ſo mouldy, black or brown,
  my comfort would be great,
Yes, albeit I took it up
  trod down in dirt and mire,
It would be pleaſing to my taſte,
  and ſweet to my deſire.
Good Lord, how happy is the hir'd,
  that labours all the day,
The drudging mule, the Peaſant poor,
  that at command do ſtay.
They have their ordinary meals,
  they take no heed at all,
Of thoſe ſweet crums or cruſts that they
  do careleſly let fall.
How happy is that little chick,
  that without fear may go,
And pick up thoſe moſt precious crums
  which they away do throw,

O that ſome pretty little mouſe,
  ſo much my food would be,
To bring ſome of the taken cruſt
  into this place to me.
But oh ! my heart, it is in vain,
  no ſuccour can I have,
No meat, nor drink, nor water eke,
  my loathed life to ſave.
O bring ſome bread, for Chriſt his ſake,
  ſome bread, ſome bread for me,
I die, I die for want of food,
  nought but ſtone walls I ſee.
Thus day and night he cried out,
  in moſt outragious ſort ;
That all the People far and near
  were griev'd at his report.
And though that many friends he had,
  and Daughters in the Town,
Yet none durſt come to ſuccour him,
  fearing the Emperor's frown.
Yet one of his Daughters dear
  .....he...
Who living in pleaſure great,
  for matching to his mind.
Although ſhe liv'd in mean eſtate,
  ſhe was a virtuous Wife,
And, for to help I .. Father dear
  ſhe ventur'd thus her life.
She quickly to her Siſters went,
  and of them did intreat,
That by ſome ſecret means they would
  convey their Father meat.
Our Father dear doth ſtarve, ſhe ſaid,
  the Emperor's wrath is ſuch,
He dies, alas, for want of food,
  whereof we have too much.
Pray Siſters, therefore uſe ſome means
  his life for to preſerve,
And ſuffer not your Father dear,
  in priſon for to ſtarve.
Alas, quoth they, what ſhall we do
  his hunger to ſuſtain,
You know 'tis death for any one
  that would his life maintain.
And tho' we wiſh him well, quoth they,
  we never will agree,
To ſpoil ourſelves, we had as leif
  that he ſhould die as we.
And Siſter, if you love yourſelf,
  let this attempt alone,
Though you do ne'er ſo ſecret work,
  at length it will be known.
Oh, hath our Father brought us up,
  and nouriſh'd us, quoth ſhe,
And ſhall we now forſake him quite,
  in his extremity ?
No, I will venture life and limb,
  to do my ...
The worſt that ... die,
  to fit a T...

With that in haſte, away ſhe hies,
  and to the priſon goes,
But with her woful Father dear
  ſhe might not ſpeak, God knows,
Except the Emperor would grant
  her favour in that caſe,
The keeper would admit no one
  to enter in that place.
Then ſhe unto the Emperor hies,
  and falling on her knees,
With wringed hands, and bitter tears
  theſe words pronounced ſhe ;
My hopeleſs Father, ſovereign Lord,
  offending of your Grace
Is judg'd unto a pining death,
  within a woful place.
Which I confeſs he hath deſerv'd,
  yet mighty Prince, quoth ſhe,
Vouchſafe, in gracious ſort, to grant
  one ſimple boon to me.
It chanced ſo I match'd my ſelf
  againſt my father's mind,
Whereby I did procure his wrath,
  as Fortune hath aſſign'd.
And ſeeing now the time is come,
  he muſt reſign his breath,
Vouchſafe that I may ſpeak to him
  before his hour of death.
And reconcile my ſelf to him,
  his favour to obtain,
That when he dies, I may not then
  under his curſe remain.
The Emperor granted her requeſt
  conditionly, that ſhe,
Each day ſhe to her Father came,
  ſhould throughly ſearched be.
No meat nor drink ſhe with her brought
  to help him there diſtreſt,
But every day ſhe nouriſht him,
  with milk from her own breaſt.
Thus by her milk he was preſerv'd,
  a twelve month and a day,
And was as fair and fat to ſee,
  yet no man knew which way.
The Emperor muſing much thereat,
  at length did underſtand
How he was fed, and not his law
  was broke at any hand,
And much admired at the ſame,
  and her great virtue ſhown,
He pardon'd him, and honour'd her
  with great preferments known.
Her father ever after that,
  did love her as his life,
And bleſt the day that ſhe was made
  a loving wedded Wife.

Sold at the *Bible & Heart*, in *Boſton*.

14. An American broadside titled *Worthy Example of a Married Daughter* (1776) shows a married daughter nursing her father through the bars of a prison. Online Early American Imprints, Series I, Evans: 1639–1800. Stanford University Libraries.

The parable as related in the three late-eighteenth-century American broadsides about the Grecian daughter emphasized one key aspect of the story: money, that most tangible symbol of love and duty. Before the father went to jail, he had been both "very rich" and on very bad terms with the Grecian daughter, who had married against his will. The wealthy father cut her out of his fortune, and the Grecian daughter and her husband were left in "mean estate." But the Grecian daughter was "a virtuous wife," and "to help her Father dear" consulted her sisters—her co-inheritors— about how to proceed. The sisters, fearing the wrath of the emperor and perhaps hoping for the father's untimely demise to recoup their share of the inheritance, advised her to stay home, as they had: "we would as soon / That he should die as we," they cried selfishly. Despite this advice, the Grecian daughter risked life and limb to help her father, or as she put it, "to reconcile myself to him / His favor to obtain." Thus saved from starvation, and pardoned by the emperor, the noble (and rich) father became more devoted to his daughter than ever and—most significantly—praised her marital state for rendering her virtuous. In the words of the broadside, he "bless'd the day that she was made / A loving wedded Wife." The masthead on the 1794 version explains the moral to children: "to be obedient to their PARENTS at all times, if they would hope for a Blessing on their spiritual and temporal Affairs notwithstanding many Parents may err in their Judgment respecting their CONNUBIAL AFFAIRS."[33]

Through the innovation of the Grecian daughter, revolutionary Americans pondered how filial piety could be reconciled with conjugal good. The new version of the ancient parable accurately described the lives of a new generation of American women, the daughters of Columbia, who had lived through the Revolution, who had navigated between demands toward patriarchal fathers, and also who had been attracted to a new ideal of marriage as a more egalitarian, republican institution.

It certainly described the life of Martha Ramsay. After becoming a wife and a mother, she ultimately mended fences with her aging father, Henry Laurens, just as the Grecian daughter did in the new American broadsides. In 1792, fearing that he might die from the latest in a long series of illnesses, she left her Charleston house for his nearby plantation, throwing herself into a carriage with her nursing baby and her favorite slave. Henry Laurens was glad she had come, and blessed her in the manner of a patriarch—by conversing "on indifferent matters"—before slipping into unconsciousness and dying a day later at the age of sixty-eight.[34] Martha could do nothing but watch: the miraculous milk of the Grecian daughter was, after all, the stuff of legend.

THE GRECIAN DAUGHTER.

15. This American broadside, titled *The Grecian Daughter* (1798), replicates the image in Rubens's *Roman Charity*. Courtesy, American Antiquarian Society.

But one woman took Roman charity a step further. As she had with the Spartan women, Judith Sargent Murray delved into new meanings for Roman charity at the radical fringe of women's republican thinking. She made concrete the ephemera of metaphor by arguing, in an essay published in 1791, that Roman charity illustrated the new idea that women had intellectual and moral capacities equivalent to those of men, that they had full access to the universal human reason promised by the Enlightenment. The persistent deficiencies exhibited by women were caused not by nature but by culture. And what better example was there of women's moral equivalence to men than Roman charity? In Murray's view, Roman charity showed that "in *every respect*" women were "equal to men":

> Filial duty—conjugal affection—persevering constancy—these receive in the female bosom the highest perfection of which they are, in the present state, susceptible. The young Roman, supporting her imprisoned parent by the milk of her own chaste bosom, if unparalleled in history, would yet, in like situation, obtain many imitators; and the feelings of a daughter would prompt, for the relief of the authors of her being, the noblest exertions.[35]

16. Pieter-Paul Rubens, *Roman Charity* (c. 1612). Oil on canvas. 140.5×180.3 cm. © The State Hermitage Museum, St. Petersburg.

Here then was a new claim for an old imperial metaphor. Roman charity now became a launching pad for women's access to the radically egalitarian legacies of revolution. For Murray, Roman charity was about access to reason, to heroic nobility of sentiment, to all of the qualities shared by republican Cincinnatus and Brutus.

VENUS (AND MINERVA)

In 1806 Nicholas Biddle (1786–1844) explained why classical art and ruins should not be viewed with women. "With females you can never see the whole of anything," wrote the dashing young Philadelphia merchant and aesthete, one of the first Americans to go to Greece for the purpose of visiting its antiquities. "The courtesies of society distract attention, & tho' many objects are seen more agreeably when seen with females, yet all are seen less profoundly & perhaps less usefully."[36]

No classical figure in early America illustrates the Biddle principle more clearly than Venus, whose beautiful shape seemed to distract attention like no other. We tend to think of Venus as a work of art, but in the

17. Rembrandt Peale, *The Roman Daughter* (1811). 1977.109. Smithsonian American Art Museum, Gift of the James Smithson Society.

eighteenth century she was also a political figure. If the Enlightenment was the age of reason, embodied by wise Minerva, it was also the heyday of reason's opposite: Venus, she of the passions and the flesh. Embodying ideal feminine beauty, she also personified the Enlightenment's major contradictions. Venus was the "natural" female body unadorned by corrupting artifice, but she was also the passion that threatened the reasoned consent on which the new American republic rested.

In the pages of early national magazines, American men and women debated the matter of passion and reason through the forms of Minerva and Venus, but it was a conversation that also had much to do with real women. The Venus conversation is notable for how it became a way for men to talk about women. This is not to say that women did not discuss— or even admire—Venus: they did, especially in a marriage market that put a premium on female youth, beauty, and fecundity. But the discussion had less of the quality of a shared set of mutual expectations, as had the discussion around the Roman matron of the 1770s. In the ever more inclusive public discourse of late-eighteenth-century classicism, the Venus conversation insisted that women naturally failed to possess the reason on which republicanism's consensual politics rested. It undermined their claim to a public presence and suggested that while their disembodied voices might now appear in public through the printed medium of books and magazines, their bodies were unwelcome on the senate floor, at the bar, and on the pulpit.

Americans had a long past with Venus, the goddess of beauty, love, and generation. For colonists deeply influenced by John Milton's *Paradise Lost* (1667), Eve had long been the model of feminine loveliness, the fountain of desire within marriage. Milton thought her a "perfect beauty," more radiant than a goddess. But there was still room left for Venus, who figured prominently in the all-purpose sex manual and midwifery guide, *Aristotle's Master Piece*, as the superintendent of sexual activity. In one image of a face in the book, her zodiacal symbol, the handheld mirror, bedecked the nose to show the ravages of syphilis, one of the "venereal" diseases that bore her name.[37] But Venus did not achieve widespread popularity until the early national period, when she rose up alongside Eve as a new model of feminine beauty. Venus could offer something more in a young nation that needed new narratives. Needing neither Adam nor garden, neither tree nor Fall, Venus offered a pleasing alternative to Eve's troubling trajectory. Lover to many, wife to no one, and mother of nations, Venus was womanhood emancipated from the narrative of sin, the empty vessel to be filled by republicans in the new Arcadia.

And fill they did. First, Venus was enrolled in a printed discussion about the proper role of republican women. The conversation took a number of forms. Sometimes Venus was the heroine, appearing as the doting mother of impish Cupid and as benevolent Nature juxtaposed to objectionable Artifice (especially in female dress). Just as often, however, Venus jeopardized Enlightenment reason and republican self-government. By suggesting that sexual attraction was fundamentally unpredictable and ungovernable, Venus endangered a republic built on men's reasoned consent. Votaries of Venus, wrote an anonymous contributor to the *Massachusetts Magazine* of 1794, had "passions" that should "soon be brought under the easy dominion of reason." As the incarnation of disarray, Venus was often cast as the frivolous opposite of brainy Minerva. In one essay in the 1807 *American Gleaner,* Minerva berates Venus for not teaching Cupid to read or write. The seat of Venus's charms lay not in her mind but rather at the center of her body, in her legendary girdle, the cestus of Venus, "Where centered all the power of love," as one magazine from 1794 put it. The cestus of Venus, also called a "zone," was envisioned as a portable garment, a veil of artificial seduction that women could borrow from the goddess and wield for their own romantic projects.[38]

When revolutionary Americans thought of Venus, they thought of one Venus above all others: the Venus de' Medici, the most venerated statue in America from the eighteenth to the mid-nineteenth century, when she was side-lined by the more athletic Venus de Milo, discovered in 1820 (see figure 18). The Venus de' Medici was an ancient Greek statue housed in the Uffizi in Florence, and it soon became one of the most copied statues of all time, and became widely known through casts and engravings. Her oxymoronic nickname, *Venus pudica* (modest Venus), reveals much about her appeal. Though entirely unclothed, she uses her arms strategically to conceal her breasts and pubic region. This gesture, what one writer in the *Monthly Anthology* of 1805 called the "modesty of the attitude," helped to sustain her popularity. On the one hand, it reflected her virtuous attempt to conceal her nakedness, while, on the other, it drew attention to those parts she apparently hoped to screen. It helped that her head (a different one than originally sculpted) was small, too; it confirmed what one American art critic called her "imbecility of mind."[39]

In statues, paintings, and prints, Venuses were especially prized by men, though exact numbers are difficult to come by since these prints and statues were by definition more private than others. A number of eighteenth-century men owned and circulated copies of Venus in the eighteenth century. The Boston painter John Smibert owned a cast as early as the mid-1750s; at the top of Thomas Jefferson's list for the statues he wanted at Monticello was a copy of the Medici Venus. The second Medici after Smib-

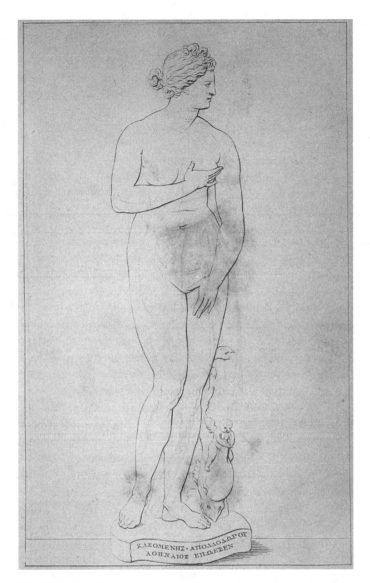

KΛEOMENHΣ · AΠOΛΛOΔΩPOY
ΛOHNAIOΣ EΠΩEΣEN

18. Although a few Americans would have seen statue copies of the
Venus de' Medici, a larger number would have known this favorite representation of the goddess from engravings like this one from 1818, which
circulated widely in the eighteenth and nineteenth centuries. The Library Company of Philadelphia.

ert's was brought to America in 1784 by Robert Edge Pine, and Charles Willson Peale borrowed it in 1795 to open his hall of casts in the new Columbianum or American Academy of Painting, Sculpture, and Architecture in Philadelphia. For the sake of propriety, it was kept shut in a case and only shown to people who particularly wished to see it.[40]

Prints dispersed the form of Venus more widely. Some hung in stately homes, like Mount Vernon, where two prints of Venus hung in the first floor passage to form a kind of visual intermission between the family portraits in the front parlor and the portraits of patriots that adorned the dining room. There seems to have been a lively private trade in Venus prints as well. "Mr. W. chose out two of our prints for which he is to give two others—Danäe and Venus," wrote Anna Maria Thornton (1775?–1865), wife of the Capitol designer William Thornton.[41]

Although women could see a Venus cast, painting, or engraving, these objects tended more often to be owned and circulated by men. When the Maryland plantation mistress Rosalie Stier Calvert (c. 1780–1821) ordered some statues from her native Belgium, she declared her preferences explicitly. "I should like so much to have two plaster casts for our north drawing room. Papa writes that they are all too indecent, but [people] have changed on that subject here. I should like to have one of the Apollo Belvedere and my husband says he must have the Venus de Medici sent too. . . . At all events, if the statues are such that I cannot put them in the drawing room, I shall put them in my husband's study."[42]

The form of the upright Venus de' Medici also became known through "sable" Venuses, representations of black women that authorized their sexual exploitation by white men by suggesting they were as desirable—and therefore as irresistible—as Venus. Venus was among the most common classical female names given to slaves in America. Sable Venuses began to appear in British and French literature, ethnology, and prints in the eighteenth century. Their beauty and sexuality were compared explicitly to white or "Florentine" Venuses, which suggested the growing concern in multiracial empires about the erotic possibilities of a black, female labor force. Americans may have been exposed to Thomas Slothard's engraving of Venus, "The Voyage of the Sable Venus, from Angola to the West Indies," which appeared in Bryan Edwards' civil and economic history of Jamaica in 1794 (see figure 19). Modeled on the popular Roman naval triumphal image of the goddess Amphitrite borne aloft across the seas, the print reworks an old imperial form for a new empire dependent on racial and sexual hierarchies. It shows a black Venus sailing gamely across the Atlantic on her half shell, pulled by dolphins and cheered by dimpled putti. The title of the print referred to a poem of the same name that suggested the sable Venus

19. Thomas Slothard, "The Voyage of the Sable Venus, from Angola to the West Indies," in Bryan Edwards, *List of Maps and Plates for The History, Civil and Commercial, of the British Colonies of the West Indies* (1794). Library Company of Philadelphia.

rode willingly over the Atlantic to enjoy a watery union with a British Neptune (who hoists the Union Jack in the print), a union from which springs a mulatto Cupid. The poem was headed by an epigram, taken from Virgil's tenth Eclogue, about the handsome, swarthy shepherd Amyntas. The quotation suggested that interracial sexuality had the imprimatur of classical authority: "Quid tum, si fuscus Amyntas? Et nigrae violae sunt, et vaccinia nigra." (So what if Amyntas is dark? Violets, too, are black and black are hyacinths.) It was also at this time that the name "Hottentot Venus" was given to Saartjie Baartman, a southern African woman whose exaggerated buttocks attracted public attention in France and England when she was publicly displayed there in the early 1800s. After her death her body was dissected by the French anatomist Georges Cuvier.[43]

The controversy surrounding Adolf Wertmüller's *Danaë and the Shower of Gold* (1787), one of the first female nude paintings exhibited in America, typifies the anxieties raised by the unclothed female form in public (see figure 20). Danaë, along with Venus, was a common classicizing pretext for the nude female. She was the daughter of Acrisius, king of Argos. Acrisius had been warned by an oracle that Danaë's son would one day kill him, so he locked the lovely Danaë in a bronze room. Despite the precaution, Zeus, besotted with her beauty, entered the chamber as a shower of gold, and impregnated her with her son, Perseus (who as an adult returned to kill Acrisius, fulfilling the oracle). Wertmüller's version is a neoclassical take on the subject, its simple lines substituting for the voluptuous roundness of Titian's Venuses. Wertmüller had completed the painting in Paris, to the applause of the likes of Jacques-Louis David, and, with the help of Charles Willson Peale, imported it into the United States in 1794. Beginning in 1806 it was exhibited in Philadelphia, and for years Wertmüller turned a considerable profit not only from the exhibited painting but also from the several copies of it he produced. Though crowds flocked to the exhibit, some male commentators attacked the picture especially for its potentially disastrous effect on women, who were allowed to see it only on Mondays in gender-segregated groups. Peale himself, while recommending the painting to artists, hesitated to show it to the general public: "I like no art which can raise a blush on a lady's cheek," he confided to Benjamin Latrobe. Thomas Cooper, a classically educated émigré from England and usually a great supporter of shoring up classical learning in the United States, nonetheless denounced the painting's "wanton delineations" and "vulgar lasciviousness."[44]

Women also expressed shock at the unclothed female form in art. Part of their alarm derived from knowing that they had crossed into what was clearly a masculine space. In 1814 Harriet Manigault of Philadelphia de-

20. This was among the first paintings of a female nude to be publicly exhibited in the United States. Adolf Wertmüller, *Danaë and the Shower of Gold.* Paris. 1787. Oil on canvas 150×190 cm, NM 1767. Nationalmuseum, Stockholm.

scribed stumbling across copies (probably engravings) of a Venus and of Wertmüller's *Danaë* in the private chambers of male relatives. "They carried us up stairs to see a certain Venus which seems to be a fine painting, & as large as life; but it struck me as being a most disgusting looking thing, & I don't think the face pretty either, for it looks impudent. This Venus is placed in Uncle Andrews room, opposite to his bed, & has a curtain over it. There is a small Danae in Uncle James' room, which is also very correctly concealed by a curtain. The attitude of it is frightful; she is on the point of receiving Jupiter in the shape of a shower of gold."[45]

For some women, however, Venus began to acquire new meanings. As educated women in the late eighteenth century began to participate in transatlantic debates about "taste" as a legitimate form of elite activity, they turned to Venus as a particular classical artifact that could show them to be arbiters of fashion and connoisseurs of a rarefied aesthetic language. This new language of "taste" helped them neutralize the sexuality of Venus and instead to accentuate her artistic beauty. Mary Stead Pinckney, second wife of the Charlestonian planter Charles Cotesworth Pinckney, wrote admiringly from Paris in 1796 about seeing a porcelain plate at the Sèvres porcelain manufactory showing "a naked Venus . . . de la dernière beauté."[46]

Abigail Adams stands out as an unusually well-documented female observer of Venus. This pillar of New England sobriety might seem like the last person in the world who would take an interest in Venus, but in fact Abigail shows how, by the late eighteenth century, an elite American woman could be exposed to Venus through cosmopolitan travel and wide reading. Abigail's letters show that over time—especially during her years in Europe in the 1780s—she began to acquire the aesthetic language of classical connoisseurship and shared among her network of friends and family a developing female language of taste and style. But she also remained enmeshed in the republican conversation about Venus, in which the goddess stood less for taste than for ungovernable, dangerous, and effeminate passion. Abigail Adams's experience with Venus over time illustrates not just the goddess's transition from sinful to tasteful, but how a woman could at once participate in conversations *with* men about Venus and be the object of men's conversations *about* Venus.

Until 1784, when, at the age of forty, she traveled to Paris with John on political duties, Abigail had never ventured more than twenty miles from her home in Braintree, Massachusetts. Her culture shock in the apparently vice-ridden Old World was extreme, and she recoiled from the luxuries of the Parisians with predictable horror. But her aversion quickly turned to tolerance, if not to delight. Writing to her sister eight months after her arrival, she declared herself astonished by how quickly she became accustomed to gauzy dresses and libertine manners. "Shall I speak a truth, and say that repeatedly seeing these dances has worn off that disgust, which I at first felt, and that I see them now with pleasure?" Such was the human tendency to decline into vice: republicans must always be on guard. "Think you that this city can fail of becoming a Cythera, and this house the temple of Venus? . . . it requires the immortal shield of the invincible Minerva, to screen youth from the arrows which assail them on every side." By 1785, now stationed in London, she was ordering classical figurines from Paris through the intermediary of Thomas Jefferson. He sent her a grouping of a Minerva, a Diana, and an Apollo, but he did not include a Venus, joking that he feared that the beautiful statue would compete with Abigail's daughter, Nabby, now twenty. "Wisdom, I know, is social," he said of Minerva, indirectly comparing her to Abigail. "She seeks her fellows. But Beauty is jealous, and illy bears the presence of a rival."[47]

In England Abigail continued to be exposed to a level of artistic cultivation and aristocratic wealth beyond her imagining. She relayed her
amazement at the paintings and statuary she saw, but her initial distaste
for the intrinsic debauchery of Venus seems to have faded as new mores
and styles expanded her visual register of appreciation. One letter, in particular, shows how Abigail, during her years in Europe, gradually acquired
a language of "taste" that helped to neutralize the dangers of Venus. In
1787 she visited Blenheim Palace, the stately home and gardens of the
Duke of Marlborough. She described the scene to her niece, Lucy Cranch,
walking her along through a setting of minutely described art objects, lac-
ing her letter with terms only a connoisseur would know. Abigail knows
whether columns and pilasters are Corinthian or Doric; she rattles off the
mythological subjects of busts and paintings; she identifies the fabrics
used on the furniture; she judges the vista created by the trees and temples dotting the garden in the language of artists ("The plain—or as artists
term it—the lawn," she writes at one point). To sum up this noble scene,
she invokes the gold standard of eighteenth-century aestheticism, Edmund Burke, whose famous aesthetic treatise, *A Philosophical Enquiry in the
Origin of Our Ideas of the Sublime and the Beautiful* (1757), was a Bible for
connoisseurs. Whether or not she had read Burke, she still knew his
renowned phrase, "the sublime and the beautiful," and she applies it to
the scene before her. The grounds are "on the scale of the sublime and the
beautiful," opines Abigail, no longer the provincial from Massachusetts.
In this tasteful landscape, a bronze of the Venus de' Medici espied in the
palace is just one statue among many, beautiful but not shocking.[48]

Behind all these words there was, of course, Abigail Adams the person, a
woman whose whole life had been wrapped in classical labels. As a young
woman writing to her friends and courting John Adams, she had liked to
call herself Diana, the virginal goddess on the hunt. During the hard years
of the Revolution, she styled herself as the long-suffering Portia, the wife
of the republican patriot Brutus. When she and John missed the children,
they were Hector and Andromache longing for Astyanax. As she prepared
to leave with her husband for the Continent, she called herself Lucretia to
describe to John her powerlessness. When John was often absent, she was
Penelope pining for her Ulysses. Now, at forty, she had earned Thomas Jefferson's highest praise: she was Minerva, goddess of wisdom and patroness
of the American Revolution.

Still later in life, a final classical identity was suggested for Abigail when
she sat for a portrait by Gilbert Stuart, as she and John Adams finished his
presidential years. The portrait, begun in 1800, was not completed until

21. No longer the "perfect Venus" of her youth, Abigail Adams is shown here in a portrait begun when she was fifty-six and completed when she was seventy-one. Gilbert Stuart, *Abigail Smith Adams (Mrs. John Adams).* Gift of Mrs. Robert Homans, Image © 2006 Board of Trustees, National Gallery of Art, Washington, 1800/1815, oil on canvas, .734×.597 (28 7/8 ×23 ½).

1815 (see figure 21). It is not her most flattering likeness. She looks worn and tired, but these had been difficult years of wearisome public service and private tragedy: she lost one son, Charles, to alcoholism in 1800, and her beloved Nabby to breast cancer in 1813. Stuart said that he wished he could have painted her when she was young, for then she would have been "a perfect Venus." John Adams heartily agreed.[49]

During and immediately after the American Revolution, a national identification with the republics of Greco-Roman antiquity catapulted classical figures into the political limelight. This was the heyday of Cicero, Brutus, and Cincinnatus, and educated men participated actively in the classicized political debates that mark this period (as the collective signature of "Publius" in *The Federalist* famously demonstrates). But rising literacy levels and an expanding world of print also enabled the first generation of women—the "daughters of Columbia"—to enter public, political conversations about the prospects and limits of republican revolution. Could women be patriots and should they bear arms in defense of the nation? To whom did women owe allegiance: fathers or husbands (or neither)? And in a republic built on reasoned consent, did women's bodies pose a threat by stirring the passions? The daughters of Columbia found that the historical and mythological women of Greco-Roman antiquity were especially relevant to discussions about women's place in the new republic. Far from representing women's exclusion from republican politics, classical figures like Minerva were women's portals of entry into the new world of publishing and politicized debates.

FOUR

GRECIAN LUXURY, 1800–1830

La mode est pour le Grec; nos meubles, nos bijoux,
Etoffe, coëffure, équipage,
Tout est Grec, excepté nos âmes.
—Nicolas-Thomas Barthe, *L'Amateur*

[Greek fashion is all the rage; our furniture, our jewelry, fine fabrics,
hairstyles, carriages—everything is Greek except our souls.]

In 1815, John Wells asked his sister-in-law, a Miss Huger, to select some furniture for him at the New York City shop of Duncan Phyfe, the most famous furniture maker in America at the time. "I leave the whole to your selection and taste," he wrote of the beautiful Grecian sophas, tables, and chairs that marked Phyfe's work.[1] John Wells's confidence in the sophisticated Grecian taste of his sister-in-law opens a window onto a major change in the verbal and visual lexicon of American women in the period 1800–1830. During these decades, their classical vocabulary shifted abruptly from a preoccupation with the austere aesthetic of Rome to a rage for Grecian luxuries. The shift in the verbal and visual lexicon is striking in its rapid onset, its dominance of the visual field, its national presence, and its longevity. This was the age of neoclassicism.

Neoclassicism, which arose in Europe around the middle of the eighteenth century, was revolutionary in two ways. Not only was it the visual idiom of political revolutions, it was also the first international aesthetic style that was fueled on the one end by the productive capacities of the industrial revolution and bolstered on the other by the rising purchasing abilities of consumers around the Atlantic. In an age of rising nationalisms, what is so striking about neoclassicism is how it was used internationally to declare separate national allegiances between 1770 and 1840. Neoclassical taste bedecks a staggering variety of buildings and objects in England, Prussia, France, and Italy. Even the Greeks adopted neoclassical aesthetics from Europe in the 1820s during their struggle to overthrow the rule of the Ottoman Turks.[2] Neoclassicism originated with the European nobility among kings in league with emerging industrial entrepreneurs. In the 1770s and 1780s, the style was co-opted as a visual system of signs that could address a revolutionary public in political terms, as it did in France especially by the painter Jacques-Louis David. After the revolutionary decades, it remained a powerful set of symbols that could be used by old elites and ambitious upstarts to wrap their legitimacy in the authority of the Greco-Roman past.

The United States was a major staging ground for neoclassicism between roughly 1800 and the 1830s.[3] Art historians often call this the "Federal" style, but this term was not used at the time and, in fact, imputes to American neoclassicism a nationalist boosterism, a republican austerity, even an incipient populism that were not its dominant characteristics. (The word "neoclassicism" was not coined until the late nineteenth century, though it is useful because it is a widely recognized term.) American neoclassicism should be seen not just as an expression of early nationalism but more broadly as a subset of the transatlantic conversation about taste and gentility, a dialogue in which women became active participants. That the dialogue concerned taste does not mean it ignored political realities. As in Europe, American neoclassicism was the idiom of elites invoking various strands of the Greco-Roman past for thoroughly modern political and cultural projects. The best way to capture the meaning of neoclassicism in early national America is to call it by the name contemporaries most often used: "Grecian." What made an object "Grecian" in America between 1800 and 1830?

The first thing that made something Grecian was France. Though England played a major role too, the epicenter of the Grecian style was France in the period of the Diréctoire, Consulat, and Empire (1795–1815). "Rome n'est plus dans Rome," went a French ditty of 1798, "elle est tout à Paris." The refrain referred to the piles of classical loot that Napoleon Bonaparte had lugged back from his campaigns in Italy and installed in the Louvre to magnify his glory. Napoleon melded these Roman antiquities with the Greek-inspired court style of dress and furnishings that defined his regime. What modern historians often call the "Empire" style (a term not used at this time) involved a fantastic amplification of the aesthetic of Grecian luxury, one that visiting Americans quickly brought back to their own country. They were assisted by French artists and intellectuals who had fled to America to escape the disruptions of the Napoleonic era. In fact, two of Napoleon's brothers, Jérôme and Joseph, actually lived in the United States during part of this period. Igniting one of the marital scandals of the century, Jérôme wed Elizabeth Patterson, daughter of the wealthy American merchant William Patterson, but he quickly divorced her and returned to Europe to be crowned king of Westphalia by Napoleon. Joseph Bonaparte, the former king of Spain, bought the elegant New Jersey estate of Point Breeze and made it a showplace for art and furnishing in the Grecian style. His gallery was both familial and classical: it included a reduced-scale copy of Canova's white marble statue of his sister Pauline Borghese as Venus Victrix lying semi-nude on a sofa (see figure 22). The sight shocked some visiting Quaker ladies expecting a rather more staid family portrait gallery.[4]

Americans' infatuation with the Grecian style revealed not just their cosmopolitan taste but also their deep ambivalence about France, a sentiment captured by James Madison in 1799. "With every thing that regards the French Republic, it is of peculiar importance that it should be accurately

22. This reduced-size copy of Antonio Canova's *Paolina Borghese as Venus Victrix* (1807) adorned the home of Napoleon Bonaparte's brother, Joseph Bonaparte, at Point Breeze. Pauline Borghese was their sister. The Athenaeum of Philadelphia.

and fully understood, because that is the Foreign Power, with which our relations have become more interesting than with any other."[5] If revolutionary American classicism had been, in part, a way to talk about Britain,
American classicism between roughly 1800 and 1830 was a way to talk
about France.

On the one hand, Americans were fascinated by the military successes
of Napoleon, the opulence of his imperial regime, and the exotic beauties
that dominated it. American republicanism, then as now, was thoroughly
compatible with an infatuation with the trappings of royalty. The unshak-
able Francophilia of the American elite could now express itself in the patronage of French craftsmen (or English craftsmen who imitated French
styles), French books and writers, and artistic training in Paris rather than
in London. John Vanderlyn (1775–1852) was among the first major American painters to train in Paris rather than in London. Illustrations from
some of the most popular English furniture guides read by Americans
were copied from French precedents like Charles Percier's *Receuil de Déco-
rations Intérieurs* (1801, 1812).

On the other hand, Americans were still deeply disturbed by the radical
legacies of the French Revolution, and were later rattled further by the
mercantile and military disruptions of Napoleon's relentless campaign
to dominate Europe. The ongoing struggles between France and England
embroiled the weak, new nation in trade disputes that culminated in the
two-and-a-half-year War of 1812, in which British troops invaded Washington, DC, destroyed such new national symbols as the presidential mansion
and the Capitol building, and blockaded ports, acts that helped plunge
the United States into a deep economic recession. Though alarmed by
British actions, Americans also feared that their own republic, like
France's, might degenerate into the debauched imperial grandeur fore-
cast by Livy and Tacitus.

The Grecian style also had distinctive aesthetic elements. One was a fusing of the Greek and the Oriental, which allowed Americans to invoke the
simple beauty of ancient Greece while also harnessing the exoticism and
grandeur of the "Orient." The simultaneity of the Greek and the Oriental
at this time reflected the modern political and cultural realities of the
Mediterranean. Greece was still under the dominion of the Ottoman
Turks until the 1820s, so that the category of Greek and Turk overlapped
easily in Americans' minds. Travelers going to Greece in search of classical
ruins discovered that these sturdy buildings had been commandeered by
Muslim Turks for modern defensive and religious projects. The Parthenon,
notably, had been converted into a mosque in the 1460s (complete with
minaret). Used later as a gunpowder store, its roof blew off in an explosion

in 1687, contributing to the ruinous look that later delighted European romantics.

The fusion of ancient Greek/pagan and modern Turkish/Muslim elements festooned the flamboyant folio editions of Greek antiquities now being published. The lavish illustrations in James Stuart and Nicholas Revett's *Antiquities of Athens* (1762–1830) revealed for European and American eyes not only the crumbling remains of Greek temples, but also the modern world of the Ottoman Turks with their distinctive cultural practices. Also fueling American interest in the Orient were the "Barbary States" of North Africa (Morocco, Algiers, Tunis, and Tripoli), which posed a persistent threat to the United States between 1785 and 1815 by preying on American commercial ships in the Mediterranean and selling some captured Americans into eastern slave markets. And, although the Oriental element was most obvious in Greece, Americans who went to Italy also encountered vestiges of earlier contacts with the Islamic east. Renaissance Venice, a frequent model for American republicans, had been a great international emporium, the nexus of European trade routes to the Levant. Its architecture and city plan still revealed to modern visitors numerous Oriental characteristics. And last, the Oriental could also refer to French imperial ambitions; John Adams half-jokingly proposed in 1810 that Americans renounce Greek and Latin to take up instead the "Asiatic writers," handbooks of world conquest from Genghis Khan to Tamerlane and would help Americans to comprehend Napoleon.[6]

Modern Greeks and Turks were very much on Americans' mind, but as they had in the eighteenth century they blended easily with their ancient counterparts in Hellas, Egypt, and Persia. This chronological fusion was promoted by internationally known style-setters such as the British aesthete Thomas Hope (1769–1831). Hope drew from his travels in Mediterranean countries and his considerable knowledge of classical archaeology to create furniture and clothing guides that publicized the forms of ancient Greece, Rome, and the Orient. (In fact, Hope coined the term "interior decoration.") American women snapped up his *Household Furniture and Interior Decoration* (1807) and *Costumes of the Ancients* (1812), and discovered in the text and ample illustrations reminders that the Greco-Asiatic aesthetic worked equally well in both the modern and the ancient worlds. "Those inhabitants of Asia," Hope told his readers without chronological specificity, "though a race totally distinct from the Greeks, had with their European neighbours some intercourse." Hope himself was a living monument to temporal acrobatics, stuffing his Surrey mansion with classical antiquities he had gathered on his Grand Tour while posing for a portrait dressed as a modern Turk (see figure 23).[7]

23. Classical tastemaker to America's elite women, Thomas Hope poses here in grand Oriental style. Sir William Beechey, *Thomas Hope* (exhibited 1799). National Portrait Gallery, London.

The second hallmark of the Grecian style was simplicity of line. "Simplify. This is for the Emperor," Napoleon Bonaparte dashed across his architect's sketch of a candelabrum, a directive intended to associate his regime's classicism with permanence and solidity. In America, the aesthetic of sweeping simplicity was eagerly embraced by rising architects such as the Englishman Benjamin Latrobe (1764–1820), who had come to America in 1795. Latrobe was deeply influenced by one of the Grecian style's most popular promoters, the English illustrator John Flaxman (1755–1826). Flaxman had gained an international reputation for his illustrations in a new edition of Homer's *Iliad* (1795). Flaxman's simple, almost cartoon-like outline figures of Homeric heroes looked as if they had been lifted intact from ancient Greek urns. "My intention is to shew how any story may be represented in a series of compositions on principles of the Ancients," explained Flaxman of his minimalist compositions. But it was not beside the point that such simple figures were more easily reproduced with new technologies of publication for a mass audience; easy reproduction was a feature exploited not just by printers but also by English potters such as Josiah Wedgwood (1730–1795), who mixed antique style with modern industrial techniques at his factory (aptly named Etruria, referring to the rage for Etruscan styles).[8]

Though simple, the lines of Grecian furniture were not easy to achieve: it was an aesthetic of moneyed minimalism, of opulent austerity, and required a craftsman skilled enough to turn out a sofa or chair with long expanses of gleaming mahogany as sleek as a porpoise's back. By the mid-nineteenth century, the simplicity of the Greek line was increasingly associated with democracy and a populist style, but in this earlier period it had everything to do with summoning the permanence and majesty of an elite's vision of antiquity. It also had everything to do with women.

Networking

Like Joséphine Bonaparte, whose generous patronage of French artists made Napoleonic France the hub of this international style, elite American women were essential conduits for the Grecian taste.[9] Their letters and diaries are full of references to these novelties and to how they eagerly snapped up luscious classical objects from across the sea. Women wrote of Grecian sofas, klismos chairs, Grecian robes, Sheraton mirrors, Sèvres and Wedgwood porcelain, Turkish turbans, not to mention stacks of books that in one way or another—through language, history, or aesthetics— evoked the wonders of a mythical Greco-Asiatic past. By the 1820s, this style had reached the *bon ton* on the western frontiers of Kentucky, Ohio, and Tennessee. Ralph Eleaser Whiteside Earl's painting of the family of the well-heeled Tennessee lawyer and politician Ephraim Hubbard Foster in 1825 captures the Grecian frontier in all its aspirations to cosmopolitan gentility and local clout (see figure 24). Foster's wife wears a yellow, long-sleeved Grecian dress while sitting upright on a Grecian-style chair. One of their little daughters has clambered triumphantly to the windowsill to show off her spectacular Greco-Turkish (even vaguely Scottish) ensemble: red shoes, Grecian gown, and, topping it all, a whimsical tartan cap spewing a fountain of feathers.

The women who navigated the transition from Roman asceticism to Grecian luxury were part of a new generation of Americans born in the 1760s, 1770s, and 1780s. Its most prominent members included Margaret Bayard Smith (1778–1844), Eleanor Parke Custis Lewis (1779–1852), Anne Willing Bingham (1764–1801), Elizabeth Patterson Bonaparte (1785–1879), Theodosia Burr Alston (1783–1813), Rosalie Stier Calvert, Dolley Madison (1768–1849), Louisa Catherine Adams (1775–1852), and Elizabeth Kortwright Monroe (1768–1830). These women had close personal access to powerful men, access they used as influence in a quasi-political fashion that one historian has called "parlor politics."[10] Denied such rights of citizenship as the ballot and office holding, they used their social and marital standing to influence the powerful men around them. The Grecian style of these women's parlors reveals the multiple aspirations of Americans in the early republic. The classicism of the Grecian style communicated the new nation's intellectual and political debts to the virtuous republics of antiquity. But the opulence of the new Grecian aesthetic, with its whiff of Oriental exoticism, conveyed something equally important in this age of rising commercialism and consumerism: it displayed elite Americans' cosmopolitanism, their knowledge of the latest aesthetic trends in Britain and France. In short, the Grecian style that elite women helped to propagate allowed Americans to be both virtuous, classical republicans and thoroughly modern consumers.

Poised at the center of this web of fashion and manufacture, these women helped to launch the careers of a new generation of American artists and designers, many of whom had studied in European centers of the Grecian style and who brought their own interpretation of this style to America. The group included Benjamin Latrobe, John Vanderlyn, Gilbert Stuart (1755–1828), and Charles-Balthazar-Julien Férret de Saint-Mémin (1770–1852). But the majestic public buildings and banks designed by architects such as Latrobe were not the primary concerns of these women. Instead, they turned their attention to filling the domestic interior, and they patronized not just portraitists but domestic furniture makers in the

24. This family portrait from 1825 shows how Grecian taste also appealed to elite women and girls in what was then the frontier state of Tennessee. The mother wears a simple, yellow Grecian robe while her daughter on the tabletop sports a rather more flamboyant version of the Grecian style. Ralph Eleaser Whiteside Earl, *The Ephraim Hubbard Foster Family* (1825). 1969.2. Oil on mattress ticking. Collection of Cheekwood Museum of Art, Nashville, Tennessee.

Grecian style. Grecian furniture became the idiom of a generation of skilled craftsmen, best known through the work of a few nationally prominent cabinetmakers like Duncan Phyfe (1768–1854) and Charles-Honoré Lannuier (1779–1819) of New York. Numerous letters and diary entries from elite women, as well as newspaper advertisements, suggest that women were central nodes in the matrix of neoclassical taste formation. They bought the furniture, read furniture catalogues, and dealt with the disposition of the completed product in their homes. Prudency Telford Morton, wife of a wealthy New York merchant, ordered a klismos chair from Duncan Phyfe that would precisely fit a small needlework seat cover she had made. Phyfe obliged, delivering an exquisite klismos in miniature just for her.[11]

If France had its trend-setting Joséphine, America had Dolley Madison, first lady during the Madison Administration (1808–1817) and reigning queen of Grecian taste for years before and after. (In fact, the term "first lady," an English translation of the more pungent term, *prima donna*, is believed to have originated, after the fact, to describe Dolley Madison's cultural and social influence.) Until the invading British torched the presidential mansion in 1814, she turned her considerable energies and her impeccable eye to converting the interior to the latest Grecian style. She corresponded frequently with the architect and designer Benjamin Latrobe to put her personal stamp on the presidential mansion. She also became an important part of a Washingtonian patronage network and had less established artists begging to be introduced to her. "Permit me to introduce to you Mr. Findlay, our Man of Taste," wrote Samuel Smith to Dolley Madison in 1809, "he wishes to have the honor of presenting to you Specimens of his work, his Object to obtain your friendly interference with Mr. Latrobe, that he may participate in the furnishing of the Presidential House." Even Latrobe, however, was willing to concede that in some matters his wife had more taste than he. "I have already bought most of the articles in the small way & Mrs. Latrobe is so good as to run about for me & aid me with her taste & judgment in those articles which she understands better than I," he confided to Dolley Madison.[12]

Though conversation and parlor visits certainly helped women to train their eyes, new books—mythologies, travel narratives, poetry—also opened the new worlds of Greece and "the Orient." That many of these titles were in French (or English translations of the French) suggests not just the entrenched Francophilia of the American elite but also women's awareness of the nation's embroilment in the Franco-British wars, of which they speak with some frequency in their letters. Their reading of French-language titles about the Greco-Oriental past, and their efforts to translate these works into English, were part of two worlds: the highly cultured world in which French was a byword for female civility and the elite social world in which women had access through influential husbands and male family members and friends to contemporary political influence.

Jean-Jacques Barthélemy's *Travels of Anacharsis* (1788) typifies the kind of Grecian book now available to women. First issued in France, the *Travels of Anacharsis* was a publishing sensation that roared through an edition a year for the first ten years and was translated into numerous other languages, including English. The premise was that a young Scythian philosopher travels through Greece in the fourth century BCE, where he meets and converses with famous philosophers and historical figures. In the style of the modern travel narrative, he gives an account of the government, customs, peoples, and antiquities he encounters. The translator of the first American edition in 1804 (which had no illustrations) recommended the readability of the book: it was so charmingly relayed that the reader could imagine that it was "a work of mere amusement, invention, and fancy." Yet each fact was footnoted so that it would appeal to "the man of real learning," or even to "such readers as can never be supposed to have any intention to consult the authorities quoted." American women read both versions. Harriet Manigault of Philadelphia read hers in French one evening in 1814. Anna Maria Thornton of Washington, DC, the wife of the Capitol designer, used the prints in an illustrated edition of the *Travels of Anacharsis* as drawing templates.[13]

25. "Sister's Cylinder Bookcase," from Thomas Sheraton, *The Cabinet-Maker and Upholsterer's Drawing-Book* (1802), plate 38. Courtesy Department of Special Collections, Stanford University Libraries.

Giving palpable form to the mania for Grecian reading was a Grecian bookcase made just for women. Around 1811, the van Rensselaer family of New York owned a marvel of female classicism pulled directly from Thomas Sheraton's *Cabinet-Maker and Upholsterer's Drawing-Book* (1802): the Sister's Cylinder Bookcase (see figure 25).[14] This hulking contraption satisfied the new vogue for female reading and writing while insisting that it be done communally and in plain view in the middle of a room. Shaped like an H, it consisted of two bookcases joined by a desk with a cylindrical top that could be opened to reveal a writing desk on either side. According to Sheraton, it was "intended for the use of two ladies, who both may write and read at it together." His illustration shows how the communal writing and reading might be pursued. One sister (clad in high Grecian style) sits at one side desk while the other sister pulls open a drawer on the other side.

As was the case for dress, the Grecian reading by these women had a particular "Oriental" component like that exemplified by Anne Willing Bingham. The wife of the spectacularly wealthy Philadelphia merchant William Bingham, she embodied the problem in the new American republic of women close to political power who were nonetheless denied its direct use, the kind of situation that caused republicans to rain down accusations of Oriental "luxury and effeminacy." A brilliant success in French and English high society in the 1780s, Anne Willing Bingham had defended the politically involved women of Paris to Thomas Jefferson in a letter in 1787.

> The Women of France interfere in the politics of the Country, and often give a decided turn to the Fate of Empires. Either by the gentle Arts of persuasion, or by the commanding force of superior Attractions and Address, they have obtained that Rank and Consideration in society, which the Sex are intitled to, and which they in vain contend for in other Countries. We are therefore bound in Gratitude to admire and revere them, for asserting our Privileges, as much as the friends of the Liberties of Mankind reverence the successful struggles of the American Patriots.[15]

Perhaps acting on these convictions that women be allowed to "interfere in the politics" of her country, Anne Bingham became a central node in the parlor-centered Philadelphia high society in the 1790s. She was so beautiful and well connected that her profile was chosen to bedeck the Liberty coin of 1795 (the coin was modeled on an image made by Gilbert Stuart). Gilbert Stuart painted her portrait again in 1797, dressed this time not as Roman Liberty but on the cutting edge of Grecian style as it was first becoming known in America (see figure 26). Her majestic black velvet

26. Anne Willing Bingham poses with Volney's *Voyage en Syrie* while wearing an early interpretation of the Grecian style of dress in America. Gilbert Stuart, *Anne Willing Bingham* (1797). Oil on canvas, 30×25 in. (76.2×63.5 cm). Private collection.

gown, lined with white gauze, opens to reveal the swell of her right breast. A massive, jeweled pendant hangs to her waist, while an exotic, single hoop earring glistens from beneath ropes of hair. Her left arm was exposed in what was considered the most alarmingly risqué fashion (espying the Bingham arm at a soirée, future chief justice John Marshall expressed shock at the "naked elbow," the "vacancy of three or four inches" visible between sleeve and glove). But what makes the portrait truly Oriental is the book Anne Bingham holds in her hand: *Le Voyage en Syrie et en Égypte* (1787). It was first published in Paris by the French geographer and Orientalist Constantin-François Chasseboeuf, comte de Volney (1757–1820); a London reprint appeared in the same year in English, and a New York edition came out in 1798. The book was a narrative of Volney's travels in Syria and Egypt in the 1780s, and it became a major source for the history of the Arab east. Volney at times compared Arab mores to those of the women of France. Syrian women, though uncorseted, remained as slender as the tight-laced demoiselles of France, Volney opined. Anne Bingham not only knew the *Voyage en Syrie et en Égypte* well, she knew Volney himself in person. Volney came to America in 1795, and, while in Philadelphia, was not only a frequent guest of the Binghams, but also French tutor to the Bingham daughters.[16] Here, in the person of Anne Bingham, was a compact fusion of elite female patronage, Grecian opulence, and French Orientalism.

Most women did their Grecian reading either in English or French, but one woman now learned to read and write ancient Greek. That woman was Theodosia Burr, the brilliant daughter of Aaron and Theodosia Burr. (The names of both mother and daughter referred to no specific historical figure; they appear to be the product of fancy, recalling Christian Byzantium, an empire centered on the east-west boundary of the Middle Ages.) History has been unkind to Aaron Burr: after he killed Alexander Hamilton in the infamous duel of 1804, his political career never recovered. But he was a man of great charm and erudition, and he was the major American patron of the artist John Vanderlyn. He made no secret of his love for intelligent, educated women. He wrote to his wife about his faith in "female intellectual powers," and he encouraged her reading of the radical English feminist Mary Wollstonecraft (1759–1797), whose *Vindication of the Rights of Woman* (1792) took America by storm. The talents of the daughter quickly became evident to both the parents; "ma Minerve," her father called her. Here was a good candidate for Latin and Greek. Burr even encouraged young Theodosia's idea of making a book of classical mythology for children.[17]

Theodosia the mother died in 1794, and Aaron Burr poured his desire for learned, flirtatious repartee into his relationship with young Theodosia, whose classical education he oversaw whether he was at home or abroad. He seemed to keep nothing from his daughter. He regaled her with tales of his amorous attempts on eligible women, and relayed the decline of his political career with ironic smirks. ("If any male friends of yours should be dying of ennui, recommend to him to engage in a duel and a courtship at the same time," he wrote in August 1804, a month after the duel in which he fatally shot Alexander Hamilton.)[18] Theodosia Burr's classicism, cultivated to the level a son might have had, seemed imperative for Aaron Burr's continued intimacy with her.

They began with a plan drawn up when Theodosia was ten. She finished Horace, began Terence, and started in on Greek grammar; the last presumed she already knew the Greek alphabet and some basic vocabulary, a remarkable achievement for a child so young. Aaron Burr's was not a subtle pedagogy. He filled his letters to her with precise commands on what to read. When she was just eleven, he wrote:

> Four pages in Lucian was a great lesson; and why, my dear Theo., can't this be done a little oftener? You must, by this time, I think, have gone through Lucian. I wish you to begin and go through it again; for it would be shameful to pretend to have read a book of which you could not construe a page. At the second reading you will, I suppose, be able to double your lessons; so that you may go through it in three weeks. You say nothing of writing or learning Greek verbs;—is this practice discontinued? and why?

But then he seemed delighted when Theodosia could communicate in the code of classicism, something so few women could do. She was to him "the metempsychosis of Madame Dacier" (Anne Dacier had translated Homer into French). In one letter he specifically alluded to the private (usually male) code of classicism and what it meant to him as a sign of intimacy: "The Greek signature, though a little mistaken, was not lost upon me." When Theodosia failed to festoon her letters with Greek and Latin, he commanded her to do it. "I hope you like Terence. Can't you lug a scrap from him now and then, apropos, into your letters? It will please Your affectionate papa."[19] Here was pedagogy and love mixed in equal measure, a father searching for a language of secret confidence in the beauties of tongues long dead.

Whether in language or aesthetics, Grecian taste was all the rage now. But two objects in particular formed the defining core of this new complex of Greco-Franco-Asiatic splendor: the Grecian robe and the Grecian sofa.

GRECIAN ROBES

When we think of women in the early republic, we often think of the peculiar style of dress that dominated the period 1800–1830: the distinctive high-waisted frocks that seem to be such a contrast to the fat skirts and pinched waists that came before and after. Called Empire dresses now, they were termed Grecian robes at the time, and they are a peculiar blip on the sartorial screen that illuminates an important aesthetic moment for American women.

Searching for women's presence in early national political life, historians have paid much attention to the appearance of women dressed like Liberty or Columbia in Fourth of July parades and festivals during the period 1800–1830. The fashionable Grecian robe probably lent itself well to looking like these nationalist goddesses in a parade or festival (and some contemporary prints of Liberty and Columbia adjust their iconic robes to look "Grecian"). But we should beware of focusing too much on the gowns women might don for a few hours once or twice a year—however political the dress might seem to us now—to the neglect of women's everyday clothing and the subtle political, intellectual, and aesthetic reasons women had for wearing them. What did these international Grecian robes mean specifically to the American women who wore them?

American women first became obsessed with Grecian dresses in the late 1790s, when reports from Americans in Paris of Parisian women dressed "à la grecque" began to trickle back. This designation included not just robes, but also hair curled into tiny face-framing ringlets and festooned with ribbons. The style—which had many names, such as *à la Titus*— might be topped with a turban and even a feather tucked akimbo like a sail. Both Greek and Turkish in aesthetic, the style was utterly transnational. For all its transatlantic popularity, its origins are obscure. It may have originated in the children's clothing of the 1780s, which, as portraits suggest, moved into a direction of loose robing. It may have originated more directly in England from the former dressmaker of the deposed French queen, Marie-Antoinette; it may have then crossed back over to France, where it was first embraced by radical revolutionaries eager to throw off *ancien régime* formalities, and was later popularized especially by the empress Joséphine.[20]

American women returning from France in the late 1790s were amazed at these innovative frocks, and brought descriptions, patterns, or even dolls, as Sally d'Yrujo did in 1796, when she described a doll from England sporting the latest fashion. Like other well-connected women in the new capital, Dolley Madison felt the influence of Alexandrine-Émelie Brongniart, wife of the French chargé d'affaires, Louis-André Pichon. Dolley Madison wrote to her sister that Madame Pichon "shews me every thing she has, & would fain give me of *every thing*—she decorates herself according to the french Ideas & wishes me do so two." The portrait of Dolley Madison made by Gilbert Stuart in 1804 captures her on the cutting edge of the new fashion in Washington, DC (see figure 27). Her hair tumbles in Grecian ringlets; her white gown is trimmed with gold and set off with a gold necklace; a gauzy shawl drapes her left arm and the right side of a sumptuous red velvet chair. Women also imported sumptuous fashion plates from England and France, such as *Ackermann's Repository* (1808–1828). This marvel of printing technology not only featured hand-colored fashion plates of Grecian robes, but even included four small fabric swatches on the cover of each month's issue, sandwiched between an allegorical engraving of Britannia and Neptune on the frontispiece.[21]

An excerpt from *Ackermann's Repository* in the Massachusetts *Repertory* from 1813 shows how thoroughly cosmopolitan such robes were. The magazine was English, some of the words are French, and the geographical representation of sartorial options melds the Greek with the Oriental to form a vague category here invoked by reference to the Circassian, Angolan, and Indian: "A Grecian round robe, or lilac or apple-blossom crape, worn over a white satin petticoat. A satin bodice, the color of the robe, ornamented with white beads and drops, *a la militaire*; the same continued down the front of the dress; short Circassian sleeves, with similar ornaments; a deep vandyke trimming of lace, or lilac Angola silk, round the bottom of the robe. An Indian turban, of silver frosted crape, decorated with pearl or white beads . . ."[22]

One element that distinguished the Grecian dress of this period from the *turquerie* and Roman garb featured in elite eighteenth-century portraits is that it was clothing worn across the class spectrum for everyday activity. Although there does seem to have been a "portrait dress" version of the Grecian robe for elite women's portraits—in which they appear in the most sumptuous velvet or silk versions, dripping jewelry and feathers—much visual and documentary evidence suggests that Grecian robes quickly moved far down the social ladder among women who made them from more modest fabrics (using muslin rather than silk, calico rather than velvet). And while French salonnières might sport transparent versions that barely concealed the bust, the style was easily adaptable for the Sunday-to-church needs of women in the American province. A shawl, for example, could both warm and conceal the ample décolletage. Engravings and paintings from this era show women bedecked in modest Grecian robes attending churches in the classical revival style promoted by such architects

27. Dolley Madison was a style-setter for the new Grecian taste, appearing here in a white Grecian robe while seated on a crimson chair. Gilbert Stuart, *Dolley Payne Todd Madison* (1804). The White House Historical Association (White House Collection)

28. Louisa Catherine Adams appears here in the posture recommended for sitting in klismos chairs. Both the posture and the klismos chair were popularized in Thomas Hope's *Costumes of the Ancients* (1812). Charles Leslie, *Mrs. John Quincy Adams* (Louisa Catherine Adams) (1816). Courtesy of the Diplomatic Reception Rooms, U.S. Department of State, Washington, DC. Photographer: Will Brown.

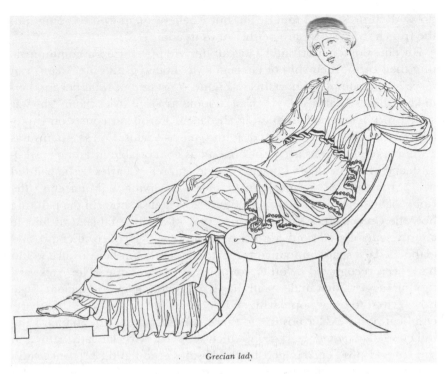

Grecian lady

29. A "Grecian lady," from Thomas Hope, *Costumes of the Ancients* (1812). Courtesy Stanford University Libraries.

as Robert Mills, who believed that the nobility, grace, and proportion of this architecture enhanced the experience of Christian veneration.[23] Painters such as John Krimmel and William Birch of Philadelphia depicted scenes of ordinary white and black women moving through city life bedecked in Grecian robes.

But the lead in bringing such styles to America came from women of the upper crust. The Charlestonian Mary Stead Pinckney exemplifies the abrupt transition to *le style grecque.* She was the second wife of the widowed Charles Cotesworth Pinckney, whose first wife, Sarah Middleton, had posed as a Roman matron in 1773 (see figure 10). In the late 1790s the Pinckneys were in Paris on diplomatic business. Here Mary Pinckney experienced the full force of the turn to the Grecian motif, with its risqué sensuality. She elaborated in a letter to her friend in 1796. "Sometimes she [Mme. Tallien] goes into public à la grecque, with drawers, and a gawze petticoat." She watched as her American friends also began to trade their more modest apparel for styles *à la grecque.* She described how a friend still dressed "at present a l'Américain, but I believe she purposes going into the french style, tho we are neither of us its admirers."[24]

For elite women, portraiture was an important vehicle for communicating their connoisseurship of Grecian style. Louisa Catherine Adams can serve as an example of how this was done. Possessed of what her mother-in-law, Abigail Adams, called "classical looks as Virgil styles them," she was raised in London and frequently abroad in European courts on diplomatic errands with her husband, John Quincy Adams. Louisa Adams was a woman of enormous accomplishment, as comfortable in French as English and a favorite of the Russian tsar and empress. Charles Leslie painted her portrait in 1816 while John Quincy was serving as Minister to the Court of St. James in London (see figure 28). Louisa shows in the painting how the Grecian robe could become part of a subtle tableau of female connoisseurship. Not only do her crimson velvet gown, coral comb, and elaborate lace shawl announce her patrician taste, but her posture would have been recognized by other connoisseurs as "antique." Her backward tipping suggests that underneath her is a klismos chair, an "ancient" style now revived to huge popularity, and one that encouraged this slightly recumbent posture. Her posture is almost an exact replica of an engraving in Hope's *Costumes of the Ancients,* which showed a "Grecian lady" sitting in the languid pose encouraged by the klismos (see figure 29). Sheraton's *Cabinet-Maker* explicitly instructed women and men in how to sit in a klismos chair. "The parties who converse with each other sit with their legs across the seat, and rest their arms on the top rail, which, for this purpose, is made about three inches and a half wide, stuffed and covered."[25]

There was enough rhetoric surrounding the Grecian robe that it is worth spending a moment dispelling some myths to show the nature and limits of women's engagement with things Greek. First, the resemblance of these frocks to actual Greco-Roman dress was hazy at best. Though described as "Grecian," they in fact bore little resemblance to garments worn by women in the ancient world. In ancient Greece and Rome women wore simple woolen or linen rectangles tied under the breasts with a band of cloth, a flimsy apparatus that would have created a rather flat silhouette. By contrast, modern Grecian dresses were feats of heroic engineering in the service of the décolletage. The dresses hid women's torsos behind an unbroken column of fabric while cinching the breasts into two high, distinct orbs, as though announcing the new republican vogue for breast-feeding. In an age when the lift of the breast depended almost entirely on the corset below, the bust line of the Grecian robe rushed to assistance with its tight cut and heavy linen lining. For American women, what made the robes Grecian was that they let women achieve an ineffable union of virtuous, republican simplicity, and cosmopolitan taste. An article extolling the virtues of the women of ancient Greece marveled at how "the simplicity of their dress harmonized with the perfection of their charms." Such paeans to the simplicity of the Grecian dress also had to do with its color, which was often white. White—the color of classical columns long stripped of their original bright coloring—had long been associated by modern aesthetic theorists with the moral virtue of the ancients. The Greeks, wrote George Turnbull in his *Treatise on Ancient Painting* (1740), "avoided the gaudy, luscious, and florid; and studied Chastity and Severity in their Colours. It was not till Painting was in its decline, that Luxury and Libertinism in Colouring, so to speak, came into vogue."[26]

It is widely assumed that the Grecian robe succeeded because it required no stays. Freed from the prison of monumental colonial-era dresses and their tight corsets, women would now be free to move about. Like the women of the free republics of antiquity, their sartorial liberty would suggest their modern political liberty. For women, however, liberty always shaded into libertinism, a danger suggested by some women's interpretation of the Grecian dress. Elizabeth ("Betsy") Patterson Bonaparte, daughter of a merchant prince at the pinnacle of American society, is often invoked as an exemplar of this phenomenon. In 1803 she shocked polite society in America and France by marrying Jérôme Bonaparte, a brother of Napoleon Bonaparte. Almost as shocking were her frocks, entirely transparent Grecian gowns that she wore without corsets. When she attended a Washington levee in 1804 in this getup, Thomas Law was moved to compose this poem:

> I was at Mrs. Smith's last night
> And highly gratified my self
> Well! What of Madame Bonaparte
> Why she's a little whore at heart
> Her lustful looks her wanton air
> Her limbs revealed her bosom bare.

But Elizabeth Patterson Bonaparte was the exception rather than the rule, and her example of using the Grecian gown to underline her personal emancipation from demure republican mores was not followed by many women. Women from this period discuss stays often in their letters (they were in the wash, getting too tight, too loose, needing new laces), and they suggested that the Grecian gown demanded the ministrations of the whalebone as much as earlier and later styles. Corsets were used as much to achieve a small waist as a regal carriage; that waists were now concealed under columnar dresses did not mean the corset had lost its social functions.

In fact, a new, longer, back-lacing corset now became popular because it helped women of all shapes and sizes to achieve the fashionable columnar shape of the torso. Gussets in front helped to heave the bosom upward into the desired twin-moon shape (there was even a "divorce corset" invented not to break marriages but to achieve the proper bustline). And despite the republican vogue for breast-feeding, evidence suggests that the bust-revealing Grecian robe was not necessarily any easier to manage for nursing mothers than previous styles. Grecian dresses buttoned or hooked at the back, so a special panel had to be fitted over the front, which a mother could raise and lower as needed to feed her child.[27]

And although part of the cross-class appeal of the Grecian dress was that it could be made cheaply out of muslin or calico, its ostensible republican simplicity could be entirely offset by such luxurious fabrics as silk, satin, and velvet. Elite women delighted in draping themselves with garlands of jewels, turbans, furs, and gold trimming. Any woman who sends away to Belgium for eight ostrich feathers, as Rosalie Stier Calvert did in 1808, is not a woman invoking the simple, free republics of antiquity through dress. Certain kinds of jewelry that meshed well with simple, classical lines became especially popular: gold and pearls, which nicely offset the white of the gowns, and black and red jewels like amber, jet, and coral, which suggested Etruscan wall paintings. A whole jewelry ensemble known as a "parure" emerged during this period. Consisting of a necklace, bracelet, earrings, and tiara, it completed the effect of the classical goddess. Dolley Madison was possibly the most famously resplendent of American women to sport the classical idiom, and she was known for looking like a "goddess" in what one critic called "a profusion of finery, Diamonds, &c." The language of luxury festooned advertisements even for modest versions of such frocks. Newspaper advertisements appealing to a broad spectrum of women described Grecian robes as being only part of a flood of scrumptious goods from London, Europe, and points east. "Grecian Robes . . . fancy colored Cambrics . . . Fine Cords and Velvets . . . A handsome assortment of India Muslins," read one of the earliest of such advertisements.[28]

Describing these robes to each other in private letters, women invented a particular variation of the word "taste" that suggests they also had a physical yearning for the bodily pleasures such frocks and jewels invited. The word "tasty" crops up as a kind of period-specific patois. Sally d'Yrujo in 1796 and Mary Boardman Crowninshield in 1816 described the new Grecian fashion as "most tasty" and "very tasty." They showed how this might evoke both the rarified aesthetic language of "taste" and the sensory physicality of tasting with the tongue, as though they might at any moment just lick one of these creamy frocks like a vanilla ice cream cone.[29]

In short, the Grecian gown was less an expression of rising nationalism or republican simplicity than a part of women's growing access to the international language of taste. That it resembled the flowing gowns of politicized female classical icons like Columbia showed that both female icons and real women could be clothed in the garb of classical antiquity while speaking to different audiences for different agendas. The classical robes of female political icons could appeal to a broad public that liked to express present political concerns by gesturing in a general way to the re-publics of antiquity. In the meantime, American women were pursuing a parallel project that sought through a highly specific form of classical in-cantation a different meaning for antiquity. Their robes invoked less the republican austerity of Columbia's iconic gowns than Grecian luxury and Turkish exoticism, safely harnessed to women's daily lives by a corset and a hatpin.

GRECIAN SOFAS

Like the Grecian robe, the Grecian sofa illuminates women's particular attraction to neoclassicism. Although daybeds and couches appear before the revolutionary period in household inventories, it was not until the late eighteenth century that elite Americans began to purchase upholstered neoclassical sofas for their drawing rooms. By the middle of the nine-teenth century, sofas had become all the rage and were sold in catalogues at all price ranges along with matching chairs and tables in an increasing array of classical and non-classical styles. Their showplace was the parlor. The parlor was an emerging symbol of middle-class refinement, a place in which Americans could be in public and at home, reading and conversing, while draped in a posture of semi-repose that, like the newly popular rock-ing chair, bespoke simultaneous comfort and decorum.[30] The varied shape of sofas suggested their diverse uses: some were meant for conversa-tion, inclining their occupants toward one another, while others were meant for reading or reclining. But, until roughly 1830, the most popular style was the Grecian sofa (or "sopha," as it was often written), with its sweeping lines and classical motifs, such as carved Greek keys, lyres, cor-nucopias, paw feet, and caryatids. It was often covered with richly hued (often crimson) damask, silk, or horsehair.

The sofa is extraordinary in being associated chiefly with women: they ordered them, bought them, looked at them, wrote about them, had their portraits made while posed on them, and of course, lay and sat on them. Why?

One reason was gentility, the term most often used by women of this period to describe the sofa. Nothing said "wealth and taste" faster than a sofa. Visiting Paris in 1809, the Quaker hatmaker's wife Margaret Boyle Harvey (1786–1832) pointed out this function of the sofa. "The people we took the house from were not moved out; meanwhile we bought furniture, not forgetting a Sofa, an article thee all know I am fond of. But persons cannot make as little furniture answer here as in America, for if there is not some degree of gentility kept up, the common orders will think nothing of us."[31]

Beyond style, some of the appeal of the sofa was sensual. The sofa was puffy and soft, a delight in an age that increasingly put a premium on physical comfort. It was a private relief for women squeezed all days into stays, though the term, *fainting couch*, did not exist at this time. So compelling were the delights of the sofa that the English poet William Cowper enshrined it as the apex of English civilization in his poem, *The Task* (1785), which was popular on both sides of the Atlantic. Household furnishing manuals recommended the Grecian sofa as an elegant, more comfortable replacement for earlier styles. One 1828 manual recommended that Americans with drawing rooms replace the "stiff, high-backed, undeviating chairs, and the clumsy, unwieldy tables of our grandfathers" with "the easy elegant curve of the Grecian chair and couch, which combined strength and lightness." But the realities of furniture technology were such that comfort levels varied widely. Some couches were great clouds of pillows and soft silk; others were mahogany nightmares covered by horsehair bolsters "hard as logs of ebony."[32]

The classicism that spurred the sofa's popularity, however, also linked it to fears of debauchery, variously construed. First was the bacchanal. Designers of neoclassical sofas drew some of their inspiration from *klinai*, couches found in ancient Greece and Rome, which became better known as archaeological digs, such as those at Herculaneum and Pompeii, uncovered the daily lives of the ancients. *Klinai* had been introduced into Rome from Greece and formed a highly prized feature of the Roman household. Although some were specifically for sleeping, more commonly they were arranged around three sides of a low dining table, following the Roman custom of dining while reclining (a practice that gave the Roman dining room the name, *triclinium*). At first, following the Greek custom, women were not allowed to lie down on *klinai* to eat, but instead sat at their husbands' feet for the evening meal. Later, however, women claimed a place next to men, and even slaves were allowed to eat recumbent on holidays. Americans might have been infatuated with many things about ancient Greece and Rome, but the practice of recumbent dining was not one of them. In fact, by the early nineteenth century the American middle-class dining room had become a forum for upright formality, a posture encouraged by high-backed dining chairs. The fact that ancient sofas had been used for recumbent dining made them guilty by association with the sofa's notorious role in orgies.[33]

The neoclassical sofa also reeked of another kind of debauchery: luxury. Luxury, of course, was in the eye of the beholder, but it was widely conceded in the early national period that the sofa not only embodied luxury, but gave it the classical spin that rendered its opulence a particular threat to a republic modeled on Rome. Already in 1790, the *New-York Weekly Museum* told the story of a greedy, lazy young widow, "educated in luxury," who gloats about her unearned wealth while "lolling one evening upon a damask sofa." (Not by coincidence, the widow was named Sempronia, a name shared by the Roman aristocratic lady condemned by Sallust for her sexual rapacity and involvement in the conspiracy against Catiline.) Neoclassical sofas retained their association with luxury even as they moved down the social ladder into middling households by the 1830s; the movement was hastened by lower prices and technological improvements, such as coiled springs, which made sofas more comfortable and durable. In the 1820s a Moravian family in North Carolina still referred to "such luxuries as sofas." Much more than just an upholstered bench, the sofa was often singled out for its particularly republic-threatening properties. In 1820, Stratford Canning, the British foreign minister, was stunned to behold the grandeur of Congress because he had presumed it would be the seat of republican austerity. ". . . Instead of the venerable simplicity . . . the H. of Representatives, besides being stoved, carpeted, desked and so-faed in the most luxurious style, rivals and indeed surpasses the Legislature of Paris in decoration and drapery."[34]

Like the Grecian robe, the Grecian sofa was thoroughly infused with Oriental associations. The word *sofa*, first used in English in the seventeenth century, was derived from the Arabic word *soffah* and referred to the raised area of floor covered with sumptuous carpets and cushions found in Eastern countries. The word even in its earliest uses evoked the mystery and dissolute exoticism of the harem, the setting for the repose and allegedly promiscuous sexuality of the sultan and his veiled wives. In a similar manner, the word *ottoman* began to be used in the nineteenth century to describe a piece of furniture (rather than a person or place). The silks and other fabrics that covered many sofas were themselves products of the eastern trade in luxury goods.

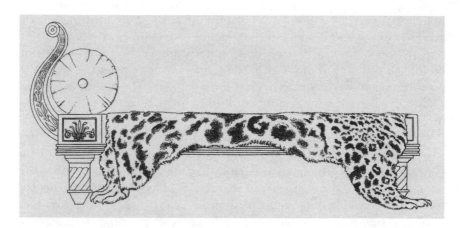

30. A "low sofa, after the eastern fashion," from Thomas Hope, *Household Furniture and Interior Decoration* (1807). Courtesy Stanford University Libraries.

Called the "gentleman of sofas" by Lord Byron, Thomas Hope was the man who most influenced American views about the sofa. One of Hope's guides described a "low sofa, after the eastern fashion," picturing one strewn rakishly with a leopard skin (see figure 30). His *Costumes of the Ancients* was filled with spare line drawings of people drawn from Greek and Roman statues and vases. The book shows several ancients recumbent on sofas. In one plate, a "Syrian" woman reclines on a sofa (see figure 31), while another plate (labeled as a Bacchanalian scene) shows a man and woman embracing on a sofa. American women spoke of the sofas in Oriental terms. Rebecca Gratz (1781–1869) of Philadelphia observed in 1821 that a wealthy woman's drawing room "was certainly more like an apartment in an eastern fairy tale, than a Phila parlour."[35]

It was luxurious; it was classical; it was Oriental. But what specifically made the sofa female, the crucial modifier in the dire republican equation of "luxury and effeminacy"? The sofa's popularity spanned the decades when the shift toward white, middle-class female domesticity—and its implied female leisure—was being made. The role of women in popularizing such a symbol of republican vice becomes clearer when we understand that leisure was a badge of familial success worth advertising in portraits and parlors, even if it did not accurately portray the realities of women's workload. Along with the parlors that contained them, sofas began to achieve popularity in America after the Revolution, during the decades of the transition to a market, wage economy. Sofas functioned ideologically as the opposite of manufactories and of the men who labored at machines, and they suggested that elite and middle-class women were delightfully

31. A "Syrian" woman recumbent on a sofa, from Thomas Hope, *Costumes of the Ancients* (1812). Courtesy Stanford University Libraries.

above such mundane matters. The reality, of course, was far more complicated. Elite and middling women did work at home despite the presence of servants or slaves; at the lower end of the economic spectrum, by the early decades of the nineteenth century, women, such as those at the Lowell Mills, were working on machines and earning wages. But while women of all classes arguably worked hard, in the realm of ideas, some women's work began to be dissociated from symbols of economic value like property and wages.[36] The soft, sinuous sofa rebuked the straight, unyielding, noisy gadgets of the machine age. The fabrics that covered it—silks and damasks—were those of women's clothing. Sofas, and especially women on sofas, embodied "luxury and effeminacy," but this could be made to mesh with an emerging republican emphasis on female domesticity.

Exotic, luxurious, debauched, and effeminate, the sofa became a perfect vehicle for commenting on the French in the early national period. This convention had a long history. Preliminary contributions to the sofa literature had, in fact, been French; the first fictional account to make the sofa the forum for erotic activity was an early anti-clerical pornographic tract, Abbé du Prat's *Vénus dans le Cloître* (1672). "Assieds-toi sur ta couche comme tu étais, je vais fermer la porte sur nous," says one young nun to another. ("Sit down on your couch as you were; I'll go close the door for us.") Better known in the English-speaking world was *Le Sopha* (1745), by the French writer Crébillon-fils, published in London in English translation as *The Sopha: A Moral Tale* (1781). In this bizarre yarn, Brahma punishes a dissolute man by forcing his soul to transmigrate into a sofa; from this new vantage point, he observes the passionate goings-on of women and men in the Oriental seraglio. "There are few chaste women on the Sopha," he says, his words setting the tone for adventures to come. The sofa is placed in a cabinet, a place of "hypocritical luxury," where many a woman "gave herself up to pleasure, but knew not what it was to love." The narrating sofa was just one of a whole genre of stories of "speaking objects" that flourished in the eighteenth and early nineteenth centuries. These stories featured favorite items of the burgeoning consumer market like fans, mirrors, wigs, umbrellas, pincushions, and stagecoaches. The sofa was the only novelty to be featured explicitly as a prop for love. The genre was durable in America: *Godey's Lady's Book* printed a number of such stories throughout the nineteenth century.[37]

Americans' simultaneous horror and fascination with French sofa-bound dissipation was exemplified by their interest in the debauched, imperial grandeur of the Napoleonic era. A central figure in the mythic construction of the Diréctoire as a decadent cultural formation dominated by women was the legendary Juliette Récamier (1777–1849). Madame Récamier self-consciously fashioned her image and delighted in the contrast between her austere, white gowns, which portrayed her as the image of feminine modesty, and the iconography of erotic repose implied by her pose on the sofa. The best-known image of Madame Récamier was Jacques-Louis David's painting made in 1800, in which she is shown reclining fully clothed on a sofa with bare feet peeking out from her snowy robe and curls framing her winsome face. The American press followed the movements of Mme. Récamier and others in the Napoleonic court with great interest. In 1806 a number of American magazines reprinted a report of her admirable retirement from the "circle of fashion," her abandonment of the "dissipation of courts," in favor of "fulfilling her first duty, that of a wife." As in the eighteenth century, class determined who sat at the apex of classicism, and the wealthiest Americans could one-up mere readers of newspapers. The Charlestonian aesthete John Izard Middleton befriended Juliette Récamier in the fall of 1807 when they were cast together in a play by Mme.

de Staël. He commissioned a small copy of François Gérard's scrumptious painting of Juliette Récamier for his display at the family Middleton Place in South Carolina (see figure 32). She sits, semi-recumbent on what appears to be a semi-sofa. She seems to be preparing to bathe in the water lapping at her bare feet; her gauzy Grecian robe, held up by the flimsiest mechanism, seems destined for the laundry basket behind her. While not exactly a scene from a Turkish bath, this is an example of how the Grecian taste could absorb Oriental eroticism.[38]

The sofa's career in the United States showed, as did the Grecian robe, women's ability to create and sustain networks of cosmopolitan taste and style that fused classical prestige with a beguiling tincture of Turkish exoticism. But wasn't all this Grecian luxury corrupting the new Roman republic? How did American women reconcile these luxuries with the endlessly repeated injunction that they selflessly raise their sons to patriotic service in conditions of bucolic asceticism? How, in other words, could they be both virtuous Romans and luxurious Greeks?

THE JEWELS OF CORNELIA, MOTHER OF THE GRACCHI

For the problem of reconciling Grecian luxury with Roman austerity, Americans—and especially American women—marshaled a major figure from the ancient Roman world: Cornelia, mother of the Gracchi, who had lived in the third century BCE. They loved one story in particular, known from Plutarch, Dionysius of Halicarnassus, Livy, and especially Valerius Maximus. This was the parable of the jewels, in which Cornelia snubs the necklace offered to her by a friend, while insisting that her children are her only ornaments. Here is the parable, distilled to its essence in the 1807 *Ladies' Weekly Miscellany*, one of numerous Cornelia nuggets collected in early national magazines and books.

> Cornelia, daughter of the great Scipio, and wife of the consul Sempronius, was one day in company with some Roman ladies, who were shewing their trinkets, and admiring their jewels, and whose minds seemed wholly occupied about their dress; observing Cornelia sit silent among them, they asked her to shew them *her* jewels, upon which, with a true maternal pleasure, she called her *children* to her, and presenting them to the company, said, "these ladies; these are my ornaments; these are my jewels, whom I have endeavoured to educate, for the good and glory of their country."[39]

This story of awesome Roman-style feminine austerity was emblazoned on a number of sumptuous objects. It was perhaps best known from Angelica Kauffman's painting of the subject in 1785 (see figure 33). The image

32. Portrait of Madame Juliette Récamier, by Pierre Guérin after François Gérard. c. 1808, oil on porcelain. The Middleton Place Foundation, Charleston, South Carolina.

dramatized the problem of how to educate girls in Roman virtues of selfless civic virtue in a society teeming with luxurious materialistic temptations. Clad in ethereal white, Cornelia stands in the center of the painting, refusing the jewels held up to her by the seated visitor. Cornelia's sons, Tiberius and Gaius, enter at left, one carrying a scroll on which the letters "ABC" appear: they have been well educated to the service of Rome by their mother, and they take her lessons to heart by staying far from the visitor. But while Cornelia can point to her sons as her proudest ornaments, her daughter's

33. This was perhaps the best-known visual representation of the beloved parable of Cornelia and the jewels. Angelica Kauffman, *Cornelia Pointing to Her Children as Her Treasures* (ca. 1785). Virginia Museum of Fine Arts, Richmond. The Adolph D. and Wilkins C. Williams Fund. Photo: Katherine Wetzel. © Virginia Museum of Fine Arts.

role is far more problematic. Cornelia holds little Sempronia's hand, but the girl has turned away and fondles the pearls that spill from the visitor's lap. Such was the female propensity to luxury and effeminacy.

The scene obviously captivated a young woman at a female academy in Massachusetts, who made it into a needlepoint based on Francesco Bartolozzi's engraving (1788) of Kauffman's painting. The parable of Cornelia's jewels also appeared on fans, in books and magazines, on a stained glass at Harvard's Memorial Hall, and in a magic lantern show in Philadelphia in the 1870s. It also crept into quotidian life in more subtle ways. In 1841, the American portrait miniaturist Thomas Seir Cummings gave his wife a necklace made of nine ivory miniature portraits of his children. He called the piece "A Mother's Pearls."[40]

The legendary parable of Cornelia and her jewels exhumed a central problem in the republican tradition and helped Americans—especially American women—reconcile Grecian getting and spending with Roman thrift and austerity. It specifically addressed how this problem would be worked out for mothers, and showed how women could combine materialism with maternity. The 1819 *Ladies' Magazine* of Savannah, Georgia, explicitly mentioned the story of Cornelia and her jewels as an object lesson for women "in a Republic like this."[41] The parable took an ancient tradition of tying women and jewelry to national health, and reworked it specifically for a republic. American women would contribute to the republic by educating their children—their ornaments—and by cultivating a republic of merit rather a nation of inherited rank.

Even in antiquity Cornelia was the star in the firmament of Roman matrons. She was the daughter of the Roman general and statesman Scipio Africanus, the Elder (237–183 BCE), who had conquered Rome's archenemy, Carthage, and laid low its famed general, Hannibal. She was also the mother of the two Gracchi brothers, Tiberius (163–133 BCE) and Gaius (153–121 BCE), renowned for their populist sympathies. She bore twelve children in all, though only three survived to adulthood (besides the two brothers, a daughter, Sempronia, also lived).

According to the historical sources, Cornelia was an exceptionally intelligent and broad-minded woman, who had been raised to unusual levels of education in the cultured Scipio family. As was typical for a woman of her station, who was expected to help her family cement political alliances, she married a prominent politician. After his death, she refused marriage to King Ptolemy of Egypt, thereby embodying the Roman ideal of *univira*, the woman forever faithful to one man. Single to the end of her days, she put her intellect first to the service of her sons and second to the service of Rome. She personally chose her sons' tutors and closely observed their adult careers as politicians who promoted populist causes like agrarian reform. If rumors are to be believed, Cornelia helped to engineer the assassination of her daughter's husband. When her two sons were killed, she withdrew to a villa at Misenum, where she opened a kind of literary salon, invited dignitaries, and regaled them nobly and tearlessly about the exploits of her sons. Chaste, fecund, intelligent, educated, and civic-minded, Cornelia was ideal Roman matronhood incarnate. She is the only non-mythological female figure in Rome to be publicly portrayed in a statue before Augustus's principate in the late first century BCE. Only the pedestal of her statue has survived, and its inscription encapsulates the reason for her enduring fame: that she selflessly promoted the men in her life for the greater glory of Rome. It read, "Cornelia, Africani f. / Gracchorum" (Cornelia, daughter of Scipio and mother of the Gracchi).[42]

By the early 1800s American women were increasingly reflecting on the problems of rising luxury in a nation that equated austerity with civic virtue. Catharine Maria Sedgwick (1789–1867) was one. In 1810 a ship had arrived laden with the latest muslins, and her friends were speculating about what they wanted from it. Sedgwick replied:

> I wish there was some philosophy in vogue that would free us from the slavery of these petty wants. Nothing less than the "genius of universal emancipation" will effect it, and I am afraid that even this wonder-working genius has no microscopic eye to discern the pigmy chains that bind us in this debasing dependence. These aspirations to heroic indifference are nothing more nor less than the consequence of a provoking disappointment of my mantua-maker; so you see I am not free from, but irritated by my chains.

The wealthy Maryland plantation mistress Rosalie Stier Calvert was another. Of noble birth, she was no friend of austerity or populism, and she loathed Thomas Jefferson, but could not see her way around the luxury-austerity dilemma. "We have all the luxury of Europe and have lost that simplicity which was worth far more," she wrote to a friend in 1810. Women tempted by the classical luxuries they saw all around them were clearly torn. In Paris in 1797, Mary Stead Pinckney relayed her conflicting desires when she visited one of France's finest porcelain manufactories at Angoulême, where she saw "cups & saucers with beautiful miniature figures rivaling the first master on ivory." But she struggled with her conscience: "ought I to be ashamed to tell you how I longed? & yet then would follow how I resisted."[43]

Whatever its modern form, the problem of reconciling a healthy polity with luxury was an old conundrum. Since the ancient period the problem had assumed the palpable form of women and jewels, and had entered political rhetoric as the cancer of luxury and effeminacy. Jewels could be good or bad: they were symbols of women's vanity and propensity to luxury but also of the wealth through dowries they brought to their marriage. The word "paraphernalia," in fact, had its root in the Latin term "parapherna," used among ancient Roman jurists to describe property over and above a woman's dowry, and over which a husband had no control without her consent. Under British common law, all personal and moveable property belonged to the husband, but *paraphernalia* referred to things like jewels and dress over which wives retained free use.[44]

Women, jewels, and national welfare were already linked by the time Cornelia was born. In 195 BCE Roman women had assembled en masse in the Forum to lobby for the repeal of the *lex Oppia*, which was passed twenty years earlier during the height of Scipio's wars with Carthage. This law limited the number of luxury goods (chariots, gold, and jewelry) that a woman could own without their being considered unlawful luxuries. Livy's version of the debate over the repeal of the law suggested the range of meanings that Romans assigned to women's ownership and display of jewels. Cato lobbied vigorously to keep the law in place, and he said that jewels were just some of the many vices of women that eroded the fragile fabric of the republic. His opponent argued for a more positive view of women's jewels: now that peace and posterity had been restored, women should be allowed to wear and enjoy the luxury goods proper to their sex. It was in this context of nostalgia for the ostensibly simple, austere days of the republic gone by that Romans began to circulate the parable of Cornelia and her jewels. Even in ancient Rome then, the story of Cornelia and her jewels carried an element of nostalgia for the simpler early days of the republic. The most popular version of the story appeared in a tale told by the first-century moralist Valerius Maximus, who saw in Cornelia's renunciation of jewels the living incarnation of the old-style republican mother more devoted to her children than to ornamentation.[45]

In the eighteenth century, an age besotted by Roman exemplars of judicious statecraft, jewels remained a favorite means of tying the household to the nation. The symbol of the decadence of the French monarchy before the revolution was the notorious "diamond necklace affair," in which Queen Marie-Antoinette was rumored to have secretly trafficked in jewels. Thomas Jefferson blamed her in part for the French Revolution, citing the exhaustion of the French treasury. By contrast, women's giving up their ornamentation to the needs of the state symbolized their virtue and patriotism. A group of female artisans in France bestowed their jewels on the revolutionary cause with these words in 1789: "One [possession] is left for our use, which vanity employs for an ephemeral triumph—these are our ornaments, so dear to beauty, so varied by fashion, so vaunted and sought after by national taste and foreign imitation. Here is the offering we must make with enthusiasm, French women. We do not need citations from the example of either the Romans or the Spartans."[46]

By the eighteenth century some political economists began to rethink the age-old link between female morality and jewelry. In the *Wealth of Nations* (1776), Adam Smith tried to show that jewels were not a symbol of a peculiarly feminine vice but that they simply embodied a certain kind of value. There were two kinds of value, he said; "exchange" value and "use" value, each of which contributed in its own way to the wealth of the nation. Water had a high use value and little exchange value; diamonds had high exchange value but were useless in and of themselves.[47]

But Adam Smith was clearly in the minority in trying to unlock jewels from female morality. In the American revolutionary period, popular and philosophical opinion continued to single out women and jewelry as particularly important symptoms of national health. In his *Spirit of Laws* (1748), a work that deeply influenced American revolutionaries, Montesquieu specifically cited the incident of the Roman women urging the repeal of the Oppian law. Montesquieu reiterated the view of the Roman moralist Valerius Maximus, that the date of the law's repeal marked the beginning of the "epoch of Roman luxury." The non-importation agreements of the American pre-revolutionary period invoked the frugality of Roman matrons to encourage women to patriotism through abstinence. In 1774 the *Royal American Magazine* called upon America's "Roman matrons" to lay aside their luxuries, among them "Fringes and jewels, fans and tweeser cases."[48]

As the revolutionary war progressed, it was not enough simply not to buy, a kind of passive virtue that had been encouraged in American women and men with the non-importation associations of the pre-revolutionary period. By 1780, with the war stretching interminably on, active patriotism was required: women should give up their money and their ornaments for the state. Esther DeBerdt Reed (1746–1780) explicitly alluded to women and their jewelry to encourage women's financial donations to the revolutionary cause. In 1780 she published the first petition on behalf of American women to urge them to give money to the revolutionary war effort, by saying that modern women would be emulating the active heroism of the Roman matrons of antiquity." "Who, amongst us, will not renounce with the highest pleasure, these vain ornaments, when she shall consider that the valiant defenders of America will be able to draw some advantage from the money which she may have laid out in these . . . ?" She then gave the specific example of a heroine of Shakespeare's play *Coriolanus:* "Rome saved from the fury of a victorious enemy by the efforts of Volumnia, and other Roman ladies." Such praise for the material renunciation of Roman matrons continued unabated well into the antebellum period, when a broadside of 1840 quoted Livy to compare the Boston women, who had raised money for the Bunker Hill monument, to the Roman matrons who had renounced their "chains and ornaments of gold" for their country.[49]

By the early 1800s, however, Cornelia's lauded rebuff of her diamonds was rubbing up against economic and social reality; rising wealth and consumer demand were causing women to buy and wear more jewelry than they ever had before. In the post-revolutionary period, Americans not only imported more jewels from abroad, they also increased their domestic manufacture. Before the second decade of the nineteenth century, organizations had been formed in many American cities to promote indigenous manufacturing. In 1817, one of them specifically addressed the question of women's ornaments as the key to national health and linked them to classical antiquity. "The fictions and fables of antiquity are realized in the short annals of our country," it began. "And you, fair daughters of Columbia . . . disdain the fashions of foreign climes; . . . let your dress be national; let your ornaments be of your country's fabric, and exercise your independent taste in suiting the array of your toilet to your own climate and your own seasons."[50]

The problem of Grecian luxury and Roman austerity was probably most ably channeled by Margaret Bayard Smith, who wrote about Cornelia's virtues because they seemed so relevant to the dilemmas facing modern American women. Margaret Bayard was born to an elite political and revolutionary family and received an education typical for a girl of her station at the Moravian Young Ladies Seminary in Pennsylvania. Against her family's wishes, she married her second cousin, Samuel Harrison Smith, a Republican, and, in 1800, moved to the new, neoclassical federal city, Washington, DC, when it still consisted of a few buildings poking up from a northern Virginia swamp. ("Voila un Capitol sans Ciceron; voici le Tibre sans Rome," remarked one early French visitor.) Here this modern Roman matron remained an avid reader with a particular interest in the history of ancient Greece and Rome; she often commented on parallels between ancient Roman parables and her own life at the center of the parlors and political life of early national Washington. In 1809 Smith visited Thomas Jefferson at Monticello and borrowed from him what she called "Greek romances." "He took pains to find one that was translated into French," she recalled. In her fiction, she footnoted authoritative works like Basil Kennett's *Roman Antiquities* (first published in 1697 and a staple of college and private libraries into the nineteenth century) and Cicero's

De Senectute (which she called "on Old Age," probably because she had read it in English translation).[51]

Like other elite women during the administrations of Thomas Jefferson, James Madison, and James Monroe, Smith was part of a wide, quasi-political, quasi-personal network in the capital city. These relationships were forged and sustained through formal, public ceremonies and more private forums like the drawing room and salon, which were now fitted out in luxurious Grecian taste and crowded with men and women dressed in silks and velvets. A veritable Versailles sprouting from the swampy banks of the new Tiber, this opulent society worried Smith. She confessed to her sister in 1807 her fear about these "splendid" drawing rooms packed with men and women who displayed "the dangers of dissipation." But there was the work of patronage and networking to be done in these luxurious drawing rooms with their Grecian sofas and klismos chairs. Smith described a private evening at the White House, sitting on the "sopha" with Thomas Jefferson, his daughter, Martha Jefferson Randolph, and her own husband, Samuel Harrison Smith, nearby:

> I was seated on the sopha which he and Mrs. R. occupied and Mr. Smith close by me, and almost fronting him. You know the effect of such a disposition of places on the free flow of conversation, and I am certain that had he been on the other side of the chimney we should not have heard half so much.[52]

For Smith, the sofa-centered, classical drawing rooms of elite Washington society afforded her—and other women in her circle—a chance for political and social influence.

Having idealized the society of early Washington, DC, as the virtuous, republican heyday of the new Rome, Martha Bayard Smith was among the first to bemoan its apparent decline into crass materialism and political and moral corruption, problems she saw heralded by the administration of President Andrew Jackson in 1829. Her diagnosis of imminent decay— Roman style—appeared in a series of six short stories that she published in the early 1830s in Sarah Hale's *Ladies' Magazine*, which was among the first American magazines to be edited by a woman. Most of the stories were set in first-century Rome during the reign of Nero (54–68 CE), the emperor notorious for plundering the national treasury and apocryphally fiddling while Rome burned, and for murdering not just his wife and mother, but also his famous teacher, Seneca. Now in her early fifties, Smith saw, in imperial Rome's "general corruption of morals" a parallel to Jacksonian America. "In no period in Roman history," she informed her female readers, "did a darker gloom invest the aspect of society, than in the time of Nero, 'when virtue,' in the words of Tacitus, 'was a crime that led to certain ruin.' "[53]

In her stories, Smith locates the bulwarks against republican decay in an idealized Roman household dominated by women and their classical paraphernalia. In Smith's villas, Roman matrons—often widowed and grieving, but always virtuous—are the pillars of republican society and candidates for heroism far more deserving than men. "Allowing however the devotedness and fortitude of these heroes to be greater than that of the Roman matron—were not their supports greater? Were they not more than rewarded for temporary pain by immortal glory?" Smith looked back nostalgically to her own days as a young Washington wife circulating in elite society to call for a return to the days when both men and women participated in learned, political conversations. "The social circles of Rome, at least those of the higher classes, were always composed of both sexes. Virtuous and learned women mingled with statesmen and philosophers, and imparted to society that refinement which they alone can impart. . . . They had ceased to be the slaves, and had become the friends and companions of men."[54]

In this pantheon of exemplary women, one stood out especially for Smith: Cornelia, mother of the Gracchi. Smith spelled out exactly the dilemma that Cornelia could help to resolve in the new Rome. Above all, Cornelia, as a paragon of virtue, exalted merit above rank, and earned her laurels by being a mother. Smith explained how modern motherhood was essentially Roman. While wealth or title might be bestowed by the outside world, maternity was something earned through individual virtues, the fruit of what she called "intrinsic worth." Looking beyond any natural talent her children might have, the Roman matron saw above all the need to educate them: the children would be perfected not by external reward but by internal effort. "These are my only jewels," she would say of this meritorious achievement.[55]

The great irony of the parable of Cornelia and her jewels, of course, was that it rose on the wings of those new luxuries that old republicans thought would corrode the new nation. The story's message of republican merit and Roman frugality was emblazoned on those objects that most loudly announced their opulence, such as silk embroideries, fans, and lavish books. Through the new, classicized language of "Grecian luxury," women could announce their wealth and renounce it at the same time, could look for a way to be mothers and buyers, republicans and consumers, Roman matrons and Grecian goddesses. Perhaps they read further in Valerius Maximus's parable of Cornelia and the jewels to find a lesson that republicans both ancient and modern could take to heart:

> Surely he has everything who craves nothing, more certainly than one who possesses all things, because ownership of objects often collapses, whereas the possession of a good state of mind is not subject to any assault of unkind Fortune.[56]

FIVE

CLIMBING PARNASSUS, 1790–1850

In 1845, Elizabeth Rogers Mason Cabot (1834–1920) described a visit she planned to make one afternoon to see the books and art at the Boston Athenaeum. "I have been very kindly invited by Mrs. President Quincy to spend the day at their house in Cambridge with Mary, and go with them to the exhibition. I have spent a delightful day in going to the exhibition, going to the Library, and also going to see the Panorama of Athens given to the College by Mr. Theodore Lyman. It is very beautifully painted."[1]

In a few words, eleven-year-old Elizabeth Cabot summed up a major change in the classical world of American women, as women's classicism moved from private homes to public institutions, where it was infused with a new, morally didactic public voice. Through classicism reconceived as a project for the elevation of morals, women found yet another way to justify their involvement in numerous voluntary activities, which also included benevolent reform movements like temperance and abolitionism. Until now, elite women had encountered antiquity mostly in the privacy of their homes and shared it among a tightly knit group largely through letters, travel, collecting, reading, and visiting. Now, publicly accessible museums and libraries suggested that classicism was less private ornament than public *art*, endowed with moral power to elevate and refine. This shift also expanded the class profile of classicism. Elite women still participated through charitable organizations and as private donors to the museums and libraries. But now middling women could play an equally important role as the public who attended the museums and female academies, and as writers and readers of published articles and books about classical art.

Aiding classicism's shift from private code to public art was a gradual change in Americans' understanding of ancient Greece, and especially of fifth-century BCE Athens. That polis, long denigrated as the seat of dangerous mobocracy, now emerged from behind the previous domination of Rome to set the standard of democratic virtue in the Age of Jackson. Lopping off the old element of plush decadence *à la turque*, Americans now viewed ancient Greece as the cradle of freedom and democracy, of sturdy farmer-warriors so modern in their virtues that they might be hoplites in coonskin caps. "What is the foundation of that interest all men feel in Greek history . . . ?" asked Ralph Waldo Emerson in 1841. "The manners of that period are plain and fierce. The reverence exhibited is for personal qualities, courage, address, self-command, justice, strength, swiftness, a loud voice, a broad chest. Luxury and elegance are not known. A sparse population and want make every man his own valet, cook, butcher, and soldier, and the habit of supplying his own needs educates the body to wonderful performances."[2]

Ancient Greece became more acceptable as democracy itself became more palatable, but philhellenism had implications that extended beyond the political sphere to the realm of the culture. Most important, ancient Greece offered women and men a new avenue to self-formation. Drawing on German Romantic ideals of ancient Greece as a font of spiritual, aestheticized self-development, educated Americans after 1820 began to study Greek art and literature as high culture rather than as private ornamentation. Hellenists imagined Greece as an antidote to the gritty realities of an emerging industrial, capitalist society, and they enlisted philhellenism to defy the materialism, machines, and rampant getting and spending that undermined republican virtues. By studying Greek art and literature, Americans would transport themselves back to an idealized ancient Greek world and purge themselves of Jacksonian toxins. Hellenism represented a new secular ideal of self-formation, compatible with Christianity and yet nonsectarian. It allowed Americans a chance to perfect themselves in the earthly sphere while also offering a glimpse of the higher spiritual truths of Hellenism and culture. Ancient Greece and its political and moral virtues became a frequent subject of discussion in lyceum lectures, political speeches, and general-interest journals. For college boys, and then girls in academies, this change appeared first in their curricula, which by the 1850s included the study of the literature of ancient Greece: Homeric epic, the Greek tragedies of Aeschylus, Sophocles, and Euripides, and the oratory of Demosthenes.[3]

With democratic ideals ascendant, Greek aesthetics now became associated less with opulence than with Everyman. The trend was perhaps clearest in architecture manuals, which, by the 1830s, were promoting the Grecian style as a democratic one. Home-building guides explained how middling Americans could adapt public classical architecture to their own homes. In his popular manual, *The Architect, or Practical House Carpenter* (1830), Asher Benjamin offered practical hints for adapting Greek and Roman public monuments to the private homes of middling Americans. While he described the design for a marble fireplace, he noted that it could be made more cheaply of wood. He urged the carpenter to indulge his "wildest fancy" in design, while also suggesting that the wood fireplace be painted black so smoke would not discolor the installation. Greek aesthetics now also increasingly competed with other vernaculars like the Tuscan villa and the Gothic manse. Andrew Jackson Downing's *Cottage Residences* (1842) declared that slavish imitation of the stately columns and porticos of "Greek temples" were signs of "ambitious display" and "false taste." Much better was a home with a "beautiful and appropriate" form compatible with domestic life and American weather. People who "talk pure Greek" would be "laughed at by our neighbours."[4]

In women's dress, the columnar Grecian robe had utterly vanished by the 1830s, as ruffly skirts once again ballooned over a mountain of petticoats and hoops that reached peak circumference during the Civil War years. So much did the new, full skirts return to pre-Grecian styles that colonial-era dresses were now plundered for their stiff brocades and crisp silks. Some of the women who had been spectacular successes as Grecian goddesses in the period 1800–1830 could not adapt to the new era, and they clung to the opulent Grecian robe and its Turkish embellishments long after these had gone out of style. William S. Elwell's portrait of Dolley Madison, made in 1848 when the former First Lady was eighty years old, showed what Elwell described as "one of the Old School," a stately widow sporting her signature black velvet gown and turban, now a half century out of date (see figure 34).[5]

These exterior changes in dress and architecture testified to major internal changes in the minds and eyes of American women. Schooled in the growing numbers of female academies, museums, and libraries, American women acquired a new classical vocabulary and, more importantly, a sense of classicism's perfectionist purposes. From the private world of ornament and luxury they inherited from their mothers, this generation of women, born in the early decades of the nineteenth century, helped create a new classical world of institutions of art and culture open not only to elites, but also to the middle classes. Some of the women schooled in these academies and reading societies turned their classical educations into platforms for social reform in the antebellum period (a development we

34. The Grecian robe and Turkish turban remained Dolley Madison's signature style of dress, even after it had long gone out of fashion, as in this portrait made when she was eighty years old. *Dolley Madison.* By William S. Elwell. Oil on canvas. 1848. Stretcher: 76.8×64.1×3.2 cm (30¼×25¼×1¼"). Frame: 90.8×77.5×8.9 cm (35¾×30½×3½"). National Portrait Gallery, Smithsonian Institution. NPG.74.6

will trace in chapter 6). But building the new Parnassus came at a price: they built it, stone by stone, in part by dismantling the old world of Roman matrons and Grecian goddesses, separating objects and paintings in family collections and forgetting the books that schooled their mothers.

CLASSICISM IN THE FEMALE ACADEMIES

Among the remarkable transformations in the early national period was the proliferation of female academies and seminaries between 1790 and 1850. Equally significant was the flourishing in those academies of the study of classical antiquity. One count suggests that up to 50 percent of women's academies and seminaries were offering young American women some exposure to a combination of Latin, Greek, ancient geography, classical history, and mythology by the middle of the nineteenth century. The gains made by young women in the area of formal education during this period are remarkable, even though women's access to classical learning still lagged behind that of boys, who could attend college and, then, by the 1820s, even began to travel to German universities to pursue the first doctorates in classical study. Female academies (there were also all-male and coeducational academies) grew alongside other novelties in female learning, such as reading societies, the first of which was founded in 1805 as the Boston Gleaning Circle.[6]

The real revolution was less the presence of classicism in female academies than the role such academies and reading circles had in gradually expanding the class contours of classicism for American women. The female academies reached more deeply down the social ladder than the parlor-centered elite female learning of the eighteenth century. Classical learning became not just a badge of middle-class, female accomplishment, but a portal of entry into a rudimentary public life of writing and speaking. The friendships that women formed in their academy years also became the foundation for local, regional, and national networks of women's reforming activities. Thus, the importance of the female academies was not just female learning, whether classical or otherwise, but the institutionalization of the idea of female learning and preparation for public life.

Before 1800 much of the debate over formal female education centered on whether women should be educated at all. Classical learning was seen as something "derogatory to the natural character" of the female sex, as one writer phrased it in 1793. By the 1830s most Americans had conceded that women should receive some kind of formal education so that they could be better wives and mothers to virtuous male citizens. Women's education should fit them for the "higher destiny" of being a mother and wife, as George B. Emerson stated in his *Lecture on the Education of Females* (1831).[7]

For all their innovations, the female academies also placed limits on the extent of female classical learning. Most commentators agreed that women should not pursue the classics as far as men did. They were not so much fearful that profound classical erudition would make emasculating pedants out of women—the earlier fear—but that such extensive learning was simply irrelevant to their domestic duties, and, consequently, a waste of precious time. When commentators did praise the two European giants of female classical learning, Elizabeth Carter and Anne Dacier, they noted that such exalted learning enabled woman "to understand her duty better." Thomas Gallaudet, in an address to an audience at the dedication of a new building of the Hartford Female Seminary in 1841, explained that Greek and Latin for girls were "valuable accomplishments" if a "young lady has time and opportunity to devote to them," but that learning English should take priority.[8]

The Litchfield Female Academy, founded in Litchfield, Connecticut in 1792, exemplified the kind of classical learning available around the nation in the growing number of female academies. Its founder, Sarah Pierce (1767–1852), was born into a middle-class family in Litchfield and attended a local school, where she learned reading, writing, English grammar, and arithmetic (only boys learned Greek and Latin). Pierce represented new trends that came to characterize the academy movement. Academy founders were often women of less-than-elite status and served a clientele of both elite and middling women, propelling classical learning well beyond the rarefied niche it had occupied earlier.

In 1783, when she was just sixteen, Pierce's father died, leaving full responsibility for his widow and nine children to her older brother, John, then thirty-one. John Pierce sent several of his younger sisters to New York City to train as teachers, knowing that it was one of the only professions considered acceptable for young, unmarried middle-class women. No record of which school she and her sisters attended is left, but, in addition to their studies, the girls also were exposed to the highest social and political circles. These new connections became invaluable to Sarah Pierce in finding young women to attend her academy. But soon tragedy struck again: John died in 1788, and the family plunged again into dire financial straits. This situation seems to have been the final inspiration for Sarah to open her academy in 1792; it may also have contributed to her decision never to marry. She confided to a friend that she wanted to live "in single blessedness." The combination of Sarah's ambition to succeed, her single status in a nation that valued marriage, and her considerable erudition caused Catharine Beecher to portray her in a poem as "Minerva wise, the warrior maid." The school opened in her dining room in 1792 with enrollments of just two or three, and by 1798 a subscription drive had raised enough money for a building to house the school and the growing numbers of female students, which eventually topped 1,400. The school attracted elite and middle-class young women between the ages of six and the mid-twenties from all over the nation and even Canada.[9]

As did many other female academies after 1800, the Litchfield school offered Greek and Latin in the desultory way that was a sign of continued ambivalence toward teaching women these languages. And, as in many other academies, like the Female Department of the Raleigh Academy in North Carolina in 1811, Latin was taught at Litchfield by a man. John Pierce Brace joined the school as a teacher in 1814 and made some attempts to teach Latin to some of the girls. Abigail Bradley, a student from Massachusetts from 1812 to 1814, wrote home asking her mother to send her a "Lattin Dictionary." Both Sarah Pierce and John Pierce Brace conceded in 1832, in their description of the school's curriculum, that the "Latin and Greek languages" were "occasionally taught."[10]

Although Latin and Greek were only minor additions to the curriculum, the classical world—its history, geography, art, and mythology—formed central features of the offerings. The diary of eleven-year-old Julia Cowles, who attended the Litchfield Academy in 1797, offers some insight into what was being offered and reveals her own struggles to become Minerva ("I cannot recollect any History that we read today only that there was one Punic war," a typical entry reads). Like many elite women since the middle of the eighteenth century, young women at the Litchfield Academy read Rollin's *Ancient History*, though it is a sign of the persistent inequality in men's and women's classical education that Rollin was now being scrapped from elite male colleges as an embarrassing fossil. Women read it rapidly: Egypt on 5 July, through the Punic wars by 12 July, and onward through the Assyrians, Babylonians, and Persians. Sarah Pierce also used Alexander Adam's *Roman Antiquities* (1791), Oliver Goldsmith's *Roman History* (1769), and Samuel Whelpley's *An Historical Compen* (1807). Students or teacher read aloud at the front of the class, and the students copied furiously into their daily journals; they were expected to memorize this information and recite the contents to the teacher.[11]

Quickly tiring of the futility of this method for teaching history, Sarah Pierce published *Sketches of Universal History Compiled from Several Authors for the Use of Schools* (1811) to accomplish the task better. Subsequent volumes were published in 1816, 1817, and 1818. As the title suggested, the *Sketches* plucked bits and pieces from favorites like Rollin and arranged them in the form of a catechism, through the question-and-answer method from which the students would learn both historical facts and moral lessons. In keeping with traditional norms, Pierce submerged the history of the "heathen" classical world in a larger narrative about biblical antiquity and transcendent Christian truths. Her summing up in a section about the history of ancient Syracuse typifies the style. "Though God does not always chastise the wicked in this life, to intimate that greater punishments are reserved for guilt in eternity; yet he has never left himself without a witness, even among heathen nations, that he is a God, who hateth iniquity, and will assuredly punish the guilty according to their works."[12]

As they had done before in the family parlor, girls in academies pursued classical feminine "accomplishments" like painting and needlework. Lucretia Champion (1783–1882), who attended the Litchfield Academy, embroidered an allegorical print around the year 1800 based on one that she had seen in the Philadelphia magazine *Literary Miscellany* (1795). The print showed Minerva ("Wisdom") leading a young woman ("Innocence") along a shaded path toward an elaborate Roman temple; the caption reads, "Innocence Protected by Wisdom, in her Road in the Temple of Virtue." Madame de Genlis's *Arabesques Mythologiques* (1810) was also useful in melding classicism with accomplishment. This little book, which could fit into the palm of the hand, gave short descriptions of the best-known Greco-Roman deities, and was specifically intended for mothers to teach to their children. Each god's name was written out in elaborate script along with its mirror image to form a pleasing design; the whole was then encased in the trappings associated with each particular deity (hunting paraphernalia for Diana, wheat for Ceres, and so on).[13] A girl could learn to read, write, and practice ornamental penmanship, all while grasping the essentials of Greco-Roman mythology.

If embroidery, penmanship, and needlework replicated traditional female activities in the curriculum, a few innovations suggested aspirations for rudimentary forms of public life. Public speaking was the most prominent of these. Plutarch called oratory the wings of public business, and in an increasing number of academies, girls gave speeches to one another and to parents at end-of-year celebrations. The Young Ladies Academy of Philadelphia was a pioneer in this regard. Founded in 1787, it was one of the earliest female academies in America, supported by such educational reformers as Benjamin Rush. Although it was not specifically committed to classical learning for women, its young students learned about exemplary women from the ancient world. Priscilla Mason, in delivering the salutatory oration at the Academy in 1793, assured the "promiscuous assembly" that the "female orator" was equal to, even superior to, the male orator. Condemning shrewish Xanthippe, the wife of Socrates, for using oratory to bully her husband rather than to promote "reason," Mason claimed that women should be orators in all the same fields as men: the church, the bar, the Senate. She concluded by invoking the example of the Roman emperor Heliogabalus, who made his grandmother a senator and established a senate of women to which he appointed his mother as president. Later, James Neal, a teacher at the school, oversaw the publication of the essays and poems of some of the students in the *Philadelphia Repository and Weekly Register*. A woman signing herself "Maria, One of your former Pupils," contributed some verse in 1801 that she dedicated to James Neal. "Hail! to the friend of virtue and of youth," it began, and went on to praise the "knowledge" she had acquired from him. As more women began to learn about oratory, treatises on oratorical gesture included illustrations of orating women. Jonathan Barber's *Practical Treatise on Gesture* (1831) urged "decorum and simplicity" on its readers and included illustrations of a woman in Grecian dress gesticulating and falling to her knees.[14]

Some academies, by offering both Greek and Latin, were more radical. The Troy Female Seminary, founded in 1821 by Emma Willard (1787–1870), remained a giant in women's education in the nineteenth century. It enrolled over 12,000 students in the first fifty years of its founding. Distressed by the substandard education she had received as a child, Willard hoped at the Troy Female Seminary to offer education essentially comparable to that of college men. The curriculum included mathematics, science, literature, history, philosophy, and Latin. Its vice-principal, Almira Phelps (1793–1884), scoffed at the prohibitions against "females pursuing what are called *masculine studies*," and urged her pupils to study Latin and Greek. Greek, she argued, was especially useful because it taught young women about botanical nomenclature at a time when botany was viewed as a venture particularly suitable to women. By the mid-1830s, a number of schools modeled on the "Troy plan" had been founded in Maryland, Ohio, South Carolina, and other areas; so influential was the Troy seminary that some of the most outspoken feminists of the nineteenth century, such as Elizabeth Cady Stanton (1815–1902), fondly remembered the "profound self-respect" inculcated by the egalitarian education they had received at Troy.[15]

Other girls simply began to attend schools founded for boys. There are no statistics about this phenomenon, but it was a strategy pursued throughout the first half of the nineteenth century in families in which the father was deeply invested in rigorous classical learning and had a daughter who was up to the challenge. One of these was Margaret Fuller (1810–1850), the fiercely intelligent daughter of the Boston lawyer and politician Timothy

Fuller. He was so intent on getting his daughter a thorough classical education that he kept her up until very late in the evenings—after he had come home from work—to practice her recitations. She woke up from nightmares about passages in Virgil, but the result of his exacting pedagogy and her hard work was a soaring classical erudition and a lifelong love for what she called "my Romans" and "the enchanting gardens of the Greek mythology." (Later, as an adult, she held a series of conversations with other women about Greek mythology.) Timothy Fuller also allowed Margaret to attend the Cambridge Port Private Grammar School, founded in 1819. Established to compete with Boston Latin as a preparatory school for Harvard, the Port School (as it was called) admitted girls, and there the young Margaret Fuller attended classes in Latin and Greek along with the boys, reciting Virgil and Cicero with the future New England literati, like young Oliver Wendell Holmes. By age ten Fuller had read, in Latin, Caesar, Horace, Livy, and Tacitus, along with Plutarch's *Lives* in translation.[16]

Still, Margaret Fuller remained exceptional. The stark collision between the worlds of women's and men's classicism became especially clear in antebellum Cambridge, Massachusetts, where a few especially well-connected young women had access to the faculty of classical scholars at Harvard College. Along with some other young women, Ellen Tucker Emerson (1839–1909), the daughter of Ralph Waldo Emerson, attended the school of Louis Agassiz, which was held in his house. Also living there was the family of the most distinguished Hellenist and philologist in America, Cornelius Conway Felton (who, according to Ellen Emerson, christened Agassiz's one-hundred-by-one-hundred foot house the "Hecatompedon," a word that also referred to the Parthenon). Felton was engaged as the Greek teacher for the young women of the Hecatompedon, but Ellen Emerson's letters suggest that he was preoccupied with other matters, not surprising given his collegiate duties and participation on the lyceum circuit. "I have the famous Professor Felton of Harvard University for my Greek teacher, but for all that Greek flourishes but poorly, because we have a recitation only once a week, and several times a holiday or vacation comes in the way," she confessed to her father in a letter. Things seem to have gone better with Latin, she noted in 1857, but still the school routine of the girls was often interrupted. "Mr Felton has gone away and left us for a composition to write in his absence an abstract of Livy from the 3rd to the 21st book, only we are to read nothing but the Arguments, and shall never read the whole. Mr Felton says we are to begin at the 21st book when he comes back. I am very sorry, for I like Livy."[17]

Anna Cabot Lowell Quincy (1812–1899), the daughter of Harvard president Josiah Quincy, was even less lucky with Felton and Greek. Her letters show how a young woman could be near one of the epicenters of male classicism and yet feel utterly deficient. The home of President Josiah Quincy was a hub for the Cambridge intellectual community. Anna Quincy recorded in her letters the frequent comings and goings of Felton and his colleague, the Latin scholar Charles Beck. She felt chronically ill at ease, however; except for one year of her life, she was educated at home. "Felt horribly stupid & remember nothing worth mentioning," she wrote in 1833 after one of Felton's visits.[18]

Though it remained overall less rigorous than what college men received, classicism could thrive in the female academies in part because of the seamless melding of pagan texts with Christian ethics that had long characterized women's classical reading. For all of the talk in boys' schooling about expurgating obscene classical texts for youthful minds, the problem seems to have been solved in advance in the female academies because of the existing, rich literature on classical mythology made just for girls. These books were readily adopted in the female academies, but also continued to be read by young women who did not attend academies. There are a few expressions of women being aware that the ancients were somehow inappropriate for Christian women, but not nearly as many as we might imagine. In 1814 Harriet Manigault of Philadelphia described her discovery of Socrates in the library of her uncle in such terms. "Mama and my Aunt played at piquet, and after I had [done my needlework] for some time, I bethought me of my Uncles library, & after considering for some time, I took courage and went into it, as I knew there were books there, that were not meant for ladies and I did not hesitate but took a volume of Socrates, found it most entertaining. I should like to read it through, but then they say that it gives one false ideas, etc."[19] But these episodes are far outnumbered by women's reconciliation of the two, a wholesome project made easy by a flood of books that encouraged a reading of pagan literature in the service of a Christian agenda.

Mary Monsigny's *Mythology* (1809) was such a text. Monsigny believed that girls should learn about classical mythology to understand classical references in poetry and painting. Her book reads as a kind of blow-by-blow of the major deities of Greco-Roman antiquity. Monsigny couched many of her descriptions in the circumspect language with which one might relate such adventures to young girls. In her telling, Jupiter "introduced himself to," or "carried off," his many lovers. Yet any girl would be able to read between the lines that much more was going on. Jupiter not only had "many wives," according to Monsigny, but her list of his other conquests of many "beauties" goes on for two pages. Where necessary, Monsigny is in fact frank: she baldly states that the "rape of Helen by Paris" was the cause of the Trojan War. Academy leaders agreed with Monsigny, and acknowledged that while these may at times be "disgusting fables," they had many uses, not the least of which was to give women a common cultural currency in a nation where classical allusion still formed a major feature of public discourse.[20]

Textbooks of history and geography pursued a similar goal, fusing the artistic glories of Greece and political virtues of Rome with a thoroughly sacred short chronology. Samuel Augustus Mitchell's *Ancient Geography*, first published in 1845 and billed on its title page as being designed for "academies, schools, and families," is listed in the syllabi of a number of female academies in the antebellum period. A monument to the Hellenists' love of Greece, Mitchell's textbook praises Athens as "the great seat of learning and the arts," and "the birth-place of the most eminent orators, philosophers, and artists of antiquity." The first half of the book is dedicated to the geography and history of classical antiquity, but a second section, entitled "Sacred Geography," makes clear that Athens must always be viewed in the context of Jerusalem. "The only credible account which we have of the origin of the world is contained in the Bible," Mitchell informs his readers, and thereafter he sticks to the short biblical chronology of an earth created in 4004 BCE. Even the Greek architecture of female academies was in the service of Christian ends. In New York, the Albany Female Academy, founded in 1834, was housed in the middle of the town in a Greek revival building of imposing Ionic columns. John Ludlow, the president of the board of trustees, assured his listeners at the opening convocation about the morality of the style of architecture. "This house . . . though modelled after the style of Grecian architecture, we dedicate to no Grecian deity—to none of the fabled muses of heathen mythology . . . [but] we do dedicate it to the All-Wise God."[21]

Though moralists promoted the view that middle- and upper-class women were benevolent creatures unsullied by passions and physical yearnings, the classical reading and art of young American women in the female academies suggest that they were in fact quite interested in learning about classicism's intellectual and sensual pleasures. A case in point is their enthusiasm for Ovid, the Roman poet whose *Metamorphoses* was a major source for Americans' knowledge of ancient mythology. Ovid's poem related the history of the earth and the gods and goddesses by showing the changes of spirit into matter over time; as Ovid makes his way through Greek and Roman mythology, one thing changes into another, and humans take the form of flowers, trees, and animals. Against the serious epic weight of Homer and Virgil, Ovid offered a frivolous and absurd romp through cool Arcadian glades, telling stories of adultery, jealousy, betrayal,

incest, and bestiality with such charm that for centuries he had been admired as a model of literary style. Ovid's, in fact, was one of the first Latin
texts to be published in the United States, but long before, lavishly illustrated Ovids had been among the most common classical books in colonial
libraries, and the texts had long formed part of boys' classical education.[22]

By the antebellum period, girls from progressive New England families
reported on their reading of Ovid—in Latin. Harriet Beecher Stowe
(1811–1896), who attended her sister Catharine Beecher's Hartford Female Seminary in the 1820s, recalled learning Latin and Ovid. "I began
the study of Latin alone, and at the end of the first year made a translation
of 'Ovid' in verse, which was read at the final exhibition of school, and regarded, I believe, as a very creditable performance." Ellen Emerson shows
how a girl could appear in letters to be utterly blasé about reading Ovid.
While attending the Sedgwick School in Lenox, Massachusetts, in her
mid-teens, she was taught Latin through several standard texts, including
Thomas Arnold's *Latin Prose Composition*, Virgil, and Ovid's *Metamorphoses*.
In her letters from school in 1853 and 1854, she told her father that at first
she loathed Arnold, but then realized Latin was the key to Ovid:

> We are going on very well in Ovid, learning alternately 60 and 90 lines a les-
> son. I can read my lesson now without my dictionary by me. The words I don't
> know I mark and look them out afterwards. I can read Latin better since I
> have studied Arnold for I know now what quin and quominus etc. mean and
> how they are used which always puzzled me before.

She decided in the end that Ovid was more "interesting" than Virgil,
though does not say why.[23] Ovid probably reached his largest audience in
Thomas Bulfinch's best-selling *The Age of Fable* (1855), a book later known
as "Bulfinch's Mythology." Bulfinch had studied classics—including Ovid—
at some of the best schools in the nation (Boston Latin, Philips Exeter,
then Harvard), and did his own bowdlerized translations of Ovid for this
compendium of mythology that he intended to be used as a "classical dictionary for the parlor," that kingdom of Victorian female propriety.[24]

Outside the careful boundaries established by Bulfinch and the female
academies, classicism could still function as a gender line in nineteenth-
century sexual knowledge. The classical nude woman, for example, became a staple of nineteenth-century pornography directed at men. Pornographic books and magazines could sell reliably by putting the word
"Venus" in their titles, and the backdrop of Cleopatra's boudoir or the Roman dining room was a dependably erotic stage-setter.[25] But if the pornography industry led classicism down one path, the improvement in women's

grasp of Greek and Latin led down another. One consequence of the female academies was that men could rely no longer on Latin as a language of exclusion, whether from the public world of print and podium or the private realm of the boudoir.

MUSEUMS: FROM ORNAMENT TO ART

Female academies educated women's classical minds; museums preached to their eyes and souls. These secular temples of art positioned classical things—neoclassical sculpture, genuine antiquities, plaster casts, or paintings of women in classical garb—in a different relationship to the viewer than had the pedestals, parlors, and niches of elite homes. Before, classical objects had been arranged according to the fancy of an owner interested in displaying familial wealth and power. Now, museums offered a second use for classical things that was dependent on the older mode of ownership and display, but had public functions quite different and new. Classical objects, lent by a private citizen to the museum, were now exhibited in a painstakingly arranged array to inform and elevate the public who came to visit them. Women were essential to the transition from private classical objects to public classical art. They are often listed as the owners of the objects, sometimes as the artists, and often as the subjects. During the antebellum period, they gained access to the language of art criticism central to this new public project of the art world. But one unintended consequence of the shift was that it dismantled the female, family-centered, elite classicism of the eighteenth century by putting portraits of Roman matrons and "Grecian" goddesses into new visual and cultural contexts. Because we have inherited the art world of this later, Victorian generation, we too have lost sight of the one that came earlier.

The Boston Athenaeum, founded in 1807, shows that women were involved in the shift from the private to public display of objects in the project of didactic, moral uplift. The Athenaeum was founded by a group of eminent Bostonians, who christened this combination literary society and museum an Athenaeum to make clear its connections to what they saw as Greek ideals of artistic refinement and public elevation in a democracy. "A nation, that increases in wealth, without any corresponding increase in knowledge and refinement, in letters and arts, neglects the proper and respectable uses of prosperity. . . . When we admit the dignity and use of the science of the learned, the taste of the refined, and the improved and cultivated character of the citizens at large, we must also admit, that these objects require a fostering care, and will not be obtained without adequate means and incentives."[26] The Athenaeum's move to the Greek revival building on Pearl Street (which it occupied until it moved to Beacon Street in 1850) cemented the association between American high culture and Greek antiquity.

Women had "at least an indirect interest" in the Athenaeum, according to the founders. First, the Athenaeum would raise the character of men, and by extension, "that of the other sex." Second, well-informed citizens made "the intercourse of the sexes the more rational and agreeable." With this lukewarm endorsement, women were invited to attend the lectures, to use the books in the circulating library, and to enjoy access to the "other apartments," presumably the "Repository of Models" that housed copies of sculptures. To do so would help women who "aim to be connoisseurs," and would allow them to "bestow praise and censure with discrimination."[27]

By the late 1820s the Athenaeum was actively soliciting the participation of women as lenders of art and as members of the viewing public. Its first public loan exhibition of paintings was held in 1827 in the hope of making the Athenaeum a rival to the successful academies of art in Philadelphia and New York. The paintings were on display in the topmost room of the Athenaeum, a huge space, 50×60 feet square and 20 feet high, lit from the top. An announcement of the opening assured the public that both men and women were welcome: "Visitors will find every attention has been paid to their accommodation; and Ladies will experience no embarrassment or difficulty in visiting the gallery without the attendance of gentlemen." Membership in the Athenaeum was limited to men, but six "lady artists" exhibited their work at the 1827 exhibition.[28]

Beginning in 1839, the Athenaeum's new sculpture gallery became a repository for classical female statuary, either marble neoclassical sculptures like those of Antonio Canova, or plaster casts of ancient originals. A few favorite casts had been housed at the Athenaeum early on—the Venus de' Medici and a Diana—but now the collection swelled to over eighty pieces and included the work of American sculptors like Hiram Powers, William Wetmore Story, and Harriet Hosmer.[29]

With its doors open to women, the Athenaeum sculpture gallery became a place for women to view classical female statuary and to discuss that art in the language of cultured taste. In a tradition begun by the German aesthete Johann Joachim Winckelmann, and continued by American romantics visiting European museums, American women in the Athenaeum's temple of art were urged to view such statuary in the rapturous quasi-religious tones of transcendent reverence. As creatures of ostensibly elevated sensibility, women were eager participants in, and creators of, the new language of art connoisseurship and criticism. One woman, writing in a magazine in

1845, explained the new role of Art. "There is pleasure, intense pleasure, in the consideration of Art as *Art*, in the exercise of a cultivated and re-fined judgment; in the faculties of comparison and nice discrimination, brought to bear on objects of beauty. This is criticism, or connoisseurship, properly so called." Anna Quincy, visiting the Boston Athenaeum with her mother and sister in 1833, saw some paintings and a Greek drinking cup. "Pictures beautiful," she announced, specimens of "the wonders of nature & art." Ellen Tucker Emerson, twenty years later, went to the Athenaeum with a female friend, saw the white marble busts of Daphne and Medusa made by Harriet Hosmer, and was overwrought with the beautiful ideas she witnessed there. "I'll go wild with delight I can't think how Hatty Hosmer survived the joy of finishing that Medusa, of realizing such a beautiful, beautiful idea. Such a face, such a position of the head, so fine an expression."[30]

The female nude as the embodiment of Truth and Beauty could never entirely suppress its obvious use as a comparison set for real women. Anna Quincy found the nude female statues at the Athenaeum disconcerting not only because of their potential for moral corruption, but because they made her self-conscious about her appearance in the eyes of men. She could not, that is, entirely separate the classical female form in statuary from her own female figure in flesh. Commenting on her encounter with a male visitor in the Athenaeum galleries, she compared herself to a Grecian statue viewed by a man. "As we flitted across the top of the Staircase—He probably would have taken us for some Grecian Statues suddenly endowed with life—which perchance had *followed him* from Italy." She described the sensation of artistic appreciation, and of apprehension, produced by view-ing Canova's semi-nude statues of Hebe and the Graces at the nearby Corinthian Hall, using the word "Grecian" to mean both artistic beauty and an alarming absence of female drapery:

> Drove first to Corinthian Hall, to see some copies of Canova's statues which Mr. Felton a few evenings before had entreated us to go & see, declaring they were the most exquisite things ever beheld, & that we "seldom saw so much of the Grecian"—As we presumed that we seldom saw so much of something be-side the Grecian, we hesitated, as to the propriety of going—but curiosity prevailed—& we drew up to the door—Mama and Margy went up first, & said if there was nothing there to shock my tender mind, they would send down for me—So in a few moments, I was summoned. And truly they are exauiste [*sic*] indeed—but cannot describe—The Hebe is rather my favorite—The Graces are grace indeed, & their beauty made me glad—& their having a few flutter-ing shades of drapery still gladder—All the specimens, are superior to any-thing of the kind we have seen.[31]

The overlap between women's perceptions of classical statuary and their perceptions of themselves was reinforced by medical and prescriptive literature that compared ideal modern beauty with ancient beauty. In 1831 Sarah Hale's influential *Ladies' Magazine* urged young women to employ "a careful observation of classical figures" to "form the taste and improve the style of dress." By way of illustration, Hale showed a bust of the poet Sappho, and held her up as a model of "coeffure." Particularly common were comparisons of the Venus de' Medici with modern women. Venus, cast as a naturally, healthfully, straight-spined women unfettered by too-tight stays, became central to the corseting debates of the 1820s and 1830s. Anticorseting tracts by physicians and moral writers showed the torso and head of a Venus to contrast the healthy, straight spine of the uncorseted, Greco-Roman woman with the sickly spine of the modern woman (see figure 35). Venus was the "natural" woman juxtaposed to what the American physician Charles Caldwell called the "artificial insect waist" of the woman stuffed into a corset. His medical contemporaries concurred. "The most elegant woman that we ever saw, had never worn a stay or a corset," wrote one contributor to the *Boston Medical Intelligencer* in 1825. "Yet, in the perfection and symmetry of her figure, she might have been modelled for a Venus."[32]

Elizabeth Rogers Mason Cabot was less baffled than disgruntled by her exposure to the female nude at the Athenaeum in 1857. That year a painting by William Page went on display; it showed Venus on a half shell, guided over water by two putti and two doves (see figure 36). Like much American statuary and painting depicting the female nude, it was given a narrative pretext that made the nudity palatable to audiences. Re-christened *Venus Guiding Eneas and the Trojans to the Latin Shore*, the painting was displayed at the Athenaeum to great fanfare. Elizabeth Cabot struggled to find "beauty" in a canvas that showed the human figure she had been schooled to endow with transcendent meaning. She was not successful:

> Went with Ellen Ward to see Page's picture of Venus rising from the sea. I decidedly do not like it. No doubt the painting is fine, and it has great beauties. The coloring is certainly rich and rare too, but I was shocked by the want of refinement, and rather surprised at the want of beauty to my eyes. Not that the entire want of drapery seems to me so bad, for there need be nothing revolting in the human figure; but it can be treated in a refined and spiritual way, or in a coarse way. Then the attitude seemed to me artificial and impossible. It was a fat handsome woman, not a spiritual goddess. To be sure Venus was not of that type, but I think it should have been so in such a picture.

Others agreed. The painting was roundly denounced for its "repellent realism" of an "animal woman," and, therefore, for its failure to embody

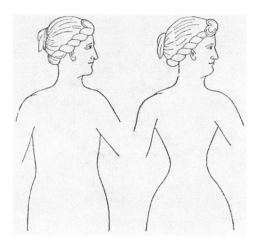

35. The healthy, uncorseted "Venus de Medici" is at left and the sickly, "well-corsetted modern beauty" is on the right. Charles Caldwell, *Thoughts on Physical Education* (1834). Young Research Library, University of California, Los Angeles.

"divine creation." The Salon of Paris, the Royal Academy in London, and the National Academy in New York all rejected the painting.[33]

Classicism at the Athenaeum was also moving in a second, equally important but more subtle direction. In its galleries were also displayed the classicized portraits of American women preserved by families from the eighteenth and early nineteenth centuries, when American women had posed in the garb of Roman matrons or in Grecian robes. Since part of the goal of the Athenaeum was to celebrate the achievements of American artists, the portraits made by such local heroes as John Singleton Copley and Gilbert Stuart were displayed in a number of highly publicized exhibitions from the 1820s onward. One effect of these exhibitions, however, was to rip their portraits of women from the familial lineage of female classicism that had characterized the earlier period. The private owners of female portraits in the Roman style of the 1770s (exemplified by Copley) and the Grecian style of the period 1800–1820 (exemplified by Stuart) now lent these paintings to the Athenaeum. Hung on walls in an array chosen by the curators, the portraits lost their earlier links to female classicism and became a forum for public elevation. It was clear that elite women still had a familial claim to these portraits: of the eight portraits by John Singleton Copley exhibited in 1828, four were owned by women. But the older meanings of these paintings were now lost. An exhibition in 1871 displayed Copley's *Mrs. Joseph Henshaw* (1770), the painting that had so clearly resembled Catharine Macaulay as a "Roman matron" (figure 8, p. 57). Loaned by a "Miss S. H. Haywood," Copley's portrait of Sarah Henshaw was hung among other portraits made by Copley, but the

36. William Page, *Venus Guiding Eneas and the Trojans to the Latin Shore* (c. 1857–1862). 1983.88. Smithsonian American Art Museum, Gift of Frederick C. Page and Lowell B. Page, Jr.

resulting emphasis was the genius and artistic progress of the artist, not the Roman virtue of the sitter.[34]

The older classical vocabulary was so obscured that explanation seemed necessary to educate the public in the peculiar rituals of a vanished, exotic tribe of "Grecian" females. In 1828 the Athenaeum held a memorial exhibition of the paintings of the recently deceased Gilbert Stuart, who had lived in Boston during his final years and had been the painter in chief to the nation's "Grecian" nabobs. The *Columbian Centinel* of 6 August 1828 applauded the 250 portraits by Stuart on display, and he noted the "many distinguished Ladies" made by Stuart's brush, such as Martha Washington, "that amiable and distinguished ornament of her sex, and the constant companion—in the darkest days—of the Americans Cincinnatus." But now that such frocks had gone out of style, the Grecian robes seemed strange. One contributor to the *Boston Daily Advertiser* explained away the Grecian dresses worn by Stuart's sitters as the oddities of an earlier age: "Those who cannot see the beauty of these heads, are blinded by prejudice—and I pity them. There are individuals who look at the short waists, and exclaim 'what horrible figures;' let them recollect the odious fashion that concealed the symmetry of the figure, and remember fashion disfigures all, more or less." He reminded his readers that the Athenaeum's display of this collection of heads had a higher moral purpose, affording "the highest treat to a cultivated taste; more so probably than any exhibition ever seen in the city."[35]

The transition of female classicism from private ornament to public art did not proceed evenly everywhere. Lending the prized classical patrimony of the family to a publicly accessible museum required a conviction that public elevation achievable through culture was as important as the lineage of the family doing the loaning. It also required a willingness on the part of social elites to mingle with the general public who viewed this art in public galleries rather than in one another's private homes. In this regard, the antebellum South—with fewer public funds, smaller cities, and elite families turned inward by a highly class- and race-defined society—showed less commitment than the North.

In Charleston, South Carolina, for example, the cultural jewel of the antebellum South, leading families failed to embrace the museum as a place of public high culture. There had been a few attempts to create local art academies, such as the Academy of Fine Arts, founded in 1821. But as an art historian has recently shown, Charleston elites were not interested in promoting the professionalization of artists, nor were they enamored of the idea of loaning their pictures to benefit the sort of people they would not invite into their own homes. They had no need to go to the academy themselves: they had all seen one another's art anyway. The museum's collections remained less spectacular than what could be seen in private homes, and it closed by 1833 for want of support. In the increasingly defensive political climate of the antebellum years, Charleston elites retreated into their homes to view canvases displaying their classical gentility, proudly displaying the patrimony of their classicized family portraiture.[36]

Charles Manigault (1795–1874) of Charleston exemplified the persistence of this older tradition of familial classicism well into the antebellum years, a tradition in which women's social status was communicated through association with Roman female virtues. The grandson of Ralph and Alice Delancey Izard, Manigault inherited not just the family's social status (though this had diminished somewhat since the revolutionary era), but also a commitment to its continued display in his mansion. His first major purchase as an adult was John Singleton Copley's portrait of his grandparents in Rome, made in 1775, in which Alice Delancey Izard hands her sketch of Papirius Praetextatus to her husband (figure 11, p. 63). Recalling this precedent of familial classicism, Manigault commissioned a portrait of his own family in a Roman setting, and it was completed by Ferdinando Cavalleri in 1831 (see figure 37). Here, with the city of Rome in the background, Manigault's wife tends to their two young children in a classical architectural setting. The moment Manigault received the two portraits from Europe, he held a dinner party to show them off. Later, he hung Copley's portrait of his grandparents "conspicuously" in the drawing room "surrounded by our numerous family portraits."[37]

Though a few other Southerners, like the Manigaults, remained willing to identify with an older tradition of familial classicism, it was a tradition rapidly losing its moorings. During the first half of the nineteenth century, the voice of female classicism began to shift from the private familial network of elites to the public, civic culture of art and elevation. Female academies shifted classical history, mythology, and even languages from the rarefied, elite family parlor and library to an increasingly diverse class of students and reached beyond the local town to summon a national population of young women. A few women even began to attend the first co-educational colleges, where they could pursue the same classical curriculum as young men. At the same time, museums such as the Boston Athenaeum moved classical objects—casts of Venus, neoclassical statues, classical paintings lent by wealthy women—into halls open to a broader civic world. What was lost in the move of female classicism from private to public were the local, familial impulses that drove a few generations of

37. *Charles Izard Manigault and His Family in Rome, 1830,* by Ferdinando Cavalleri (Italian, 1794–1861). Oil on canvas, Gibbes Museum of Art/Carolina Art Association, 2001.13.

early American women to identify deeply with Greco-Roman womanhood by taking on pseudonyms of Roman wives or posing flamboyantly as Grecian goddesses. What was gained, as the next chapter will show, was a radically new sense by a few women of how the women of classical antiquity could be used to reform self and society.

SIX

THE GREEK SLAVE, 1830–1865

In the 1840s, more than one hundred thousand Americans flocked to view one of the most controversial art works of the day: Hiram Powers' white marble statue, the *Greek Slave* (1841) (see figure 38). The statue depicts a nude, modern Greek slave, her hands bound in chains by Turkish captors. A few symbols clothe her in the language of Victorian virtue. A cross suggests her Christianity and a locket her fidelity to one person. Her pose recalls the modest posture of the Venus de' Medici. But the *Greek Slave* was far more than a statue, as was clear when the abolitionist press compared her to "a Virginian slave," which, if displayed, would have "a better moral effect."[1] The statue derived its power from collapsing into the familiar classical female form three overlapping American preoccupations of the period 1830–1860: black chattel slavery, women's rights, and the liberation of modern Greeks from Turkish rule.

Taken separately, these concerns were hardly new. Eighteenth-century American women had known that the ancient Greeks and Romans had held slaves and that many of those slaves were women. How could they not? Many of the women filling the most beloved and revered literature of ancient Greece and Rome had been slaves or captives. The *Iliad* alone is a compendium of such heroines: Helen of Troy, abducted by Paris, and Andromache, enslaved by the Greeks after they torched Troy. Other widely circulating parables featured women traded as war booty, as in the story of the Continence of Scipio, in which a young bride is traded in the contest of empires. The public praise of Roman matrons often stemmed from their dignified bearing despite enslavement. In 1790, when Edmund Burke

38. Hiram Powers, *Greek Slave* (1841–1843). 1920.3.3. Smithsonian American Art Museum, Gift of Mrs. Benjamin H. Warder.

lauded Marie-Antoinette as a Roman matron as she was toppled from her throne, he praised the French queen's "dignity" despite her "captivity." American women had also been long fascinated by the women bought and sold in the slave markets of the modern Orient. A fascination with the eastern slave market remained a feature of nineteenth-century women's Oriental travel narratives, as in Sarah Haight's *Letters from the Old World* (1840), which described a "slave market" in Egypt full of black and white women destined for the harems. It was also figured in new renditions of the "Roman play" set in Turkish-ruled Greece, like Mordecai Noah's *Grecian Captive* (1822).[2]

What was new in the 1830s was not women's awareness of female slavery in the classical past, but their mobilization of classical slavery in the service of the modern antislavery or proslavery cause. From the polite, ornamental classicism of the eighteenth century sprang this new, polemical classicism of the nineteenth century, pressed into service for the social reform movements of the antebellum period. Fired by fierce moral convictions, a few highly educated women now searched the classical past for common threads of a universal female oppression that would help them to knit black chattel slavery, the traffic in Oriental women, and the oppression of white American women into a cloth. For some, the new, morally urgent classicism fueled a lifetime of public protest against all kinds of slavery. For others, classicism affirmed the rightness of black and female submission. Whatever their paths, these women could assume a national audience of women, educated by female academies, books, and magazines about classical history, mythology, and literature, who would understand the easy parallelism between ancient and modern institutions.

For this new public project of female classicism, the Roman matron was less necessary than earlier as a form of self-identification. Unlike the elite women of the revolutionary generation who had identified with the dignity and stoicism of Roman matrons like Portia to grope toward a sense of women's politicization, women of this new generation—with a few exceptions—found their own identities sufficient, and they published under their own names. Their classicism was of a new, public kind, more open to women of the middling, evangelical classes than was the elite, ornamental classicism of the eighteenth century. It is significant that women's self-identification with the Roman matron endured longest in the proslavery South, where her elitism—and implicit slaveholding—was the most rhetorically necessary.

The early nineteenth-century philhellenic movement also encouraged the tendency to merge ancient and modern female slavery into a reformist agenda. Philhellenism involved not just the love of the artistic beauties and political perfections of ancient Athens, but also a commitment to the "liberation" of the modern Greeks from Ottoman Turkish rule. In the 1820s philhellenes in Europe and America rallied around the modern Greeks' revolt against the centuries-old dominion of the Ottoman Turks. Americans likened the Greek revolution (1821–1829) to their own uprising against British tyranny half a century earlier. They hoped that the modern Greeks, whom they considered degraded and enslaved by Turkish oppressions, would return to the glorious ancient Greek past, when artists and philosophers, Truth and Beauty, flourished in democratic institutions under the mild Mediterranean sun. Lyceum lecturers, college professors, and reform-minded women in the North and South drummed up funds and material support for the Greek Revolution.

A giant in this group was Emma Willard, who saw in Greek liberation an opportunity to educate the women of Greece, who endured the "vilest slavery" from men who wanted to "possess them." The founder of the progressive Troy Female Seminary (1821), Willard and her supporters also founded the Troy Society for the Advancement of Female Education in Greece in 1833. Here they would educate their Greek "sisters" and bring to them the light of Christianity. The cause met with some ridicule. Some critics pointed out the irony of supporting Greek liberation at a time when black slaves still wore shackles in America. Speaking to a group of Virginia women making clothing for the Greek relief effort, Congressman John Randolph was said to have pointed to gangs of black slaves, remarking, "Ladies, the Greeks are at your doors."[3]

Women's use of the classical past in abolitionist and proslavery arguments differed in important ways from the Greco-Roman world summoned by men in the antebellum era, when northerners and southerners turned to classical and biblical arguments to defend or attack slavery. In an act of bravura projection, the northern antislavery Democrat George Bancroft envisioned the Roman world as one torn between the degraded male slave and the liberty-loving "free laborer" or "yeoman" who plowed his own land, the very image of self-mastery beloved by Northern democrats.[4] Against this male world of slavery and free labor, antebellum women offered a Greco-Roman world of women, who, by virtue of their sex, could never be fully "free" in the masculine terms envisioned by George Bancroft. The classical world envisioned by antebellum female reformers was one of smaller spaces, of households, looms, and shrunken horizons, of finely parsed degrees of unfreedom. But this antiquity had a rhetorical power of its own, and through it antebellum women addressed some of the most significant questions of the decades before the Civil War. Had women in ancient Greece and Rome been less or more free than women in the modern American republic? Did Greeks and Romans treat their female slaves better or worse than modern Southerners treated their slaves? Did Roman categories of heroism, such as dying for liberty, apply to modern female slaves who fled to the free North? Could black women who fled to freedom be compared to heroic women dying for freedom in Carthage, a city now thought by some to have been populated by blacks in antiquity? Might these fleeing slave women indeed be noble enough to qualify as Roman matrons, or could only white women claim those laurels?

WOMEN, CLASSICISM, AND THE ANTISLAVERY ARGUMENT

The most vocal and influential American woman to condemn modern slavery through classical history was the antebellum reformer Lydia Maria Child (1802–1880). Today most Americans remember her—if they remember her at all—only from her children's ditty ("Over the river, and through the wood"), but in her day Child was lauded by her admirers as the "first woman in the republic." Child was among the first Americans to launch a sustained abolitionist assault on black slavery by reference to classical antiquity. In a series of publications in the 1830s that crossed genres from pamphlet to history to novel, Child connected the modern enslavement of blacks to the oppressions of women past and present, oppressions that also included female slavery and the traffic in female captives. For Child, these oppressions could be eliminated through an interracial solidarity movement. It was essential to her progressive view of history that American slavery be shown to be a severe historical aberration, a departure from the trend of constant, upward improvement.

Child's class background reveals the shift in the social location of female classicism that had occurred since the late eighteenth century, when extensive classical learning had been confined to the most elite women. By contrast, Lydia Maria Child was the daughter of a baker, and her childhood was filled with the grueling chores required to run a household and family farm. Throughout her life, she remained proud of her lowly origins and made no secret of despising what she called "aristocracy." Her bestselling household advice book, *The Frugal Housewife* (1829), was dedicated "to those who were not ashamed of economy" and was the only domestic advice book of this period that did not take for granted the presence of servants.[5]

Child also knew the deprivations of sex. Her older brother, Convers, was allowed to attend an elite college preparatory academy before matriculating at Harvard in 1811. By contrast, she attended what she called the "common town school, where Tom, Dick, and Harry, everybody's boys, and everybody's girls, went as a matter of course." But once at Harvard, Convers continued to encourage her reading of Samuel Johnson, Addison, Gibbon, Milton, and Shakespeare, and after her graduation he introduced her to key intellectuals in the Boston area. In 1826 she married the aspiring politician David Lee Child, who was not only fluent in a number of modern languages, but also knew Greek and Latin, accomplishments that doubtless attracted her to him. Especially useful to her budding literary career was the connection Convers helped her to make with George Ticknor, professor of modern languages at Harvard College and a star in the emerging Brahmin literary firmament. Through these contacts she was able to get free access to the library of the Boston Athenaeum, a privilege given to only one other woman at the time.[6]

From books borrowed from the Boston Athenaeum's library Child taught herself about ancient and modern slavery. She read a number of books on the place of women in classical and biblical antiquity: William Alexander's *History of Women,* which she checked out several times between 1833 and 1834, Madeleine Scudéry's *Female Orators,* and an English translation of the Jewish historian Josephus. In these books she found fuel for her emerging abolitionist beliefs. Alexander's history links the decadence of aristocratic women to the decline of civilization; when Greek and Roman women gave their babies away to be suckled by slaves, they "became alive to the feelings of luxury, and less to those of nature." She also checked out William Cowper's new English translation of Homer (1791), in which she also would have found a Greece alive to the enslavement of women: Helen of Troy wonders if her beloved Paris will make her his "wife . . . or perchance his slave." She supplemented these classical texts with a gallery of modern works that drew attention to slavery in the New World, such as John Stedman's *Narrative* (1796), which was about the slave revolt in the Dutch colony of Surinam, and James Alexander's *Transatlantic Sketches* (1833), which documented the "starved and ragged negroes" and "exhausted tobacco-fields" in the U.S. slave states. Stedman's *Narrative* contained some of the most wrenching illustrations of manacled and tortured female slaves to circulate in the early years of the British antislavery movement. Child checked out the book twice. Child's readings during this brief period at the Boston Athenaeum fueled a lifetime of abolitionist and feminist agitation.[7]

Although Lydia Maria Child had been publishing antislavery pieces for some time in newspapers and magazines like William Lloyd Garrison's newly founded *Liberator,* her first major antislavery work was *An Appeal in Favor of that Class of Americans Called Africans* (1833). If its form—at 230 pages—smacked of the long-winded scholarly treatise, inside it was purely in the tradition of the revolutionary pamphlet. "Read it," she taunted her readers in the preface, "if your prejudices will allow."[8] Its flinty directness established Child as one of the major voices in the abolitionist movement and gave the fledgling group its first major historical analysis of the slavery question.

In the *Appeal*, Child laid out the views of ancient Greece and Rome that undergirded her later publications and influenced her most important female followers. First, she argued that Greece could be divided into two relevant camps: the Athenians, who owned slaves but treated those slaves well; and the Spartans, who, in the manner of planters in the antebellum South, trumpeted their own freedom while reducing slaves to the most abject conditions. She also reiterated the well-known, zero-sum equation of the slavery calculus that saw the institution of slavery moving in lockstep with freedom. She asserted that societies with the greatest stated dedication to freedom concealed the greatest dependence upon slavery.

> Between ancient and modern slavery there is this remarkable distinction—the former originated in motives of humanity; the latter is dictated solely by avarice. The ancients made slaves of captives taken in war, as an amelioration of the original custom of indiscriminate slaughter; the moderns attack defenceless people, without any provocation, and steal them, for the express purpose of making them slaves.

> Modern slavery, indeed, in all its particulars, is more odious than the ancient; and it is worthy of remark that the condition of slaves has always been worse just in proportion to the freedom enjoyed by their masters. In Greece, none were so proud of liberty as the Spartans; and they were a proverb among the neighboring States for their severity to slaves. The slave code of the Roman Republic was rigid and tyrannical in the extreme; and cruelties became so common and excessive, that the emperors, in the latter days of Roman power, were obliged to enact laws to restrain them. In the modern world, England and America are the most conspicuous for enlightened views of freedom, and bold vindication of the equal rights of man; yet in these two countries slave laws have been framed as bad as they were in Pagan, iron-hearted Rome; and the customs are in some respects more oppressive; *modern* slavery unquestionably bares its very worst aspect in the Colonies of England and the United States of North America.

Convinced of the effect of historical circumstance on individual behavior, she argued that slavery corrupted both black slaves and the white women who lived in slave-holding states. At the end of the *Appeal*, Child brought her historical survey into the present, launching one of the first female abolitionist attacks on the white female aristocracy of the South, on women whose "lady-like hands" whipped their slaves into submission.[9]

Calling for the immediate abolition of slavery in the United States, Child's *Appeal* catapulted her to the front of the abolitionist movement and of American female public influence. But the book also cost her many friendships and alienated her from the Brahmin literary establishment. Loyal readers boycotted her other works and canceled their subscriptions to her popular children's magazine, the *Juvenile Miscellany*. The Boston Athenaeum rescinded her free library privileges. Even when her abolitionist friend Maria Chapman raised one hundred dollars to buy Child a paying membership to the Boston Athenaeum, the directors would not reopen its doors to her.[10]

Rather than discouraging her, this opposition seems only to have galvanized Child's commitment to using the remote past to show the misguided historical and moral trajectory of the slaveholding United States. Her next two major publications of the 1830s used the same strategy as her *Appeal*, mustering the example of classical and biblical antiquity to use in the service of a modern feminist, abolitionist agenda.

The first of these was the first general history of women written by an American woman: the *History of the Condition of Women* (1835). In this two-volume work, Child wove together the history of women and the history of slavery, moving from the ancient Hebrews to the women of the modern American South. Her historical gaze was a chilling one. Her readings in ancient history convinced her that in all ages and nations, in all religions and social classes, women had been slaves or captives, bought, kept, traded, and sold. Especially prominent in her work was the link between wife and slave: the categories for Child are often indistinguishable. Some of these slave wives were well treated, such as the favorite "khatoun," the highest-ranking beauty in the Oriental harem; others knew no end to misery. Toward the end of the second volume, Child launches her indictment of slavery's effect on modern women, showing that the emancipation of slaves and the moral reform of modern women could occur only through abolitionism. "Slavery everywhere produces nearly the same effect on character," she announced. No slavery was viler than Southern slavery. Even in ancient Athens slave women could take refuge in a temple; the Turks emancipated many slaves after six years. But in the South, nothing lightened the load of slavery. Southern slavery corrupted elite white women, making them indolent. "Ladies thus educated consider it a hardship to untie a string. . . . They are far less capable, industrious, and well-informed" than women who lived in a "healthy system," wrote Child. Southern women had "a certain aristocratic bearing, acquired only by the early habit of commanding those who are deemed immeasurably inferior."[11]

Child forged ahead with her classical, abolitionist message in her novel, *Philothea* (1836), which places the drama of female perfectionism and slave emancipation in a classical Greek setting. The choice of this particular literary genre was not accidental. Like her female counterparts in the eighteenth century, Child struggled to find an appropriately "feminine" medium to deliver a political message. Mercy Otis Warren had settled on the venerable Roman play to comment on the dangers besetting the new republic in *The Sack of Rome* (1790). Child, nearly half a century later, turned to the historical novel, a form of literature finding new respectability and a large following among American women. She was also finding that her carefully crafted literary voice, acquired through a series of popular novels, such as *Hobomok* (1824) and *The Rebels* (1825), was being lost in the overtly political, abolitionist works to which she had turned in 1833 and 1835. Her novel, *Philothea*, was her attempt to come to terms with this awkward division between her political sympathies and her literary aspirations. Child also had to navigate between her aspirations to scholarly precision and the reality of her inferior female education. She did so by claiming that, as a woman who possessed refined sensibilities, she could retrieve the spirit of ancient Greece even though she lacked philological expertise. She dedicated the novel to her classically educated brother, Convers, and apologized for "an entire want of knowledge in the classical languages." She excused herself: "But, like the ignoramus in the Old Drama, I can boast, 'Though I *speak* no Greek, I love the *sound* on't.'" She proudly parted with "scholars" when she needed "freedom of description." An appendix at the end of the novel—with definitions and citations to various eminences—wrapped the book in the authority of the scholarly treatise. At once a novel, a classical history, and an abolitionist treatise, *Philothea* straddled genres and revealed the many scholarly and literary impulses driving antebellum female reform.[12]

Child's *Philothea* transported the modern abolitionist agenda onto fifth-century BCE Greek soil. Athens represented the free North and Sparta the slaveholding South. Child spared no ink in praise of the Athenians, describing Athens as a "free Commonwealth." Athenian political liberty found expression in an aesthetic of "graceful simplicity" and transcendental philosophy. Like others at this time, Child believed that national character found expression in art. She contrasted the unchanging, stiff forms of Ethiopian and Egyptian sculptors with those in Greece. Greece had "a sculptor who can mould his thoughts into marble forms, from which the free grandeur of the soul emanates like a perpetual presence." Athenians held slaves, she conceded, but "the Athenian slave laws were much more mild than modern codes." Still, all was not well in Athens. In a barely

veiled critique of Jacksonian politics, she argued that Athens could be easily corrupted by "that love of power which hides itself beneath the mask of
democracy."[13]

By contrast, Sparta was the picture of southern slave-holding debauchery. The Spartans believe that the Athenians "disgrace" themselves by "industry" and "mechanical" employment. To liberate themselves from these
disgraceful activities so they could spend time in "dancing, feasting, hunting, and fighting," the Spartans enslaved thousands of helots. "They seek
to avoid the degrading love of money, by placing every citizen above the
necessity of laborious occupation," observes one of Child's characters.
The men of Sparta thought of themselves as "the only real freemen," living where "courage and virtue" thrive. Spartans' views of slavery and slaves
resembled precisely those of the antebellum South. Child informs her
readers that "there was a Spartan law forbidding masters to emancipate
their slaves." Helots were utterly degraded by this treatment. Originally "a
brave people," Spartan slavery made them "servile and degraded." When
asked what reward the poor helots received, a Spartan replies, "They are
not scourged; and that is sufficient reward for the base hounds."[14]

Each of the main three female characters in the novel exemplifies a
moral attribute through the medium of classical geography. The heroine
of the story is the golden-haired Athenian, Philothea, who embodies
middle-class ideals of domestic American womanhood. Educated by her
grandfather, the philosopher Anaxagoras, she views Greek mythology as
an allegory of pure Platonic thought, a pre–figuration of Christian mono-
theism. She expounds upon these ideas to her "dark" friend Eudora, a
foundling from Persia who has been made a household slave. Like many of
the other slaves in the novel, Eudora is a non-Greek and lacks the "un-
mixed Athenian blood" that characterizes the "fair" citizens of Athens. Although inferior in morals and mind to Philothea, Eudora is still a speci-
men superior to the villainess of the novel, the corrupt, sensual, bejeweled
Persian, Aspasia, whose moral debauchery is communicated through her
recumbence on a "crimson couch." Whereas mild Athenian laws allow
women to achieve their full capacities, Persian women learn early on that
"woman's whole duty is submission."[15]

Philothea was well received by Child's contemporaries in both North and
South and brought her back into the fold of literary fame. Although he
took her to task for being insufficiently knowledgeable about historical
details, the Harvard Greek scholar Cornelius Conway Felton praised the
book in the *North American Review* as the "inspiration of genius." Even
Edgar Allan Poe, writing in the proslavery *Southern Literary Messenger,* recommended that students in the women's academies study *Philothea* because

of the "spirit" of Greek antiquity with which it was "wonderfully imbued." Poe noted that because of the remoteness of antiquity from modern sensibilities, it would be difficult for the book to become a popular novel. But Child's ability to unite the modern and ancient mind by evoking emotions and passions would surely win the novel a wide following, he argued. Child evoked "passions the sternest of our nature, and common to all character and time."[16]

Child's works utterly galvanized other female abolitionists. By the middle of the 1830s they joined Child in her condemnation of elite female luxury as a barrier to the spread of abolitionism. The sofa, in particular, came in for repeated bashing as a symbol of debauched femininity that might have been pulled straight from *Philothea.* The abolitionist Juliana Tappan was typical in seeing the sofa as the platform of aristocratic, female, moral sloth. When she found it difficult to drum up support for abolitionism in New York City in 1837, she lashed out at the rich society matrons whose minds were so stuffed with fashion and frivolity that they had no room for a political conscience. "Ladies," she said, "sitting on splendid sofas, in the midst of elegance, looked at us, as if they had never before heard the word *Texas.*"[17]

For Sarah Grimké (1792–1873), who was born and raised in a wealthy Charleston slave-holding family before turning to Quakerism and abolitionism in the 1830s, Child's new brand of reformist classicism was a revelation, a way to use classicism to prepare women for citizenship and the professions. She deeply admired Child's *History,* which she quoted a number of times on classical history in her *Letters on the Equality of the Sexes* (1837). It was "a valuable work . . . worth the perusal of every one who is interested in the subject." From Child's *History* Grimké pulled her comparisons between classical and modern women. She agreed with Child that American men ("our clerical brethren") echoed Greco-Roman oppressions of women because they were "endeavouring to drive women from the field of moral labor and intellectual culture." Child also drew Grimké's attention to the oppression of modern Greek women. "In Greece," Grimké wrote in her *Letters,* "even now the women plough and carry heavy burdens, while the lordly master of the family may be seen walking before them without any incumbrance." She quoted an English physician who "visited a slave market, where he saw about twenty Greek women half naked, lying on the ground waiting for a purchaser." The women were poked, prodded, and then purchased.[18]

Latching onto Child's new brand of reformist classicism required Grimké to renounce her glittering Southern world of opulent, private classicism. She did so with glee. "During the early part of my life, my lot was cast among the *butterflies* of the fashionable world," she wrote in her *Letters*. Her brothers were taught Greek and Latin to prepare them for useful professions, while she was denied the classical languages:

> Forgive me, if I intrude upon you a chapter of my personal experience. With me, learning was a passion, and under more propitious circumstances, the cultivation of my mind would have superseded every other desire. In vain I entreated permission to go hand in hand with my brothers through their studies. The only answer to my earnest pleadings was "You are a girl—what do you want with Latin and Greek etc? You can never use them," accompanied sometimes by a smile, sometimes by a sneer. Had I received the education I coveted and been bred to the profession of the law, a dignity to which I secretly aspired, I might have been a useful member of society, and instead of myself and my property being taken care of I might have been a protector of the helpless and the unfortunate, a pleader for the poor and the dumb.

Grimké proposed that women be taught Greek and Latin because learned women contributed to the growth of free institutions. "Our republic might be enlightened by the study of ancient history," she wrote in her unpublished essay, "The Education of Women." "In Greece women were admitted to the priesthood, enjoyed its highest dignities and were regarded with great veneration; so were the vestal virgins of Rome, who were an order or priestesses." Only the full development of women's faculties would liberate them from being the "*property*" of men.[19]

Grimké's reading of Lydia Maria Child's *History of the Condition of Women* influenced her own attack on slavery, especially her opposition to the biblical defense of modern slavery. By the 1830s proslavery apologists were turning to the Bible—with its many references to slavery—to defend the institution of southern slavery. But Grimké thought their reasoning was flawed and turned to a philological explanation to refute them. A published philological refutation of slavery—by a woman—was truly a novelty, a woman meeting men on the level playing field of linguistic erudition. She wrote that the Bible had been warped in "false translations" by men. "I am inclined to think, when we are admitted to the honor of studying Greek and Hebrew, we shall produce some various readings of the Bible a little different from those we now have."[20]

In her *Epistle to the Clergy of the Southern States* (1836), Grimké showed how knowledge of classical and biblical languages could be used by a woman as an instrument of social reform. The lack of a word for "slave" in ancient Hebrew suggested to her that "no such condition as that of slave was known among the Jews of that day." English translations of the Bible that implicated Abraham and others in slaveholding were themselves the product of England's entry into the slave trade. Translators sympathetic to the English slave trade consciously tried "to cast upon Abraham the obloquy of holding his fellow creatures in bondage, in order to excuse this nefarious traffic." Slaves in America must distinguish the moral truth of Christianity from the corrupt linguistic vessels of the translated Bible.[21] Like Lydia Maria Child, Sarah Grimké was one of the first women to see that women's knowledge of the ancient world could prepare them not for ornamental accomplishment but for civic activism and reform on the national stage.

WOMEN, CLASSICISM, AND THE PROSLAVERY ARGUMENT

Just as it was possible to use classical history and modern Greek female slavery in the service of feminism and abolitionism, precisely the opposite could also be the case. The Greco-Roman past and the Oriental female slave could be used to reaffirm racial hierarchies and traditional female roles of submission.

The most sustained consideration of the place of classical antiquity in defining modern roles for women and blacks came from the South Carolina slaveholder and essayist Louisa McCord (1810–1879). Only eight years younger than Child, and of essentially identical classical erudition, she was worlds apart in outlook. She owned approximately two hundred slaves, who worked the fields at her plantation, Lang Syne. A woman of towering intelligence and fierce convictions, she deployed these attributes in the systematic defense of Southern slavery, female submission, white supremacy, and inherited black inferiority. She published these views in such Southern literary bastions of proslavery thought as *DeBow's Review* and the *Southern Quarterly Review*. She identified strongly with the elitism, stoicism, and dignity of the Roman matron at a time when this ideal was losing favor among northern women. The bust of McCord sculpted by Hiram Powers in Italy in 1859, four years after she was widowed, casts McCord as a Roman matron, a modern reincarnation of Cornelia, mother of the Gracchi.[22]

McCord received some formal education when, starting from the age of nine, she attended William Grimshaw's school for young ladies in Philadelphia. Family legend had it that her real education began when she was discovered hiding behind a door while her brothers were being tutored, and was then allowed by her father to be instructed in subjects usually taught to boys (which probably meant she learned mathematics and ancient history). Throughout her life, she read deeply in translations of the classics and scholarly commentary on the classics. Her taste ran in the heroic mold and she scoured the classical past for models of exemplary courage and fortitude. Her efforts to remain up-to-date in classical reading are reflected in her reading of B. G. Niebuhr's *History of Rome*, translated from German into English beginning in 1828. Niebuhr published his multivolume work in German in 1811 and 1812, and it established him as one of the new generation of German historians who rejected the historical validity of early Roman legends related by sources like Livy. Niebuhr substituted what he called "searching criticism" for "poetical ingredients." But McCord constantly despaired that her own scholarly abilities rested on an inadequate female education. She sent some of her work for criticism to William Porcher Miles, a professor of mathematics at the College of Charleston, with this lament: "My misfortune is, that I am most wofully [*sic*] ignorant, and the not knowing even *where* to look for the information that I want, find it now, rather late in the day, to begin my groping in the dark." Even after reading Niebuhr, she considered herself "lamentably difficient [*sic*] in information."[23]

McCord believed that northern feminists derailed female development by pursuing goals to which the natural progression of things did not assign them. Just as Lydia Maria Child used classicism to bolster her abolitionist arguments, Louisa McCord turned to the most recent works available to make the opposite case. For McCord, both women and black slaves were naturally unfitted to enjoy the same rights as white men; the difference between "the negro" and "woman" was in degree, not in kind. Both needed protection because of inferior intellects and morals, and in the case of women, inferior and weak bodies.[24] She was a strong believer in a progressive view of history, in which civilization progressed upward to a Christian perfectionism. Deviations from this natural order—either by misguided women or emancipated slaves—threatened to topple Southern civilization and to usher in depravity and barbarity. Black societies were exceptions to the otherwise universal rule of historical progress. Despite contact with "civilizations" like the Egyptian, Phoenician, and Roman, they failed to develop those arts that defined civilization. She used Thomas Arnold's edition of Thucydides' *History of the Peloponnesian War* (1830–1835) to argue that even in ancient Greece racial mixture was a bad idea unless one race completely dominated the other. "The mixture of persons of different races in the same commonwealth," Arnold had written, "unless one race had a complete ascendancy, tended to confuse all the relations of life, and all men's notions of right and wrong." Slavery was the only way to safeguard morals and manners among whites (what McCord called "the Saxon"), a race "entirely opposed" to "the negro."[25]

Yet she made no bones about the enslavement of women. In many respects, in fact, she agreed with feminists' claims that women in all ages and climates had been enslaved. "In every government, and under every rule, woman has been placed in a position of slavery . . . in as much as she is deprived of many rights which men enjoy, and legally subjected to the supremacy of man." She acknowledged that many women suffered under such oppressive systems, especially those women of "dominant intellect." But society required its members to abandon certain rights in exchange for protection from those abler and stronger. Women should give up their "natural rights" in exchange for male "protection." She compared feminists, who "strip themselves" and "wrestle in the public arena," to "the half-barbarous, half heroic Spartan maid." These "monster-women" were "Amazons." True to her time period in combining classical references with Oriental ones, she attacked the novelty of the bloomer. These trousers, worn by feminist dress reformers beginning in 1851, were labeled "Turkish trousers" in the national press and frequently compared to the dress of "Oriental" women. McCord actually thought wearing pants was not such a bad idea, and, indeed, "a great improvement upon the dirty length of skirt wherewith our fashionables sweep the pavements and clear off the ejected tobacco of our railroad cars." But because Turkish trousers symbolized rebellion against established usage, she dismissed them altogether, condemning them as "no eastern dress" but simply "vicious."[26]

At a time when few Northern women were still publicly identifying themselves as Roman matrons, McCord identified with Cornelia, mother of the Gracchi. She loved the Gracchi, calling them "my *bona fide* heroes." She derived her esteem largely from the description by Plutarch, who devotes a whole section of his *Lives* to Tiberius and Caius. For McCord, a woman like Cornelia embodied the ideal of intelligent but subordinate womanhood that was women's proper place in the republic. Women should remain subordinate to adult white men, even their sons. But they should sacrifice their own luxuries for the support of their dependents. McCord cited the parable of Cornelia and the jewels when referring to her own slaves. When asked why she wore no jewelry, Louisa McCord replied as Cornelia: "that a woman with two hundred children [slaves] could hardly afford diamonds."[27]

McCord's five-act Roman play, *Caius Gracchus* (1851), exalted the benevolent influence of Cornelia, mother of the Gracchi. Just as the choice of the genre of the novel had been important for Lydia Maria Child, the choice of the venerable form of the Roman play signaled McCord's literary and political ambitions. While her contemporaries were choosing the increasingly acceptable form of the historical novel, McCord seems to have chosen the now rather antiquarian form of the Roman play as a vehicle because it looked inward to the domestic world even while taking on larger political themes. "As to my productions being *closet dramas*, what else can a Woman write," she explained to William Porcher Miles in 1848. "The *world of action* must to her be almost entirely a closed book." In the play, McCord pits the virtuous Roman populist Caius Gracchus against his self-serving enemies. Equally important in the play is Caius's mother, Cornelia, the picture of ideal motherhood. The Rome McCord creates for Cornelia is entirely confined to a private dwelling. Only twice does she step out. In one scene she is in the street, where her grandson exclaims that "women should not run in the street." In another—her final appearance—she goes specifically to the Temple of Diana to urge her son to fight his political enemies. And though Cornelia's only action is the education of her son, he attributes his worldly success to her:

> May heaven so bless you, as your son shall strive
> To prove the honor and the love he bears you,
> By working out the noble thoughts you teach.[28]

The play was at once a public statement of her own maternal and republican principles and a private gift to her only son, Langdon Cheves McCord (1841–1863), who was named in honor of her adored father. She dedicated the play to him with a poem in which she describes herself as being "in bondage" to her love for him. As Louisa was caring for Langdon, who was injured and later died fighting for the Confederacy, her long-time friend Mary Boykin Chesnut bestowed upon Louisa the highest compliment she could: "mother of the Gracchi."[29]

LIBERTY OR DEATH: THE CLASSICAL HEROISM OF BLACK WOMEN

While white women in North and South used classical history to debate the slavery question, black women became the center of a national debate about whether they could be heroines in the classical mold. One sort of heroism in particular appealed to nineteenth-century Americans: the famous injunction of Patrick Henry, who in the revolutionary period was thought to have paraphrased a Roman senator in Joseph Addison's beloved play, *Cato*: give me liberty or give me death. If black slaves died trying to escape to freedom, did they become as heroic as the ancient Romans and revolutionary patriots? The question was especially relevant for black female slaves, who were doubly stigmatized by their sex and their race, and, therefore, most spectacularly ennobled by the crown of classical heroism.

Fueling the debate over the classical heroism of black men and women were rising education levels among free blacks. In schools, debating societies, and reading circles, free blacks were now gaining access to levels of classical learning unimaginable a few decades earlier. The importance of classicizing free blacks was recognized not just by reforming whites but also by blacks themselves, especially urban elites who saw that classical learning was the key to entering into white public culture.

The earliest sustained efforts were black literary societies, which began to be founded in the early 1830s. Because of the gender conventions of the day, most of the literary societies were segregated by sex. Men met in public buildings while women met in homes. Yet they were united in their pedagogical and reformist goals. Many of the names of these societies reveal the ambition of a certain sector of the urban, free, black elite in America to attain what they called "cultivation of taste," as the Philadelphia Colored Reading Society put it, through classical learning. The male members of this society agreed that from classical literature "a fund of ideas is acquired on a variety of subjects; the taste is greatly improved by conversing with the best models; the imagination is enriched by the fine scenery with which the classics abound; and an acquaintance is formed with human nature, together with the history, customs, and manners of antiquity." In 1833 a group of free blacks in Washington, DC, held a program to raise money for a slave on the verge of being sold South away from his family. Among the scheduled orations were "Plato and the Immortality of the Soul," "Brutus—On the Death of Ceaser [sic]," and "Epilogue to Addison's Cato." By the 1850s schools in large cities like Philadelphia were offering a classical education to black students. The coeducational Institute for Colored Youth, for example, offered a "classical course" that included "the reading of Virgil's Aeneid, the Odes of Horace, Cicero's Orations, the Greek Testament, and Xenophon's Anabasis."[30]

The classical knowledge that black women acquired in the literary societies allowed them to pursue several interrelated goals. First, they used these societies as a way to become educated while remaining within the boundaries of feminine meekness and subservience that also confined white, middle-class women. Black women were encouraged to cultivate the mind (Minerva) rather than the body (Venus); it was a dichotomy that would have been familiar to any middle-class white woman from the last half century. This was surely on the mind of the group of free black women in Philadelphia who founded the Female Minervian Association in 1832, naming the society for "the daughters of the goddess whose name they bear." Rehearsing the familiar distinction between women's minds and bodies, the association added that "the cultivation of a woman's mind [is] all important, and far more so, than the adornment of the body."[31]

There was also another urgent goal for black women: to speak out against slavery in a language that would allow them to be heard at a time when Greco-Roman allusions were practically required from national public speakers. The Female Literary Association of Philadelphia, founded by black women in the early 1830s, was an example of the kind of society that would cultivate such goals. It urged its members in the early 1830s to emulate Demosthenes and Hannibal to do battle against prejudice.

> By perseverance the great Demosthenes was enabled to overcome a natural defect in his pronunciation, so great, that on his first attempt to speak in public, he was hissed: to rid himself of it, he built a vault where he might practice without disturbance. His efforts were crowned with the most brilliant success, he became the first orator of the age, and his eloquence was more dreaded by Philip than all the fleets and armies of Athens. By perseverance Hannibal passed the Alps in the depth of winter, with an army of 110,000.[32]

Classical education for slaves and free blacks met with great resistance. Some whites, threatened by black access to this symbol of white civilization, opposed and even ridiculed black classicism. "Of what benefit can it be for a waiter or coachman to read Horace?" asked a Southern opponent in 1831. "We are only making them classical and literary to make them more unhappy." In Philadelphia, some whites used classical motifs to ridicule blacks. Edward William Clay published a satire of fashionable Philadelphia in the late 1820s that mocked high society by showing fourteen etchings of blacks parading around in fashionable clothes. In one plate a black woman says admiringly to her black companion, "You look just like Pluto de God of War." These negative views could also be robed in the authority of ethnological science, with familiar classical motifs deployed as shorthand for "civilization." Josiah Nott and George Gliddon's *Types of Mankind* (1854), among the most influential ethnological tracts of the nineteenth century, typifies in its abundant illustrations how classicism and science could consign blacks to a barbaric underclass. One image arrayed the bust of the white Apollo Belvedere atop an inferior, black head. Another compared the enormous protuberance of the "Hottentot Venus" to the bumps of a camel (see figure 39).[33]

Not just whites opposed black classical education; some blacks perceived it as a premature luxury that should, instead, await the achievement of more basic gains in education. Joseph Wilson, a southern black commentator on the "higher classes of colored society" in Philadelphia, made such a claim for blacks in a pamphlet he published in 1841. Even in

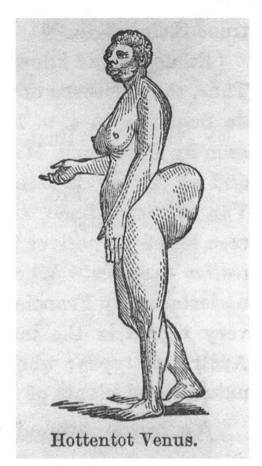

39. "The Hottentot Venus," from Josiah Nott and George Gliddon, *Types of Mankind* (1854). Courtesy Stanford University Libraries.

Philadelphia, he wrote, it was "almost impossible for them to obtain, in an open, honorable way, a thorough classical education." In a similar manner, the black reformer Martin Delany (though he used classical tropes in his own writing) urged blacks in the early 1850s to get what he called "a good business practical Education" because a "Classical" education was "only suited to the wealthy, or those who have a prospect of gaining a livelihood by it." Once the community was ready to patronize and use black classical education, it should be encouraged, but until then it would serve only to "cripple the otherwise, praiseworthy efforts they would make in life."[34]

Sarah Mapps Douglass (1806–1882), a member of the Female Literary Association, was possibly the first free black American woman to sign a published article with a classical female pseudonym. She was unusually well educated for her time and place, and she exemplified the new, reformist possibilities of black female classicism. Her mother, Grace Douglass, had founded a school with the free black philanthropist James Forten in Philadelphia. Forten's daughter, Sarah, like Sarah Mapps Douglass, was a member of the Female Literary Association. It is not clear what Sarah Douglass studied at the school, but she probably learned something about classical history because James Forten was a huge fan of Addison's *Cato* and occasionally used "Cato" as a pen name.

By 1832 Sarah Douglass was writing for the abolitionist cause in the pages of William Lloyd Garrison's *Liberator*, which had a "Ladies Department" for women's contributions. Douglass contributed three essays in 1832, not on classical themes, but under a highly suggestive pseudonym: "Sophanisba," a princess of Carthage who dies for her freedom. It is unclear what Douglass meant precisely by using this pseudonym, but the ancient city of Carthage had become a central debating point among black and white Americans over the scheme, promoted by the American Colonization Society, to export free blacks to Liberia. In this debate, Carthage was used in any number of rhetorical forms. The city was used as proof that an ancient "black" nation could stand up to Roman might, or as a clear lesson that Carthage would be destroyed in the end by Rome, a fate predicted by the Roman senator, Cato, in his famous words, "Carthago est delenda" (Carthage must be destroyed). Douglass may have been obliquely joining this debate by casting her lot with a freedom-loving heroine of an ancient—and perhaps black—Carthage. In several of the letters signed as Sophanisba, she identifies herself as "a young lady of color."[35]

The result of rising black classicism in America was that by the 1830s blacks could join one of the major debates of the fledgling abolitionist movement: the degree to which slaves escaping from bondage were courageous enough to qualify for heroism in the classical mold. During the 1830s antislavery activists began to enlist the classical past to make claims about the heroism of escape. Were these escaping slaves pursuing freedom or just running away? This might appear to be a minor debate, but the stakes were high. Abolitionists knew that setting the debate in a classical context heightened its moral tone, wrapping a thoroughly modern conversation in the garb of the venerated classical past. For black abolitionists who participated in this debate, it was especially important to retrieve the nobility of the classical past for their own uses. White masters had long demeaned their slaves by giving them classical names like Scipio, Cato, and Venus, mocking the lowliest of Americans by giving them the most exalted names. But now—with rising education levels and a newly acquired knowledge of classical antiquity—blacks could claim a place of dignity in

America's public, classical conversation. An article in the abolitionist *Anti-Slavery Record* of 1837 put the matter succinctly, comparing the act of escape to the noble retreat of the Greeks under the general Xenophon. "To escape from a powerful enemy, often requires as much courage and generalship as to conquer."[36]

The 1850 Fugitive Slave Act thrust this question into the national limelight by raising the legal and moral stakes of slaves' flight into free northern territory. Passed by Congress in 1850 as a concession to the slaveholding interests of the South, the act exposed fleeing slaves and their white and black accomplices to the most ruthless prosecution. The law created a force empowered to pursue fugitive slaves in any state and return them to their owners. It also imposed heavy fines and imprisonment on people who harbored fugitive slaves; it denied arrested fugitive slaves a trial by jury and the right to *habeas corpus*; and it granted special incentives to commissioners who ruled in favor of slave holders.[37] Like no other ruling on slavery before, the 1850 Fugitive Slave Law forced northerners to choose whether they opposed or supported slavery.

Slave mothers, already reluctant to flee bondage because of fear of losing their children, were especially stricken by the Fugitive Slave Act. Mothers who fled slavery often brought their children with them, and the onerous punishments spelled out in the law practically ensured that a woman's children would be separated from her as a means of punishment if the family was returned to slavery.[38]

The questions raised by the flight of slave mothers and by the fugitive slave law received their most dramatic enactment in and around Cincinnati, Ohio. By the 1850s the major trade artery of the Ohio River had become the symbolic edge of the American debate about slavery and freedom, in part because it exposed so clearly the human dynamics of taking flight. Straddling slave Kentucky and free Ohio, the booming river port city of Cincinnati became a major destination for escaped slaves.[39] For escaping slave mothers and children of the Upper South, Cincinnati offered a realistic nearby destination, and the city became a major entrepôt of the Underground Railroad. But with slave catchers in hot pursuit, the escape might end in capture, and some women resisted by killing themselves or their children.

Black writers for the abolitionist press quickly enshrined these women as heroines, sometimes even as Roman heroines. Stories of slave women's heroism began to filter into the Ohio Valley press with greater frequency in the 1840s and 1850s. In 1848, Martin Delany, the editor of the *North Star*, an abolitionist newspaper published by and for blacks, told of an incident in Covington, Kentucky, in which a "heroic mother" "cut the throat of her child" rather than return to slavery without him. Delany lauded her as a then-famous Carthaginian heroine, the wife of the general Asdrubal, who kills herself and her children rather than submit to Roman capture. "A noble woman!—more deserving of fame than the . . . noble wife of Asdrubal!" Frederick Douglass called another such woman a "slave heroine" in 1855.[40]

Many whites opposed such attributions of Roman heroism to black women. One of the first explicitly racial categorizations of the Roman matron came in the 1830s from Charles Darwin in a publication that was also read in the United States. Recounting his journey around Rio de Janeiro in the *Beagle*, he told of watching as a patrol recaptured a party of escaped slaves. An old black woman leaped suddenly from the cliffs rather than return to slavery. "In a Roman matron," he wrote in his journal, "this would have been called the noble love of freedom: in a poor negress it is mere brutal obstinancy."[41]

Even abolitionist whites had difficulty envisioning a black Roman matron. Writing in the *North Star* in 1849, the white reformer Edmund Quincy told the story of a Massachusetts slave named Coelia. At one point in her life, her master had offered to emancipate her, but she had declined. Now, on her deathbed, the master reflected that she was better off dying in the comforts of his family than free and alone. "No sir," she replied, "no sir, for then I should have died FREE!" Quincy wrote in the newspaper that had Coelia been white her words would have been remembered and revered as those worthy of a Roman matron. "If these replies had been made by a Roman matron, carried captive to Carthage, or into Pontus, historians would have inscribed them upon their pages, and Coelia would have been as honored a name upon the lips of all posterity, as those of Arria or Cornelia."[42]

Accustomed to trying to comprehend the heroism of slave mothers along classical lines, residents of Cincinnati recruited these stories to comprehend what became one of the most notorious fugitive slave cases in the nation's history: the case of Margaret Garner. In January 1856 Margaret Garner and her husband, Simeon, fled with their four children from Boone County, Kentucky, across the frozen Ohio River to Cincinnati. They were pursued by a posse of armed men who tracked them down to a free black hideout in Cincinnati. When the posse broke down the door, they stumbled into a scene of shocking carnage. Margaret Garner, preferring death to slavery for her children, had nearly sliced the head off her two-year-old daughter Mary, who now lay dead on the floor, and had begun to attack two of her other children, her sons Thomas and Samuel. The Garners were promptly jailed, tried, and returned to slavery. On her way back south, Margaret Garner attempted suicide by jumping into the river.[43]

Immediately abolitionists in the black press promoted the view that Garner had acted as a Roman heroine. James Bell's poem, "Liberty or Death," soon appeared in the Canadian *Provincial Freeman*, casting Garner's choice of death over slavery a "Roman" exemplar:

> Why did she with a mother's hand,
> Deprive her child of breath!
> She'll tell you, with a Roman's smile,
> That slavery's worse than death.

In a similar manner, the black poet Francis Ellen Watkins Harper (1825–1911), in a poem called "The Slave Mother: A Tale of the Ohio," published shortly after the Garner incident, invoked Margaret Garner as a Roman heroine. Harper was one of the giants of black female reform in the mid-nineteenth century, and her remarkable education at Baltimore's William Watkins Academy for Negro Youth—which emphasized biblical studies, Greek, Latin, and elocution—imbued Harper's writings and public speaking with biblical and classical allusions that appealed to black and white audiences. Calling Garner a "heroic mother," she contrasted the total depravity of modern slavery with the possibility for brief slave refuge in ancient Rome, where racial categories were unknown: "E'en Rome had altars: 'neath whose shade / Might crouch the wan and weary slave." She then knit Garner to Patrick Henry and *Cato*, showing how she chose death over enslavement:

> Then, said the mournful mother,
> If Ohio cannot save,
> I will do a deed for freedom,
> She shall find each child a grave.

Such heroic, Roman paeans to Margaret Garner enraged proslavery agitators. The day after Garner had murdered her child, the proslavery *Cincinnati Enquirer* railed against abolitionists' support of Garner. "The Abolitionists regard the parents of the murdered child as a hero and heroine, teeming with lofty and holy emotions, who, Virginius like, would rather imbue their hands in the blood of their white offspring than allow them to wear the shackles of slavery." Virginius was a Roman man who murdered his daughter, Virginia, rather than have her enslaved.[44]

By the end of the Civil War the austerity and emotional restraint of Roman heroism seemed unable to contain the magnitude of the national carnage. On each side, the depth of suffering was so great, the damage to lives and bodies so total, that a new kind of heroine, a woman who

achieved greatness for the depth of her sorrow rather than her stoic renunciation of suffering, seemed necessary. Although Roman tropes would
always remain popular, now Greek tragic heroines rose up alongside Roman matrons as new models.

The dedication of the cemetery at Gettysburg in 1863 provided the opportunity to cast the Civil War as a battle that was Greek in its nobility and
meaning. If the American Revolution had been cast in the language of
Roman antiquity, the Civil War would be the victory of brave Greeks
against the almost overwhelming forces of "Oriental" Persia in 490 BCE.
This feat was accomplished not by Abraham Lincoln in his famously terse,
three-minute "Dedicatory Remarks" (which we know as the Gettysburg
Address), but, instead, in the fluid, Latinate amblings of Edward Everett's
two-hour "Oration," which preceded Lincoln's short speech.

Among the most erudite classical scholars in America, a star in the pantheon of orators (Ralph Waldo Emerson called him "our Cicero"), Everett
had inaugurated the rage for the Greeks in America as a young man returning from Göttingen besotted by philhellenism. Now nearly seventy, he
returned to his early love of Greek glory and its resonance in modern America. He opened his speech by likening the fallen soldiers at Gettysburg to
the Athenians who fell at Marathon in 490 BCE. He saluted the assembled
crowd by equating them with the mourning matrons and daughters of
Athens. By setting the Civil War into a classical frame, Everett hoped to transcend the immediate tragedy of war and endow the struggle with higher
moral meaning.[45]

For American women the heroines of the ancient tragedies of Aeschylus,
Sophocles, and Euripides represented new emotional possibilities for making sense of the Civil War. Medea, Antigone, and Clytemnestra achieved
their greatest moments through suffering and the cathartic release they
brought to their audiences. Medea, for example, was the princess from beyond the Black Sea who murders her two sons rather than see them live with
her Greek husband Jason, who has abandoned Medea for another woman.
Medea—the outsider, alone, murderously angry—was in many ways the an-
tithesis of the dignified, stoic Roman matron who nurtured her children.
But it was Medea and other Greek tragic heroines who gradually supplanted
the Roman matron in the imagination of American women in the nineteenth century. The bloodshed and destruction of the Civil War only fueled
this trend. Mary Boykin Chesnut, the South Carolina plantation mistress
who watched as her farm was besieged by advancing northern armies, saw
that only the suffering of Medea described her own plight. "They say they
hold Port Royal," she wrote in March 1862. "So we are to be exterminated
and improved, *à l'Indienne*, from the face of the earth. Medea, when asked:

THE MODERN MEDEA—THE STORY OF MARGARET GARNER—Photographed by Brady, from a Painting by Thomas Noble.—[See Page 318.]

40. In this widely circulating print, the escaped slave Margaret Garner is immortalized as a heroine from Euripides' tragedy, *Medea*. "The Modern Medea," *Harper's Weekly* (18 May 1867). Library of Congress.

'Country, wealth, husband, children, all are gone; and now what remains?' answered: 'Medea remains.' "[46]

Margaret Garner, too, became Medea in the national memory after the Civil War. She, who had once epitomized the austere heroism of the Roman matron, received her lasting fame as the Greek heroine Medea. She was enshrined as such in a famous engraving in *Harper's Weekly* on 18 May 1867 with an accompanying caption and story called "The Modern Medea" (see figure 40). The image, reprinted in a number of periodicals, was based on a painting titled *Margaret Garner* (1867), by the American artist Thomas Satterwhite Noble, a canvas that was exhibited to great acclaim in New York City at the National Academy of Design in 1867. It was then photographed by the Civil War photographer Matthew Brady; the engraving made from this photograph was the one that circulated in *Harper's*.

Noble had posed Garner as the virtuous Roman elder Horatius in a scene lifted straight from Jacques-Louis David's lauded painting, *The Oath of the Horatii* (1784).[47] But with its new caption, "The Modern Medea," the engraving changed the classical frame from Roman soldier to Greek tragic heroine, from stoic renunciation to overwhelming passion and catharsis.

As it had in the revolutionary period, the classical world helped structure some of the major national debates of the Civil War era. Far more than they could ever have been in the eighteenth century, women were now major participants in these debates. With better educations and a public world of print open to them, women could influence national debates about the slavery question by invoking historical examples from the classical past. Classically educated women like Lydia Maria Child, Louisa McCord, and Sarah Mapps Douglass, with their national audiences of readers, focused in particular on the condition of women in slave societies like Greece, Rome, and modern America. Some also gradually moved away from an identification with the matrons of ancient Rome. That identity, which had always had slaveholding as an implicit though seldom articulated component, now became more problematic for abolitionist women. With ancient Athens now identified as the home of democracy and freedom, abolitionist women's debates about their own freedom found richer soil in Greece than they did in Rome. Ancient Greece also offered up a new kind of classical exemplar, the heroines of Greek tragedies like *Medea*. Ancient Greek tragic heroines offered a different range of emotional possibilities for nineteenth-century women that seemed better to fit the condition of modern women than the stoic, austere Roman matron. As we will see in the next chapter, the Greek tragic heroine Antigone became the crux of one of the major questions of the post–Civil War period: Could women be political actors, and on what grounds?

SEVEN

ANTIGONE AND THE TWILIGHT OF FEMALE CLASSICISM, 1850–1900

Of the many Greek tragic heroines beloved by Victorian Americans, none was more popular than Antigone. The heroine of Sophocles' Greek tragedy *Antigone*, she was a dutiful sister who defied the state to attend to her family and religious conscience. After 1840 she began to appear in American scholarship and college courses, in general interest and women's periodicals, and in novels, short stories, art, and poetry. Her popularity peaked in the early twentieth century, when *Antigone* became the most frequently performed classical play on American college campuses, where, by 1910, women formed 40 percent of the student body.[1]

Antigone was popular, in part, because she dramatized clearly how Americans might accept female political participation in an age that still insisted on the essentially apolitical nature of women. But her career also traces an important irony in the feminization of classicism. She rose to popularity just as classicism—always construed as having particularly public, political qualities—became a vehicle less for public action than for internal self-perfection, for private struggles of emotion and conscience, and for a retreat from public action. In the twilight of the heyday of the distinctive female world of classicism, Victorian Antigone was a heroine for women born in the middle decades of the nineteenth century who ultimately turned away from classicism as a form of political, public engagement.

The play *Antigone*, written in the fifth century BCE, was one of the three so-called Theban plays in which Sophocles spins out the fate of the doomed house of Oedipus, king of Thebes. The incestuous union of

Oedipus and his mother Jocasta has produced four children: the brothers Eteocles and Polyneices, and the sisters Ismene and Antigone. After Oedipus leaves Thebes in horror of his own crime, the brothers Eteocles and Polyneices are instructed to share the throne peacefully with their uncle (Jocasta's brother), Creon. Instead, the three men fight bitterly for many years. Eventually, the two brothers are killed in their attempts to reclaim the throne of Thebes, and Creon becomes king.

The action of *Antigone* begins at this point. Creon has refused the right of burial to Polyneices, whom he regards as a traitor to Thebes. Among the ancient Greeks, burial of the dead was an important religious rite that allowed them to pass into the world beyond. Against Creon's wishes, and against the advice of her sister Ismene, Antigone symbolically buries her brother and casts sand on his exposed body. Creon's men discover her, and she is walled alive in a rocky tomb. There she kills herself. Horrified by the result of the king's edict, Creon's wife, Eurydice, and his son, Haemon, who is Antigone's betrothed, also kill themselves. Creon is filled with anguish and remorse.

Like other classical myths, the Antigone story was a compelling and malleable one. There appeared over one hundred translations and interpretations of Antigone between the Middle Ages and the twentieth century, and she was also the frequent subject of paintings and sculpture. This was especially so in the nineteenth century, when many educated Europeans held that Sophocles' *Antigone* was the most perfect work of art ever produced. The ubiquity of Antigone in the European imagination stemmed from the essential dilemma she represented: the duty to family, religion, and private conscience against the demands of the state. The other major characters also fueled discussion, none more so than Creon, king of Thebes, as representative of the state. George Steiner has observed that the play might more rightly be called *Antigone and Creon* because of the several fruitful dualisms that these two characters suggest.[2]

ANTIGONE AND AMERICAN DEMOCRACY

Americans had not always been intrigued by Greek tragedy or by Antigone in particular. Her popularity rose in the 1830s when she began to appear in men's college textbooks and curricula; she gradually permeated general interest periodicals, and then women's magazines, and coeducational and women's college curricula by the post–Civil War era. The conviction that Athens was a model democracy gave *Antigone* broad political implications and helped explain first of all why this particular play, which broods laboriously over a female heroine, could attract both a male and female audience—indeed, why it penetrated men's college curricula rapidly in the 1840s and 1850s. It was not necessarily Antigone herself who would attract attention for those uninterested in a female heroine, but the political conditions of Periclean Athens that inspired the reading of this noble literature in mid-century America.

American commentators spelled out *Antigone*'s lessons for American democracy in general interest journals from the 1830s through the 1850s. It was not Thebes, the subject of the play, but Athens, the home of the playwright, that offered political instruction to modern Americans. Looking beyond the catastrophes of Thebes, American writers argued that it was the democracy of Periclean Athens that produced political conditions enabling the rise of a noble, cultivated literature in Sophoclean plays. Among some writers, *Antigone* became a pamphlet for American political and individual liberty. "Have not Grecian classics a special claim on the attention of American youth?" asked a Southern writer rhetorically in 1839. "Were not their authors *freemen*, and their thought beating high with the fervor of liberty?" An anonymous reviewer recommended Sophocles' *Antigone* to American audiences in 1851 and assured readers of the importance of Athenian literature to their democracy. "To the American citizen, above all others is it important that he become familiar with the history of Athens. . . . The similarity of their institutions to our own, the intense love of individual and national freedom which pervaded all ranks of society, render the study of Athenian life of more than ordinary interest to the American citizen." What was more, Americans should not simply read "her laws and her political history," but should also "become conversant with her poets, her historians, her philosophers, and her orators" to understand the "character of her leading men." Another counseled American readers to acquire "mental citizenship of Athens" to connect the Greek and the American experience. The age of Pericles, agreed a third, showed how "the power of the democracy . . . created and sustained the widely-diffused and magnificent public spirit . . . of every imaginative and cultivated Athenian."[3] Readers, then, were not to take away from *Antigone* a moral about monarchy, but rather they were to learn a lesson about the importance of democracies for fostering noble literature like *Antigone* that would, in turn, allow them to perfect themselves.

Not just a model for democracy, Antigone was an exemplar of true womanhood. For nineteenth-century commentators, these were just two sides of the same coin. As states jettisoned property requirements for suffrage in the first half of the nineteenth century, and extended suffrage to black men after the Civil War, it became necessary to defend women's continued disenfranchisement by arguing that women were fundamentally different from men. The 15th Amendment of 1870 had extended the vote to black men. It left women as the only large constituency of adults to be denied the franchise, and was a mark of the continued suspicion that women's ostensibly softer and more virtuous natures would be sullied by the sordid work of politics. Many Americans during the later decades of the century turned to notions of inherent, biologically rooted sex differences to show that women were unfit by nature for the sordid work of direct political action such as office holding or voting. The notion did not, however, exclude women from going public by indirect means, actions that, of course, they had been taking since the revolutionary era, and that they now did in ever greater numbers. As pious and selfless creatures, women safeguarded the republic through their benevolent influence in the home, clubs, and other voluntary organizations in which their activities on behalf of the state were made acceptable by being defined routinely as apolitical. A number of historians have argued that an expansive concern for the family lay at the core of many of these late-century debates over women's political participation. "At a fundamental level," Rebecca Edwards has argued, "elections were disputes about faith and family order, and campaigns rested on opposing views of the family's relationship to the state."[4]

Antigone, an ancient princess trapped in a moral and political dilemma, offered a familiar classical form through which Victorian Americans could debate the propriety of feminine public action. The vast majority of American commentators on Antigone, from 1841 (the appearance of the first American college edition of the play) to the early twentieth century, cast Antigone as a hyper-feminine, domestic figure, the incarnation of Victorian ideals of true womanhood. Women, these writers argued, were, by nature, emotional creatures whose innate sense of duty to family and God aimed their political compass. It was a timeless truth: Antigone was as bound to her biology as were Victorian women. When asked to make a choice about state and family, Antigone put religion and family first. According to many nineteenth-century writers, she had no choice: she literally could not—by instinct, by nature—act in any other way. Antigone, argued one author in 1873, had "an intuitive sense of right . . . she never allows herself to think that she *could* have acted differently." Her irreducible femininity determined her action. Such incarnations put Antigone squarely in the middle of Victorian concerns for defining the essential nature of true womanhood as emotionalism rooted in biology, as a scenario that threatened doom (disease and death) to women who violated it. "Her native disposition," argued the Yale Greek scholar Theodore Dwight Woolsey (1801–1889), first to publish an American edition of

Antigone from a German text, "was conceived of as exquisitely tender and feminine."[5] In stressing her essential piety and familial devotion, and her inability to imagine other ranges of action, nineteenth-century American writers cast the play less as a conflict between citizen and state—it was that too, but only secondarily, they believed—than as a battle between divine and human law. With a woman as heroine, it could not be a play only about politics; it must be a play about subjects like religion, family, and duty that suitably justified energetic feminine mobilization. Nineteenth-century Antigone represented the religious, the moral, and the divine element far more than she did the possibilities of every citizen, man or woman. In fact, Victorian Antigone was almost never called "citizen"; instead, she was routinely called a "maiden," and as maiden she embodied womanly qualities more than she represented universal qualities of citizenship.

Biologically shackled to her emotions, Victorian Antigone became a study in the selfless quality of appropriate feminine public action. The political sphere remained masculine, according to nineteenth-century commentators on Antigone, and women only alighted there as occasional, exotic guests. How then to justify Antigone's sustained revolt against Creon? The answer was to make Antigone the reluctant politician; she enters the public sphere only under intolerable duress, and then not to pursue her own agenda, but to pursue her brother's. Writers overwhelmingly emphasized the tethers of family that animated her action even as they restrained it: it was for family, not for herself, that Victorian Antigone acted. Antigone, wrote Pamela Helen Goodwin in the *Ladies' Repository* of 1875, had a "self-forgetfulness" in pursuing "right and truth." By acting in the political sphere, Antigone abnegated herself: every independent agenda dissolved in the alembic of duty to family and to the gods. Goodwin held out counter-examples of political women gone wrong, like Medea or Lady Macbeth, whose "ambition" and "unscrupulousness" marred their "daring exploits" in the political sphere.[6] Antigone, by contrast, dragged herself into conflict with the state with extreme reluctance, and only when it threatened family and conscience. Among the few visual representations of Antigone in nineteenth-century America was William Henry Rinehart's life-size, white marble statue, *Antigone Pouring a Libation over the Corpse of Her Brother Polynices* (1870) (see figure 41). It captured Antigone at a moment of a protest, made on behalf of her dead brother, against political authority.[7]

Politically self-sacrificing, Antigone was also selfless on the home front. Her love for her family, though all-embracing, was "disinterested": she loved spiritually and not passionately. Antigone differed from some of the other women of antiquity and literature, who were sullied by carnal urges

41. William Henry Rinehart, American, 1825–1874. *Antigone Pouring a Libation over the Corpse of Her Brother Polynices.* 1867–70; this version, 1870. Sculpture; Marble. 70¼×24×39½in. (178.4×61×100.3cm). The Metropolitan Museum of Art, Gift of the Family of John H. Hall, in his memory, 1891 (91.4). Photograph by Jerry Thompson. Image © The Metropolitan Museum of Art.

and irresponsible surpluses of comeliness. Unlike Helen of Troy, whose legendary beauty had launched the Trojan War, or lovelorn Medea and Dido who were undone by their pursuit of "pleasure or passion," Antigone, while also steadfast in her obligations to her loved ones, remained pure in beauty and innocent in her affections. Her name became a byword in popular fiction for a woman's tireless devotion to father or brother. "Oh! my Antigone," cries a young man in a short story in 1846, in praise of his beloved for scorning marriage rather than abandon her ailing parents. Women's magazines echoed these pieties. "Like Antigone," wrote Grace Thalmon in the *Ladies' Repository* in 1858, ". . . every daughter, through the gloom of adversity . . . should remain near and dear to him who sustains the high relation to her of father."[8]

Americans held up a living Antigone in the person of the French mystical writer Eugénie de Guérin (1805–1848), hailed as "The Antigone of France." But they admired her not as talented author or defiant citizen, but rather as a supremely dutiful sister and reluctant public figure "sublimed and ennobled by Christian faith." In the same way, Americans defused the erotic potential of Antigone's love for her fiancé, Haemon, by rendering it chaste and spiritual. Antigone embodied "virgin womanhood," according to Margaret Fuller. The feelings were reciprocated. Haemon, according to the Marshall College philosopher Friedrich Augustus Rauch (1806–1841), did not feel for Antigone the "power of subject passion . . . in the sense of a modern passionate lover." Antigone's potentially passionate love for Haemon was checked further by its bittersweet quality: we know the two are doomed to die with their love unconsummated. In the words of an 1875 poem, "Antigone's Farewell to Haemon," she knew love for Haemon not as possibility, but as denial, "by its depth . . . by what it was denied."[9]

Antigone was so perfect—so virginal and so martyred—that religious rhetoric seemed somehow apt to describe her. Without batting an eye, Victorian writers held up this Greek pagan as the purest expression of Christian devotion to God. Though ultimately she chose between two goods—duty to God and duty to state—Antigone, as befitted a Christian heroine, elects the higher of the two goods. One author admired "the halo of the martyr's crown which encircles the Theban maiden's head." Another author affirmed that Antigone was "Christ-like."[10]

But there was one problem: in rebelling against Creon, she ultimately acted alone. In contrast to the ideal woman, who was tethered to her web of family obligations, rebellious Antigone became "alone," "anarchic," and "secluded." Victorian commentators characteristically resolved the dilemma by defusing its political implications, stressing Antigone's feminine and religious side. For one thing, Antigone's trajectory of doom fulfilled Victorian expectations for the childless woman. Respected medical opinion in the mid-nineteenth century held that childless women—"maiden ladies"—courted physical and emotional disaster by spurning their maternal destinies. By renouncing motherhood and wifehood, maidenly Antigone had invited calamity.[12]

Authors also stressed that her solitary action, culminating in near-Christian martyrdom, vaulted her safely beyond masculinity into hyper–femininity. While her aggressive public action, argued Woolsey, made her "masculine," her selflessness rendered the gesture "exquisitely tender and feminine." "Verily she is the man" rather than Creon, agreed Augustus Taber Murray (1866–1940), professor of classical literature at Stanford University, who was speaking of Antigone at the moment she defies the king. The moments of Antigone's masculinity made her most feminine because they ended in death for her cause—they catapulted her beyond masculinity into true, heroic womanhood because they were expressed for duty to family and were religious. Antigone was "no virago," affirmed E. S. Shuckburgh in 1902, "but a true woman" for "doing a deed for which she knows she must die."[11] Biology and religion conspired to make Antigone's solitary suicide a fitting, feminine conclusion to her rebellion.

Where did Creon fit in this Victorian scheme? He became less an embodiment of the overweening state than the patriarch gone awry, a man who might be good except for the excessive power that has corrupted him. To Victorian writers, Creon embodied what remained a familiar type in the female landscape: the patriarch, conceived as a highly personal, familial manifestation of unchallengeable authority. The case of Antigone, argued one writer in 1873, was "of a woman disobeying the man who has over her the authority of a father." Creon's struggle with Antigone, argued Murray in 1902, was personal and not political, and it doomed Antigone at many personal levels. The king's flaws illustrated a chestnut of republican thinking, that is, the ease with which power corrupted. Creon had the potential to be a good king, "but his nature is a narrow one, and his point of view only too apt to be personal . . . how characteristic of a narrow nature!"[13] Having made Antigone the maiden, nineteenth-century Americans made Creon the tyrant, king in name only, riddled with flaws of character that doomed him to lose his family. Writers inevitably enlisted impassioned adjectives to describe Creon: he was angry, irritable, lacking in self-control, angry that he had been disobeyed by a woman, full of pride and passion, self-willed, stern, savage, purely selfish, haughty, and annoyed. Victorian Creon, like Antigone, represented the domestication of the play, its representation of an essential personal, familial dilemma rather than an overtly political one.

ALTERNATIVE ANTIGONE

Enshrined by the late nineteenth century as the mythical incarnation of feminine ideals of domestic piety, Victorian Antigone, like other cultural symbols that appeal to multiple audiences, also offered a means to resist her orthodox form, to attack the prison of Victorian feminine ideals. The American writer Elizabeth Stuart Phelps (1844–1911), one of the best-selling authors of the late nineteenth century, recruited Antigone for this mission. In her 1891 short story, "The Sacrifice of Antigone," Phelps used Antigone to embody the traditional career trajectory for women while drawing attention to the limitations of those expectations. Phelps's strategy was common among Victorian writers seeking subtly to overturn gender conventions.

Nineteenth-century novels written by women often served as vehicles of protest, a way for women publicly to express opinions without straying beyond the bounds of feminine propriety. Phelps deployed Antigone to rail against the inadequate female education that not only hindered women's future political, economic, and social equality, but also blocked them from realizing their full potential as human beings. It is a testament to Antigone's popularity by the late nineteenth century that Phelps could deploy Antigone as cultural shorthand for true womanhood, as an easy referent for her readers that she could then complicate with her own interpretation. She was not the only Victorian writer to use Antigone as both feminine archetype and feminist accomplice. A great admirer, and sometime correspondent, of George Eliot (1819–1880), Phelps may have modeled her own Antigone after the character depicted in Eliot's *Middlemarch* (1871). Like Phelps, Eliot frequently criticized women's exclusion from classical learning. In 1856 she had published an essay suggesting the timelessness of the Antigone myth for dramatizing modern dilemmas. *Middlemarch* is the story of Dorothea, whom Eliot calls "a sort of Christian Antigone" struggling to find intellectual fulfillment in a world that denies education—especially in Greek and Latin—to women.[14]

Elizabeth Stuart Phelps came to Antigone because she was concerned about the problem of women's limited opportunities for self-fulfillment in Gilded Age America. She was best known for her three-novel series, *The Gates Ajar* (1869), *Beyond the Gates* (1883), and *The Gates in Between* (1887). All three novels were veiled social criticism showing how women, after death, found release from earthly prisons of grounded intellects and the "perversion of the great Christian theory of self-sacrifice" that made their marriages spiritual and intellectual deserts.

Phelps's own life mirrored some of the blocked ambitions she portrayed in her novels. Born and raised in Andover, Massachusetts, a college town teeming with educated boys, Phelps was the granddaughter of Moses Stuart, one of the most famous biblical scholars in America. Her own education, however, typified what was available for middle-class girls in the North. She attended the Abbott Academy and Mrs. Edwards's School for Young Ladies; the curriculum included all subjects except Greek and trigonometry. She ultimately married a man seventeen years her junior. The May-December arrangement was her effort to find equality in a romantic relationship. Her attempt was unsuccessful; the marriage was a failure.[15]

In the early 1870s, Phelps turned her social criticism into political engagement by publishing overt, sarcastic attacks on the ideology of women's natural sphere. She wrote a scathing attack on Dr. Edward H. Clarke's notorious pamphlet, *Sex in Education* (1873), which had asserted the incompatibility between menstruation and lofty cerebration. She also denounced Horace Bushnell's *Women's Suffrage; The Reform against Nature* (1869), which had argued that women's innate delicacy rightly disqualified them from political participation. In fact, between 1871 and 1873, Phelps published fourteen articles in women's magazines that attacked the ideal of the true woman. "The 'true woman,' we are told," wrote Phelps, "desires and seeks no noisy political existence. To the 'true woman' the whirr and bustle of public life are unattractive."[16]

Women's inadequate educations further impeded their public ambitions. In the *Independent* in 1873, Phelps lampooned what she called the "female education" of women—that is, the segregation of knowledge in schools by sex—by deploring educations that claimed only to reaffirm what nature had already decreed. "Lest the Creator should not be able, unassisted, to carry out his own intentions, let us help him to put then into execution," she wrote caustically. She then attacked female colleges like Mt. Holyoke Seminary and Vassar, which gave women a "second-rate" education by diluting the curriculum of elite men's colleges like Harvard. In particular for Phelps, Greek loomed as the final symbol of women's inferior educational status because classical learning had long been a symbol of male privilege and exclusivity. Greek was not a requirement at Vassar, she wrote, because Vassar was for women; yet when given the opportunity to pursue classics, as at the University of Vermont, "the lady students . . . have this year received all the Wheeler prizes offered for the best classical examinations." The best education was equal education, "human" rather than simply "female."[17]

Phelps's ruminations on the insidious effects of educational inequality on women's entry into the public sphere took fictional form in her 1891 short story, "The Sacrifice of Antigone." The plot was simple. Poor, young

Dorothy Dreed (whom we are to read as Antigone) manages, by working slavishly as a laundress and a waitress, to support herself at a coeducational college. After heroic efforts, she masters her Greek lesson and presents it at a competition in which she and several young men must recite some lines from an ancient Greek author. The four young men produce their Alexander and Plato in "creditable Greek syntax, and very natural New England accent." But Dorothy steals the show:

> A hush preceded the announcement, in full Greek, of the last contestant for the occasion, Miss Dorothy Dreed. She would address the audience upon the plaintive and beautiful topic of Antigone. From the shoulders of a little figure, trembling very much, the old waterproof cloak dropped slowly. There glided to the front of the platform a lovely creature, slim and swaying, all in white, clinging white, and Greek from the twist of her dark hair to the sandal on her pretty foot and the pattern on her *chiton's* edge. The costume was cheese-cloth, and cost five cents a yard—but who knew? who cared? It was studious, it was graceful, it was becoming, it was perfect, it was Greek—it was Antigone. . . . She took the prize—of course she took the prize.

Although Dorothy had ascended to the apex of erudition by reciting ancient Greek, she soon died from overwork. "No hope," declared the physician. "The constitution has succumbed to want and work."[18] As a modern Antigone, Dorothy Dreed pursues her education out of duty to her impoverished family, and she conquers the masculine fortress of Greek only by giving up her life. Antigone for Phelps embodied the ideal of Victorian woman, while also drawing attention to its tragic limitations. Phelps's Antigone, nevertheless, remained squarely within the nineteenth-century tradition of making the Antigone story especially relevant to women. Phelps undermined the rigid polarity of Victorian sexual mores by casting Antigone as an accomplished classicist, yet did not universalize Antigone to speak for human truths that transcended both time and gender.

Antigone and the Privatization of Classicism

It is in the college performances of Sophocles' *Antigone* beginning in the late nineteenth century that we can see most clearly the process by which classicism was privatized, how it was transformed from a prerequisite for entry into public life to a platform for the perfection of the inner self. These college performances show how it was possible for women to make huge strides in publicly visible classical learning while turning it away from the overt public, political uses that had marked classicism in the eighteenth and early nineteenth centuries. In the college curriculum, the natural and social sciences were displacing classicism as the new centers of civic and moral authority, and men in public life increasingly rested claims to civic authority on the social and natural sciences. Women became fully classicized just as classicism was slipping away from its central place in political life.

There were 349 college plays performed in the first half century after 1881. These plays thrust women into public performance in ways inconceivable for middle-class young women earlier in the century. *Antigone* was performed at high schools, colleges, and universities across the nation, at coeducational, men's, and women's schools, and at Protestant and Catholic schools. The first performance was at the University of Notre Dame in 1882, and was soon followed by stagings at Beloit College in Wisconsin, Swarthmore, Vassar, Olivet College, Ripon College, Stanford, Drake, the Peabody College for Women, Syracuse University, Wabash College, and Washington University, to total seventy-five.[19]

Moreover, the college Greek plays emerged just as women's education in classics was beginning to rival men's and constituted an extraordinary example of educational parity in a discipline historically laden with implications for defining who could properly enter public life. The most spectacular increase in women's knowledge of antiquity came after the Civil War, when the women's and coeducational colleges such as Cornell University, the University of Michigan, and Bryn Mawr College began to offer a curriculum modeled upon those of men's colleges, and they offered a classical curriculum studded with classical tragedies. One example of this new classical parity illustrates a national trend. In 1885 the Greek and Latin language admission requirements to Harvard and Bryn Mawr were identical (translations of Cæasar's *Gallic War*, Virgil's *Æneid*, and Xenophon's *Anabasis*), and students at both schools read Greek tragedies (*Antigone* at Bryn Mawr, *Iphigenia* at Harvard).[20] It was an extraordinary and profound shift that was reflected in similar undergraduate offerings in classical study at the elite men's and women's colleges around the nation by the late nineteenth century. It is significant, moreover, that the college plays self-consciously departed from historical accuracy by encouraging women to play the part of Antigone (men had played the role of women in ancient Greek productions). What the dramatic performances of *Antigone* symbolized was revolutionary. For a woman to play Antigone in a college play was for her to be fully Greek: to have learned the Greek language, to have studied a masterpiece of Greek literature, and to have walked in the footsteps of one of the great heroines of Greek mythology. American women in performing *Antigone* were now for the first time as fully classical as men.

But the college performances of *Antigone* reveal the pyrrhic victory of women's classicism in the late nineteenth century, as it was transformed from a vehicle for political participation into a forum for internal self-perfection. Women had achieved parity in classicism in an arena that, while public, was not intended for political preparation but rather for self-culture, for the internal perfection of the self. The whole phenomenon of Greek plays on American campuses, in fact, testified to classicism's retreat from the political to the private sphere. During the late nineteenth century, art museums and college campuses had become discrete sites of high culture. The culture of classicism that had permeated American life into the mid-nineteenth century had begun to pool in these custodial hot-houses of culture. Morally and intellectually elevated by classical culture, Americans could purge themselves of the corrupting materialism and philistinism of the Gilded Age.

Victorian classicism as self-culture marked a change from the revolutionary era, when classically inspired plays like Joseph Addison's *Cato* operated as nurseries of political agitation against Britain. Although Greek tragedies began to be performed in urban theaters with growing frequency after about 1830 as part of the general rise of Hellenism in America at the time, they were efforts at entertainment rather than either politicization or ennobling culture, and made no effort at historical authenticity or scholarly rigor. Euripides' *Medea*, staged at least fourteen times in New York City between 1845 and 1881, was never shown in Greek, but rather in operatic form and in English translation. Nor were these performances notable for the almost funereal grandeur that would characterize the college plays. At the one recorded performance of *Antigone* in New York City's Palmo's Opera House in 1840, a man in the audience climbed to the stage to launch a wad of chewing tobacco onto an actor's shield.[21]

By contrast, the collegiate Greek plays that emerged after 1881 were not political pamphlets or entertainment as much as they were a moral education through immersion in the authenticity of the ancient past. Through these strenuously didactic efforts by students and faculty to recreate ancient drama in all its authenticity, Americans polluted by the factory age would be ennobled by the sublime, purifying spirit of antiquity. The majority of the college tragedies were performed in ancient Greek, which students learned with the help of classics professors and elocution instructors who sometimes played supporting roles. That the audience was largely uncomprehending only added to the pedagogical effect because, at the conclusion of the play, the departing audience would have "much the feeling with which the Greeks must have risen on the slopes of the Acropolis," according to the producer of the Stanford *Antigone* in 1902.

Students and faculty expended huge efforts to create authentic scenery and costuming. Often the only concession to modernity was the routine use of modern music (usually Felix Mendelssohn's choral ode, *Antigone*) to supplement the chorus. By all accounts, these plays were earnest rather than entertaining: it was high culture as medicine. "To sit for nearly three hours without a break, without relief save that afforded by the chorus, absorbed in the culmination of sorrows which the Greek tragedian elaborated for the King of Thebes, supplies the best proof of a desire to discover something in the theater beyond titillation of the senses," wrote the reviewer of the Stanford production of *Antigone* in Los Angeles in 1902.[22] A scholarly, cultured celebration of a quasi-Christian martyr in a bucolic Greek setting under open skies, Antigone was here less a preparation for political life than a secular religion in the name of self-culture.

Greek plays on college campuses, just like classical artifacts in museums and Greek language in the curriculum, had by 1900 receded from the realm of the immediately politically relevant to the merely cultivated. There were many publicly accessible museums by this time: the Metropolitan Museum of Art (1870), the Boston Museum of Fine Arts (1870), and other venues in which women and men could view classical and Oriental art. Gilded Age fortunes were also spent on making a few especially opulent interiors into galleries of Greek and Roman art; some homes, as the artist Frederic Edwin Church's eclectic house on the Hudson River, Olana, even became temples of Orientalia.[23] But the ostentatious profusion of classicism in the sphere of institutionalized high culture masked its gradual recession from women's political life. Women achieved classical equity just as classicism's importance in the political life of America was declining.

In the college curriculum, the natural and social sciences displaced classicism as the most authoritative branches of knowledge for political policy. Moreover, men preparing for careers in public service increasingly turned away from classicism as preparation to the social sciences because the latter substituted an urgent immediacy for the authority of antiquity. Woodrow Wilson, the scholar-president of the early twentieth century who attended Princeton in the late 1870s, sought political instruction not from the ancients, but from modern British history and political economy. Charles W. Eliot, president of Harvard during the Gilded Age, reaffirmed that it was modern history rather than ancient that was "so useful to a legislator, administrator, journalist, publicist, philanthropist, or philosopher."[24] In politics more generally, classical republicanism receded as an ideology; in the broader culture other interests besides antiquity overtook a public preoccupied by a rapidly commercializing economy.

Antigone also began to lose her hold on the American imagination by the early twentieth century. She has, of course, remained an extraordinarily popular figure in twentieth-century America, a favorite theme for playwrights, painters, scholars, and others. But the acclaim she enjoyed during the nineteenth century has not been repeated. We can see this in the decline of college performances of Antigone in the early twentieth century: she reached a height of 33 percent of all performances between 1893 and 1903, and tumbled to just half that in the decade after 1915. In the same way, the ultrafeminine Antigone of the late nineteenth century gradually faded from the scene to give testament to the waning of her usefulness for articulating a set of historically specific concerns about women.

With Victorian Antigone, Americans took an overtly political story and made it a study in feminine self-perfection, a study of martyrdom to biologically rooted domestic ideals. During these decades, Antigone spoke less for a universal *human* dilemma of choosing between self and state (as she often has in the twentieth century) than for a peculiarly *female* moral story of religious obligation, family duty, and martyrdom to true womanhood. In addition to symbolizing ultra-femininity, Victorian Antigone became a figure for private, internal contemplation rather than for civic pageantry. In contrast to the classically inspired women favored in American civic iconography since the eighteenth century—Minerva, Ceres, Columbia, and Liberty—Antigone did not capture Americans' visual imagination, but, instead, permeated more cloistered venues such as literature and scholarship as the incarnation of womanly feeling.

We can speculate on the reasons for the twilight of Victorian Antigone. Heavily freighted by Victorians with qualities of womanly virtue, she could not be a model for the rising generation of "New Women" in the early twentieth century. Highly educated, publicly active women like Jane Addams (1860–1935) and M. Carey Thomas (1857–1935), both of whom knew a great deal about the classical world, did not find in Antigone a compelling model for their struggles to secure equal education and equal access to public life. As president of Bryn Mawr College, Thomas looked rather to Sappho to define the educated women, while Addams admired powerful women such as Cassandra the prophet, and Isis, the brooding mother goddess. George Steiner has argued that after 1905, under the influence of Freudian psychology, Europeans and Americans turned from *Antigone* to *Oedipus Rex* to describe a new set of concerns.[25] By the third decade of the twentieth century, a new, relatively ungendered Antigone began to emerge. It was an emergence which reflected the decline of the Victorian conception of a binary opposition between the sexes. Antigone began to represent less the specifically female qualities enshrined by Victorians and more the qualities deemed common to both sexes.

Twentieth-century Antigone, embodying an essential humanity that transcends the exclusively feminine, has represented a collective defiance by both sexes to an overweening state. In the 1940s she became a figure of individual defiance against the totalitarian state in the renditions of *Antigone* by Jean Anouilh and Bertolt Brecht. In the last twenty years, political scientists and philosophers have turned to Antigone as representative of a human rather than a female condition.

The feminist theorist Jean Bethke Elshtain has brought the discussion back full circle to a focus on Antigone's gender in a way that erases binary oppositions. She bemoans Antigone's failure to become "a feminist heroine" to late-twentieth-century women. While criticizing feminists who exalt women's participation in public life at the expense of their sensitivity to a more general "social" life, Elshtain has called for women to see themselves as the daughters of Antigone by tapping into "a deeply buried human identity" of family common to both men and women.[26] The new attention to Antigone-as-human rather than Antigone-as-woman is testament to her enduring appeal over the centuries, but it also marks the decline of nineteenth-century Antigone and the American women who found in her a mirror of themselves.

THE NEW COLOSSUS

The Statue of Liberty, erected in New York City's harbor in 1886, was as much a tombstone for the vanishing world of women's classicism as she was a beacon for a new America. By the twentieth century, Greece and Rome became increasingly irrelevant for American women; the mirror of antiquity no longer so clearly reflected modern women's concerns. Emma Lazarus (1849–1887), the classically educated daughter of the prosperous New York sugar refiner Moses Lazarus, saw this clearly. Though she herself was deeply immersed in the literature of Greece and Rome, she saw that for many Americans around her the relevance of antiquity was anything but obvious. Immigrants of every religion, race, and class, who fled from hunger, want, and persecution, poured into New York's harbor. What to them were Greece and Rome?

In 1883 Lazarus wrote a sonnet, "The New Colossus," to raise money for the pedestal of the statue. The sonnet was the work of a moment, but the words, later stamped into a bronze plaque mounted in the statue's pedestal, have endured. Lazarus saw that this America was poised at the dawn of a new world of new immigrants and of the new pasts they would bring with them. These new people would create a *novus ordo seclorum* as revolutionary as the one built a century earlier. Lazarus saw that their beacon, the Statue of Liberty, would not lead them back to old worlds long vanished. She would lead them forward to a new future. She would be a new colossus.

42. The Statue of Liberty. Photo by Derek Jensen.

THE NEW COLOSSUS

Not like the brazen giant of Greek fame,
With conquering limbs astride from land to land;
Here at our sea-washed, sunset gates shall stand
A mighty woman with a torch, whose flame
Is the imprisoned lightning, and her name
Mother of Exiles. From her beacon-hand
Glows world-wide welcome; her mild eyes command
The air-bridged harbor that twin cities frame.
"Keep ancient lands your storied pomp!" cries she
With silent lips. "Give me your tired, your poor,
Your huddled masses yearning to breathe free,
The wretched refuse of your teeming shore.
Send these, the homeless, tempest-tost to me,
I lift my lamp beside the golden door!"

NOTES

Introduction

1. *Oxford English Dictionary*, s.v. "classic"; James I. Porter, "Introduction: What Is 'Classical' about Classical Antiquity?" in *Classical Pasts: The Classical Traditions of Greece and Rome*, ed. James I. Porter (Princeton: Princeton University Press, 2006), 1–30; Simon Hornblower and Antony Spawforth, eds., *The Oxford Classical Dictionary*, 3d ed. (Oxford: Oxford University Press, 1999), s.v. "classicism."

2. John Adams to James Warren, 21 March 1783, *Warren-Adams Letters: Being Chiefly a Correspondence among John Adams, Samuel Adams, and James Warren, 1743–1814* (Boston: Massachusetts Historical Society, 1917–25), 2:199; James Fordyce, *Sermons to Young Women*, 2 vols. (London, 1775), 1:173.

3. The debate over the relative effects of republicanism and liberalism has been summarized in Daniel T. Rodgers, "Republicanism: The Career of a Concept," *Journal of American History* 79 (June 1992): 11–38.

4. Richard L. Bushman, *The Refinement of America: Persons, Houses, Cities* (New York: Vintage, 1992); Cary Carson, Ronald Hoffman, and Peter J. Albert, eds., *Of Consuming Interest: The Style of Life in the Eighteenth Century* (Charlottesville: University Press of Virginia, 1994); T. H. Breen, *The Marketplace of Revolution: How Consumer Politics Shaped American Independence* (New York: Oxford University Press, 2004); I have also found useful Craig Clunas, *Superfluous Things: Material Culture and Social Status in Early Modern China* (1991; Honolulu: University of Hawai'i Press, 2004); and Pierre Bourdieu, *Distinction: A Social Critique of the Judgement of Taste*, trans. Richard Nice (1984; Cambridge: Harvard University Press, 2002).

5. Edward W. Said, *Orientalism* (New York: Pantheon, 1978). Several scholars have since revised his binary, including Said himself in *Culture and Imperialism* (New York: Knopf, 1993); see also "Between Metropole and Colony: Rethinking a Research Agenda," in *Tensions of Empire: Colonial Cultures in a Bourgeois World*, ed. Frederick Cooper and Ann Laura Stoler (Berkeley: University of California Press, 1997), 1–56; Suzanne Marchand, "Philhellenism and the *Furor Orientalis*," *Modern Intellectual History* 1 (Nov. 2004): 331–58; Maya Jasanoff, *Edge of Empire: Conquest and Collecting in the East, 1750–1850* (London: Fourth Estate, 2005), 63–71;

Charles de Secondat, Baron de la Brède et de Montesquieu, *The Spirit of Laws,* trans. Thomas Nugent (London: J. Nourse and P. Vaillant, 1750), 322.

6. The terms "republican mother" and "republican wife" have been important analytic terms for historians of this period, but unlike the "Roman matron" neither was in fact used at the time. For the republican mother, see Linda K. Kerber, *Women of the Republic: Intellect and Ideology in Revolutionary America* (Chapel Hill: University of North Carolina Press, 1980); for the republican wife, see Jan Lewis, "The Republican Wife: Virtue and Seduction in the Early Republic," *William and Mary Quarterly* 44 (Oct. 1987): 689–721. On some historical origins of the idea of the republican mother, see Rosemarie Zagarri, "Morals, Manners, and the Republican Mother," *American Quarterly* 44 (June 1992): 192–215.

7. A number of historians have analyzed these female icons and the ways they symbolized the exclusion of women from politics. See Maurice Agulhon, *Marianne into Battle: Republican Imagery and Symbolism in France, 1789–1880,* trans. Janet Lloyd (Cambridge: Cambridge University Press, 1981); Lynn Hunt, *Politics, Culture, and Class in the French Revolution* (Berkeley: University of California Press, 1984); Marina Warner, *Monuments and Maidens: The Allegory of the Female Form* (London: Weidenfeld and Nicolson, 1985); Joan B. Landes, *Women and the Public Sphere in the Age of the French Revolution* (Ithaca: Cornell University Press, 1988); Mary P. Ryan, *Women in Public: Between Banners and Ballots, 1825–1880* (Baltimore: Johns Hopkins University Press, 1990); Joan B. Landes, *Visualizing the Nation: Gender, Representation, and Revolution in Eighteenth-Century France* (Ithaca: Cornell University Press, 2001).

8. For the European tradition of female monarchs and aristocrats posing as classical goddesses, see Catharine MacLeod and Julia Marciari Alexander, *Painted Ladies: Women at the Court of Charles II* (London: National Portrait Gallery, 2001), and Annette Dixon, ed., *Women Who Ruled: Queens, Goddesses, Amazons in Renaissance and Baroque Art* (London: Merrell in association with the University of Michigan Museum of Art, 2002).

1. The Female World of Classicism

1. Eliza Lucas Pinckney to Mary Bartlett, ca. March–April 1742, in *The Letterbook of Eliza Lucas Pinckney, 1739–1762,* ed. Elise Pinckney (Chapel Hill: University of North Carolina Press, 1972), 33.

2. Walter Ong, "Latin Language Study as a Renaissance Puberty Rite," *Studies in Philology* 56 (1959): 103–24; Anthony Grafton and Lisa Jardine, *From Humanism to the Humanities: Education and the Liberal Arts in Fifteenth- and Sixteenth-Century Europe* (Cambridge: Harvard University Press, 1986), 33; Margaret L. King and Albert Rabil, Jr., eds., *Her Immaculate Hand: Selected Works by and about the Women Humanists of Quattrocento Italy* (Binghamton, NY: Center for Medieval and Early Renaissance Studies, 1983); *virilis femina*: Natalie Zemon Davis, "Gender and Genre: Women as Historical Writers, 1400–1820," in *Beyond Their Sex: Learned Women of the European Past,* ed. Patricia H. LaBalme (New York: New York University Press, 1980), 158; *homasse*: Bonnie Smith, *The Gender of History: Men, Women, and Historical Practice* (Cambridge: Cambridge University Press, 1998), 16.

3. On colonial women's literacy, see E. Jennifer Monaghan, "Literacy Instruction and Gender in Colonial New England," in *Reading in America: Literature and Social History,* ed. Cathy N. Davidson (Baltimore: Johns Hopkins University Press, 1989), 53–80; Gloria Main, "An Inquiry into When and Why Women Learned to Write in Colonial New England," *Journal of Social History* 24 (1991): 579–89; Catherine Kerrison, *Claiming the Pen: Women and Intellectual Life in the Early American South* (Ithaca: Cornell University Press, 2005); on adventure schools, see Margaret A. Nash, *Women's Education in the United States, 1780–1840* (New York: Palgrave Macmillan, 2005), 36; Lawrence Cremin addresses women's education briefly in *American Education: The Colonial Experience, 1607–1783* (New York: Harper and Row, 1970); see also Thomas Woody, *A History of Women's Education in the United States,* 2 vols. (New York: Science Press, 1929).

4. David Shields, "British-American Belles Letters," in *The Cambridge History of American Literature,* vol. 1: *1590–1820,* ed. Sacvan Bercovitch (Cambridge: Cambridge University Press, 1994), 339; Lawrence E. Klein, "Politeness and the Interpretation of the British Eighteenth Century," *Historical Journal* 45 (Dec. 2002), 889.

5. The term "female world" is used in this sense in "How to Converse with Mankind," *Boston Weekly Magazine,* 9 March 1743, 10; "On the Style of Dr. Samuel Johnson," *Universal Asylum* (April 1791): 237; "The History of Narcissa," *Massachusetts Magazine,* March 1792, 179; Carlos, "Useful Hints and Advice to the Ladies," *Weekly Museum,* 5 May 1792, n.p.; Terpander, "Thoughts on the Neglect of Morality in Choice of Husbands," *Massachusetts Magazine,* April 1795, 56; Misogamos, "Arguments in Favor of Celibacy," *American Universal Magazine,* 6 March 1797, 302. On French salon culture see Carolyn Lougee, *"Le Paradis des Femmes": Women, Salons, and Social Stratification in Seventeenth-Century France* (Princeton: Princeton University Press, 1976); Dena Goodman, *The Republic of Letters: A Cultural History of the French Enlightenment* (Ithaca: Cornell University Press, 1994); *The Wonders of the Female World* (London: Printed by J. H. for Thomas Malthus, 1683), frontispiece.

6. "Of Illustrious Women," *American Magazine and Historical Chronicle,* June 1745, 245, 248; "Advice to a Young Lady Just after Her Marriage," *American Magazine and Historical Chronicle,* Dec. 1744, 699.

7. Hester Chapone, *Letters on the Improvement of the Mind, Addressed to a Young Lady* (London: II. Hughes, 1773), 2:188–89; Chapone, *Letters on the Improvement of the Mind, Addressed to a Young Lady* (1773; Hagerstown, MD: William D. Bell for Gabriel Nourse, 1818), 2:195.

8. Madeleine de Scudéry, *The Female Orators; or, The Courage and Constancy of Divers Famous Queens, and Illustrious Women, Set Forth in Their Eloquent Orations, and Noble Resolutions: Worthy the Perusal and Imitation of the Female Sex* (London: T. Tebb, 1714), 3 (the 1728 edition is illustrated); Esther Edward Burr to "Fidelia," 24 May 1757, in *The Journal of Esther Edwards Burr, 1754–1757,* ed. Carol F. Karlsen and Laurie Crumpacker (New Haven: Yale University Press, 1984), 262.

9. Harriet Simons Williams, "Eliza Lucas and Her Family: Before the Letterbook," *South Carolina Historical Magazine* 99 (July 1998): 265–66; Eliza Lucas Pinckney to Mary Bartlett, ca. May 1743, in *Letterbook,* 62; Darcy R. Fryer, "The Mind of Eliza Pinckney: An Eighteenth-Century Woman's Construction of Herself," *South Carolina Historical Magazine* 99 (July 1998), 216; Mary Beth Norton, *Liberty's Daughters: The Revolutionary Experience of American Women, 1750–1800* (1980; Ithaca: Cornell University Press, 1996), 262.

10. Eliza Lucas to Mary Bartlett, ca. Apr. 1742, in *Letterbook,* 35–36.

11. For the pastoral tradition in American republicanism, see Carl Richard, *The Founders and the Classics: Greece, Rome, and the American Enlightenment* (Cambridge: Harvard University Press, 1994), 159–68; and Drew R. McCoy, *The Elusive Republic: Political Economy in Jeffersonian America* (1980; New York: Norton, 1982).

12. John Adams (hereafter JA) to Abigail Adams (hereafter AA), 18 Feb. 1776; AA to JA, 16–18 March 1776; JA to AA, 17 Feb. 1794, all in Adams Family Papers, Massachusetts Historical Society online (hereafter AFP); JA to JQA, 11 Aug. 1777, in *The Book of John and Abigail: Selected Letters of the Adams Family, 1762–1784,* ed. L. H. Butterfield, Marc Friedlaender and Mary-Jo Kline (Cambridge: Harvard University Press, 1975), 188.

13. JA to Benjamin Rush, 13 Oct. 1810, in *The Spur of Fame: Dialogues of John Adams and Benjamin Rush, 1805–1813,* ed. John A. Schutz and Douglass Adair (San Marino: Huntington Library, 1966), 170.

14. Eliza Lucas Pinckney to Mrs. Boddicott, 3 May 1740, in *Journal and Letters of Eliza Lucas* (Wormsloe, GA: privately published, 1850), 6. Some eighteenth-century libraries explicitly use the phrase "he or she" when outlining procedures, as the New-York Society Library did; others, such as the Charlestown Library Society, neither explicitly mention women nor explicitly ban them; the Library Company of Philadelphia lists women as "members." *The*

Charter, and Bye-Laws, of the New-York Society Library (New York: H. Gaine, 1773), 13; *The Rules and By-Laws of the Charlestown Library Society* (Charlestown, SC: 1762); *A Catalogue of the Books, Belonging to the Library Company of Philadelphia* (Philadelphia: Zacharia Poulson, 1789).

15. Kevin Hayes, *A Colonial Woman's Bookshelf* (Knoxville: University of Tennessee Press, 1996), 9; Louis B. Wright and Marion Tinling, eds., *The Secret Diary of William Byrd of Westover 1709–1712* (Richmond: Dietz Press, 1941), 461.

16. Hayes, *Colonial Woman's Bookshelf*, 10–16; Edwin Wolf, 2nd, *The Library of James Logan of Philadelphia, 1674–1751* (Philadelphia: Library Company of Philadelphia, 1974), ix; Frederick B. Tolles, "Quaker Humanist: James Logan as a Classical Scholar," *Pennsylvania Magazine of History and Biography* 79 (1955), 418–19; James Logan, *Cato's Moral Distichs. Englished in Couplets* (Philadelphia: Benjamin Franklin, 1735), 11.

17. *My Dearest Julia: The Loveletters of Dr. Benjamin Rush to Julia Stockton* (New York: Neale Watson Academic Publications, 1979), 42–43.

18. Temple Stanyan, *Grecian History* (1707, 1739; London: J. and R. Tonson, 1751), 1, unpaginated preface, 266.

19. *My Dearest Julia*, 43; Hayes, *Colonial Woman's Bookshelf*, 12–13; John Hawkesworth, *Almoran and Hamet: An Oriental Tale* (London: H. Payne and W. Cropley, 1761), 1:2; Mary Wortley Montagu, *Letters of the Right Honourable Lady M——y W——y M——e: Written, during her Travels in Europe, Asia and Africa* (London: T. Becket and P. A. De Hondt, 1763), 2:172.

20. Carrie Rebora Barratt, *John Singleton Copley and Margaret Kemble Gage: Turkish Fashion in 18th-Century America* (San Diego: Putnam Foundation, 1998), 25, 27; Carrie Rebora et al., *John Singleton Copley in America* (New York: Metropolitan Museum of Art, 1995); Elizabeth Mankin Kornhauser et al., *Ralph Earl: The Face of the Young Republic* (New Haven: Yale University Press, 1991), 104–8; on the circulation of colonial portraiture, see Margaretta Lovell, *Art in a Season of Revolution: Painters, Artists, and Patrons in Early America* (Philadelphia: University of Pennsylvania Press, 2005).

21. Jonathan Richardson, *Essay on the Theory of Painting* (London: W. Bowyer, 1715), 186–87; Leslie Reinhardt, " 'Dress and Dissipation': Costume in Henry Benbridge's Charleston Paintings," in Maurie McInnis et al., *Henry Benbridge: Charleston Portrait Painter (1743–1812)*, catalog and transcription by Angela D. Mack (Charleston: Carolina Art Association, 2000), 21–29; Gill Perry, "Women in Disguise: Likeness, the Grand Style, and the Conventions of 'Feminine' Portraiture in the Works of Sir Joshua Reynolds," in *Femininity and Masculinity in Eighteenth-Century Art and Culture*, ed. Gill Perry and Michael Russington (Manchester: Manchester University Press, 1994), 18–40; Aileen Ribeiro, "The Dress Worn at Masquerades in England, 1730 to 1790, and Its Relation to Fancy Dress in Portraiture," Ph.D. diss., Courtauld Institute of Art, 1975, 264–74; James H. Johnson, "Versailles, Meet Les Halles: Masks, Carnival, and the French Revolution," *Representations* 73 (Winter 2001): 89–116; Stephen Greenblatt, *Renaissance Self-Fashioning: From More to Shakespeare* (Chicago: University of Chicago Press, 1980).

22. Rebora, *John Singleton Copley*, 290; Barratt, *John Singleton Copley and Margaret Kemble Gage*, 38–39.

23. Anne Bermingham, *Learning to Draw: Studies in the Cultural History of a Polite and Useful Art* (New Haven: Yale University Press, 2000), chap. 5; Lovell, *Art in a Season of Revolution*, 204–5.

24. Esther Edward Burr, n.d., in *Theodosia: The First Gentlewoman of Her Time*, ed. Charles Felton Pidgin (Boston: C. M. Clark, 1907), 96.

25. "M. Crevier's Answer to Mr. Voltaire," *American Magazine*, Dec. 1745, 541; Charles Rollin, *Ancient History*, 9th ed. (London: C. Bathurst, 1795), 1:3, 8, 11.

26. Charles Francis Adams, *Familiar Letters of John Adams and His Wife Abigail Adams, during the Revolution* (New York: Hurd and Houghton, 1876), xi; Lynne Withey, *Dearest Friend: A Life of Abigail Adams* (New York: Free Press, 1981), 12; Charles Rollin, *Ancient History* (London:

J. Rivington, 1768), 1:cxxxix. Although Abigail does not mention which edition of Rollin she read, the library of John Adams contained the 1768 edition; see *Adams Family Correspondence*, ed. L. H. Butterfield (Cambridge: Harvard University Press, 1963), 1:143 n. 2.

27. AA to JA, 19 Aug. 1774, in *Adams Family Correspondence*, ed. Butterfield, 1:142–43.

28. Alice Izard to Ralph Izard, Jr., 5 Jan. 1803, Ralph Izard Family Papers, 1778–1826, Library of Congress.

29. Frank Luther Mott, *Golden Multitudes: The Story of Best Sellers in the United States* (New York: Macmillan, 1947), 316.

30. Julia Rush Williams, commonplace book (1810), Historical Society of Pennsylvania (Collection # Am. 13521); Betsy Ring, *Girlhood Embroidery: American Samplers and Pictorial Needlework, 1650–1850* (New York: Knopf, 1993), 1:215. I am grateful to Ann Lowry, e-mail communication 22 May 2006, for sharing images of her family's British and American early nineteenth-century samplers, including the one from Pesta Gates.

31. Caroline Gilman, *Letters of Eliza Wilkinson* (New York: Samuel Colman, 1839), 60–62; Sally Wister, 3 June 1778, in *Sally Wister's Journal: A True Narrative*, ed. Albert C. Myers (Philadelphia: Ferris and Leach, 1902), 165, 168; Elizabeth Drinker, 4 Dec. 1759, in *The Diary of Elizabeth Drinker*, ed. Elaine Forman Crane (Boston: Northeastern University Press, 1991), 1:40.

32. Lord Dartmouth signed presentation copies of Alexander Pope, *The Iliad of Homer* (London: J. Whiston, 1771), Rauner Special Collections Library, Dartmouth College; Julian Mason, *The Poems of Phillis Wheatley* (Chapel Hill: University of North Carolina Press, 1989), 3–4.

33. Catherine Bishir, "Black Builders in Antebellum North Carolina," *North Carolina Historical Review* 61 (Oct. 1984), 460. There is some debate about the degree to which slaves participated in classical naming patterns. Mechal Sobel has suggested that classical names were a "humiliating badge of servility," but others, such as Peter Wood, have proposed that apparently "classical" names resulted from a fusion of Anglophone and African names (Cubena, which meant Tuesday, could be construed as Venus, for example). John Inscoe has shown that some slaves and free blacks used classical names to bestow honor upon relatives. See Mechal Sobel, *The World They Made Together: Black and White Values in Eighteenth-Century Virginia* (Princeton: Princeton University Press, 1987), 158; Peter Wood, *Black Majority: Negroes in Colonial South Carolina from 1670 through the Stono Rebellion* (New York: Knopf, 1974), 183; J. L. Dillard, *Black English: Its History and Usage in the United States* (New York: Random House, 1972), 129–30; John Inscoe, "Carolina Slave Names: An Index to Acculturation," *Journal of Southern History* (1983), 543.

34. Frederick Douglass, *My Bondage and My Freedom* (New York: Miller, Orton, and Mulligan, 1855), 67.

35. Journal entry for 5 March 1774, in *Journal and Letters of Philip Vickers Fithian, 1773–1774: A Plantation Tutor of the Old Dominion*, ed. Hunter Dickinson Farish (Williamsburg: Colonial Williamsburg, 1943), 96; Thomas Jefferson, *Notes on the State of Virginia* (London: J. Stockdale, 1787), 232, 234; *Thomas Jefferson's Farm Book*, ed. Edwin Morris Betts (Princeton: Princeton University Press, 1953), 49, 50, 148; Lucia C. Stanton, *Free Some Day: The African-American Families of Monticello* (Charlottesville: Thomas Jefferson Foundation, 2000), appendix; Barbara J. Heath, *Hidden Lives: The Archaeology of Slave Life at Thomas Jefferson's Poplar Forest* (Charlottesville: University Press of Virginia, 1999).

36. Jefferson, *Notes*, 234.

37. Jefferson, *Notes*, 237.

38. Ibid., 235–37; Stanton, *Free Some Day*, 41.

39. The first English translation as *The Adventures of Telemachus, the Son of Ulysses* appeared in London in 1699; the first American edition was published, with engravings, in New York by T. and J. Swords in 1794. At least forty editions were published in the United States between 1794 and 1900, eleven by 1800. By 1773, a London edition with French and English on opposite pages was available. *National Union Catalog*, 169:352, 356–59.

40. James Herbert Davis, *Fénelon* (New York: Twayne, 1979), 42–45; François de Salignac de La Mothe-Fénelon, *Instructions for the Education of a Daughter* (London: Jonah Bowyer, 1707), 231.

41. Davis, *Fénelon*, 90–111; Jay Fliegelman, *Prodigals and Pilgrims: The American Revolution against Patriarchal Authority, 1750–1800* (Cambridge: Cambridge University Press, 1982), 46–49.

42 Wolf, *Library of James Logan*, 169; Hayes, *Colonial Woman's Bookshelf*, 10.

43. Martha Slotten, "Elizabeth Graeme Fergusson: A Poet in the Athens of North America," *Pennsylvania Magazine of History and Biography* 108 (1984), 260, 262.

44. Slotten, "Fergusson," 271, 267; Anne Ousterhout, *The Most Learned Woman in America: A Life of Elizabeth Graeme Fergusson* (University Park: Pennsylvania State University Press, 2004), 295.

45. Ousterhout, *Most Learned Woman*, 321; David Shields, "The Manuscript in the British American World of Print," *Proceedings of the American Antiquarian Society* 102 (1992): 403–16.

46. Rario, "The Pedestrian. Number IX," *Companion and Weekly Miscellany*, 11 Jan. 1806, 83. On the work of female conversation in the salon see Goodman, *Republic of Letters*, 103–4.

47. On the shell grotto, see Susan Stabile, *Memory's Daughters: The Material Culture of Remembrance in Eighteenth-Century America* (Ithaca: Cornell University Press, 2004), 20–22.

48. West's *Calypso* is discussed in "The Calypso," *Port Folio*, 11 Feb. 1804, 46; *Philadelphia Repository*, 5 Jan. 1805, 7; "The Artist—No. II. Benjamin West, Esq. President of the Royal Academy," *Port Folio*, Oct. 1811, 334–35; Campbell's embroidery is reproduced in Wendy Cooper, *Classical Taste in America 1800–1840* (New York: Abbeville Press, 1993), 257; Télémaque wallpaper is reproduced in Catherine Lynn, *Wallpaper in America: From the Seventeenth Century to World War I* (New York: Norton, 1980), 205, 211, 219; also in Doris A. Hamburg, "The In-Situ Conservation Treatment of a Nineteenth-Century French Scenic Wallpaper: Les Paysages de Télémaque dans L'Ile de Calypso," *Journal of the American Institute of Conservation* 20 (1981): 91–99.

2. The Rise of the Roman Matron

1. Oliver Wolcott, Sr., to Laura Wolcott, 11 May 1776, Oliver Wolcott, Sr., Papers (Subseries 1.ii, Folder I.14), Connecticut Historical Society.

2. Oliver Wolcott, Sr., tabulation of lead cartridges made by women of Litchfield, n.d., Oliver Wolcott, Sr., Papers (Subseries 1.i, Folder I.2), Connecticut Historical Society; The portrait of Laura Wolcott is reproduced in Elizabeth Mankin Kornhauser et al., *Ralph Earl: The Face of the Young Republic* (New Haven: Yale University Press, 1991), 148.

3. On the adoption of classical pseudonyms by men, see Eran Shalev, "Ancient Masks, American Fathers: Classical Pseudonyms during the American Revolution and Early Republic," *Journal of the Early Republic* 23 (Summer 2003): 151–72; on the possibilities of the collective pseudonym "Publius," shared by James Madison, Alexander Hamilton and John Jay in *The Federalist*, see Daniel Walker Howe, "The Political Psychology of *The Federalist*," *William and Mary Quarterly* 44 (July 1987): 485–509.

4. On the influence of Scottish philosophy on American women, see Rosemarie Zagarri, "Morals, Manners, and the Republican Mother," *American Quarterly* 44 (June 1992): 192–215.

5. Charlton T. Lewis, *A Latin Dictionary for Schools* (Oxford: Clarendon Press, 1889), s.v. "matrona"; Mercy Otis Warren to Abigail Adams [hereafter MOW and AA], 28 Jan. 1775, in *Adams Family Correspondence*, ed. L. H. Butterfield (Cambridge: Harvard University Press, 1963), 1:181.

6. Elaine Forman Crane, *Ebb Tide in New England: Women, Seaports, and Social Change, 1630–1800* (Boston: Northeastern University Press, 1998); Karin Wulf, *Not All Wives: Women of*

Colonial Philadelphia (Ithaca: Cornell University Press, 2000); Michael O'Brien, ed., *An Evening When Alone: Four Journals of Single Women in the South, 1827–67* (Charlottesville: University Press of Virginia, 1993), 1–49.

7. James Wilson, "On the Natural Rights of Individuals," in *The Works of James Wilson*, ed. Robert Green McCloskey (Cambridge: Harvard University Press, 1967), 2:599; William Alexander, *The History of Women, from the Earliest Antiquity to the Present Time*, 3rd ed. (London: C. Dilly, 1782), 1:203–4.

8. Jane F. Gardner, *Women in Roman Law & Society* (Bloomington: Indiana University Press, 1986), 5–11; Sarah B. Pomeroy, *Goddesses, Whores, Wives, and Slaves: Women in Classical Antiquity* (1975; New York: Schocken Books, 1995), chap. 8; Ian Morris, "Remaining Invisible: The Archaeology of the Excluded in Classical Athens," in *Women and Slaves in Greco-Roman Culture: Differential Equations*, ed. Sandra R. Joshel and Sheila Murnaghan (London: Routledge, 1998), 193–220.

9. Catharine Macaulay, *The History of England from the Accession of James I to that of the Brunswick Line* (London: Edward and Charles Dilly, 1767), 3:187–88.

10. Macaulay, *History*, 1:vii; Elizabeth Carter to Catherine Talbot, 27 August 1757, in *A Series of Letters between Mrs. Elizabeth Carter and Miss Catherine Talbot, from the Year 1741 to 1770* (1809; New York: AMS Press, 1975), 2:260; Catharine Macaulay, *Letters on Education* (London: C. Dilly, 1790; Oxford: Woodstock Books, 1994), 129–30, 142. For more on Macaulay as a female history writer see J. G. A. Pocock, "Catharine Macaulay," in *Women Writers and the Early Modern British Political Tradition*, ed. Hilda L. Smith (Cambridge: Cambridge University Press, 1998), 243–58; Philip Hicks, "The Roman Matron in Britain: Female Political Influence and Republican Response, ca. 1750–1800," *Journal of Modern History* 77 (March 2005): 35–69.

11. Macaulay, *Letters on Education*, 129–30, 142.

12. Philip Hicks, "Portia and Marcia: Female Political Identity and the Historical Imagination, 1770–1800," *William and Mary Quarterly* 62 (April 2005), 13; *My Dearest Julia: The Love Letters of Dr. Benjamin Rush to Julia Stockton* (New York: Neale Watson, 1979), xii, 43; AA to Isaac Smith, Jr., 20 April 1771, in *Adams Family Correspondence*, 1:77.

13. Rosemarie Zagarri, *A Woman's Dilemma: Mercy Otis Warren and the American Revolution* (Wheeling, IL: Harlan Davidson, 1995), 54–55.

14. Edith B. Gelles, *Portia: The World of Abigail Adams* (1992; Bloomington: Indiana University Press, 1995), 25; AA to John Adams (hereafter JA), 14 July 1776, Adams Family Papers, Massachusetts Historical Society online (hereafter AFP).

15. AA to JA, 4 May 1775; AA to JA, 13–14 July 1776; AA to JA, 12 April 1784, AFP; Hicks, "Portia and Marcia," 17–18.

16. Rosemarie Zagarri, "The Rights of Man and Woman in Post-Revolutionary America," *William and Mary Quarterly* 55 (April 1998): 203–230; Jan Lewis, "Representation of Women in the Constitution," in *Women in the United States Constitution: History, Interpretation, and Practice*, ed. Sibyl A. Schwarzenbach and Patricia Smith (New York: Columbia University Press, 2003), 23–29; AA to JA, 17 June 1782, AFP; MOW to AA, 15 Oct. 1776, *Adams Family Correspondence*, 2:142.

17. John Adams, autobiography, part 2, "Travels, and Negotiations," 19 May 1778; AA to JA, 25 May 1781, AFP.

18. AA to JA, 10 April 1782, AFP.

19. AA to JA, 19 Aug. 1774; AA to JA, 15 Dec. 1783, AFP. The story is from Livy: Lucretia's husband, Collatinus, brags to a group of soldiers led by Sextus Tarquinius that Lucretia is the most chaste woman. Incredulous, the men go off to find her, and indeed discover that while other women are attending a banquet, Lucretia is quietly spinning wool with her women. Upon espying Lucretius, however, Sextus Tarquinius is inflamed by lust for her. He returns late one night to rape her and threatens that if she resists he will lay a dead slave by her side

to suggest that she had committed adultery with a man of low birth. She resists Tarquinius, but still commits suicide to show that no woman could ever appear unchaste by invoking the example of Lucretia. Her exemplum is also a founding myth of the Roman republic: Lucretia's act so fired the patriotism of the Romans that they threw off the rule of the Tarquins and established their republic.

20. Zagarri, *Mercy Otis Warren*, 43; Hicks, "Portia and Marcia," 1, 23, 24.

21. Lester H. Cohen, "Mercy Otis Warren: The Politics of Language and the Aesthetics of Self," *American Quarterly* 35 (Winter 1983), 490–91.

22. Julie Ellison, *Cato's Tears and the Making of Anglo-American Emotion* (Chicago: University of Chicago Press, 1999); Joseph Litto, "Addison's *Cato* in the Colonies," *William and Mary Quarterly* 23 (July 1966), 435.

23. Zagarri, *Mercy Otis Warren*, 135.

24. Mercy Otis Warren, *The Sack of Rome: A Tragedy in Five Acts*, in *Poems, Dramatic and Miscellaneous* (Boston: I. Thomas and E. T. Andrews, 1790), 88, 43, 83, 30.

25. Warren, *Sack of Rome*, v, 13.

26. Ibid., iv; "Epilogue to the Sack of Rome," *Massachusetts Magazine*, Sept. 1790, 564. Here is a partial list of American "Roman plays": Mercy Otis Warren, *The Sack of Rome: A Tragedy* (1790); Margaretta Van Wyck Bleecker Faugéres, *Belisarius: A Tragedy* (1795); Charles Stearns, *Zenobia: A Tragedy in Five Acts: On Future Retribution* (1798); Mordecai Noah, *The Grecian Captive: Or, the Fall of Athens* (1822); David Paul Brown, *Sertorius: Or, the Roman Patriot* (1830); Charles Jared Ingersoll, *Julian: A Tragedy in Five Acts* (1831); Joan Phillips, *Camillus; Or, the Self-Exiled Patriot: A Tragedy in Five Acts* (1833); Robert Bannister, *Gaulantus: A Tragedy in Five Acts* (1836); Alexander Hill Everett, *The Grecian Gossips, Imitated from Theocritus* (1845); Louisa McCord, *Caius Gracchus* (1851); J. P. Quincy, *Lyteria: A Dramatic Poem* (1854); Louisa Medina, *The Last Days of Pompeii: A Dramatic Spectacle taken from Bulwer's Celebrated Novel of the Same Title* (1856); and Eliza Oakes Smith, *The Roman Tribute; Or, Attila the Hun* [lost play]. These are in addition to British Roman plays read, performed, or reprinted in the United States.

27. Joshua Reynolds, *Seven Discourses* (London: T. Cadell, 1778), 319–20; Gill Perry, "Women in Disguise: Likeness, the Grand Style and the Conventions of 'Feminine' Portraiture in the Works of Sir Joshua Reynolds," *Femininity and Masculinity in Eighteenth-Century Art and Culture*, ed. Gill Perry and Michael Rossington (Manchester: Manchester University Press, 1994), 18–40; Aileen Ribeiro, "Muses and Mythology: Classical Dress in British Eighteenth-Century Female Portraiture," in *Defining Dress: Dress as Object, Meaning, and Identity*, ed. Amy de la Haye and Elizabeth Wilson (Manchester: Manchester University Press, 1999), 104–113; Aileen Ribeiro, "The Dress Worn at Masquerades in England, 1730 to 1790, and Its Relation to Fancy Dress in Portraiture," Ph.D. diss., Courtauld Institute of Art, 1975, 264–74.

28. David D. Hall, "Learned Culture in the Eighteenth Century," in *A History of the Book in America*, vol. 1: *The Colonial Book in the Atlantic World*, ed. Hugh Amory and David D. Hall (Cambridge: Cambridge University Press, 2000), 414.

29. For the identification of Joseph Henshaw as a Son of Liberty, see William Palfrey, "An Alphabetical List of the Sons of Liberty who Dined at Liberty Tree, Dorchester, Aug. 14, 1789," *Massachusetts Historical Society Proceedings* 11 (1869–1870), 141; Carrie Rebora et al., *John Singleton Copley in America* (New York: Metropolitan Museum of Art, 1995), 133, 266–68.

30. Edgar P. Richardson, Brooke Hindle, and Lillian B. Miller, *Charles Willson Peale and His World* (New York: Harry N. Abrams, 1983), 30, 38–43. A different reading of the Latin inscription is also plausible: see Sidney Hart, "A Graphic Case of Transatlantic Republicanism," in *New Perspectives on Charles Willson Peale: A 250th Anniversary Celebration*, ed. Lillian B. Miller and David C. Ward (Pittsburgh: University of Pittsburgh Press, 1991), 73–81. On the reception of Thomson's play, *Sophonisba*, in eighteenth-century England, see Ellison, *Cato's Tears*, 60–67.

31. Marie Elena Korey, *The Books of Isaac Norris (1701–1766), at Dickinson College* (Carlisle, PA: The College, 1976); James W. Phillips, "The Sources of the Original Dickinson College Library," *Pennsylvania History* 14 (1947): 108–17.

32. Richardson et al., *Charles Willson Peale*, 48.

33. "Mrs. Robert Shewell" [Sarah Boyer], c. 1775; "John Purves and His Wife [Ann Pritchard]" c. 1775; "Mrs. Charles Cotesworth Pinckney [Sarah Middleton], c. 1773; Mrs. John Peyre [Margaret Cantey]; "Lady of the Middleton Family", c. 1786; Sarah Hartley in "The Hartley Family," 1787; Mrs. James Gignilliat [Charlotte Pepper], n.d.; "Mrs. William H. Gibbes" [Elizabeth Allston], c. 1786; "Mrs. William Allston, Jr." [Rachel Moore], c. 1784. All reproduced in Maurie McInnis et al., *Henry Benbridge: Charleston Portrait Painter (1743–1812)*, catalogue and transcription by Angela D. Mack (Charleston: Carolina Art Association, 2000), 14, 60, 82, 95, and passim.

34. Frances Leigh Williams, *A Founding Family: The Pinckneys of South Carolina* (New York: Harcourt Brace Jovanovich, 1978), 55.

35. Eliza Lucas Pinckney, *Letterbook*, quoted in George Lane, "The Middletons of Eighteenth-Century South Carolina: A Colonial Dynasty," Ph.D. diss., Emory University, 1990, 167; Mac Griswold, "American Artists, American Gardens," in *Keeping Eden: A History of Gardening in America*, ed. Walter Punch (Boston: Bulfinch Press, 1992), 167–87; Barbara Wells Sarudy, *Gardens and Gardening in the Chesapeake, 1700–1805* (Baltimore: Johns Hopkins University Press, 1998), 15; Maurie McInnis, "Our Ingenious Countryman Mr. Benbridge," in *Henry Benbridge*, 14–15.

36. Alice Izard quoted in Jeffrey Robert Young, *Domesticating Slavery: The Master Class in Georgia and South Carolina, 1670–1837* (Chapel Hill: University of North Carolina Press, 1999), 118.

37. The identification of the sketch and statue of Papirius Praetextatus in Copley's painting is from William B. Dinsmoor, "Early American Studies of Mediterranean Archaeology," *Proceedings of the American Philosophical Society* 87, 1 (July 1943), 75; on Ferguson's *Art of Drawing in Perspective* in the family library, see Robert F. Neville and Katherine Brelsky, "The Izard Library," *South Carolina Historical Magazine* 91 (1990), 15; on ideals of female artistic "accomplishment" in the eighteenth century, see Anne Bermingham, *Learning to Draw: Studies in the Cultural History of a Polite and Useful Art* (New Haven: Yale University Press, 2000), 185; for the view that the sketch was made by Alice Izard and a confirmation of the identification of the statue, see Maurie McInnis, "Cultural Politics, Colonial Crisis, and Ancient Metaphor in John Singleton Copley's *Mr. and Mrs. Ralph Izard*," *Winterthur Portfolio* 34 (Summer/Autumn 1999), 95, 102–4.

38. Annis Boudinot Stockton, "On Seeing Mrs Macauly Graham," in *Only for the Eye of a Friend: The Poems of Annis Boudinot Stockton*, ed. Carla Mulford (Charlottesville: University Press of Virginia, 1995), 131.

39. Mulford, ed., *Only for the Eye*, 152–53; Carl J. Richard, *The Founders and the Classics: Greece, Rome, and the American Enlightenment* (Cambridge: Harvard University Press, 1994), 69–70.

40. Catherine La Coureye Blecki and Karen A. Wulf, eds., *Milcah Martha Moore's Book: A Commonplace Book from Revolutionary America* (University Park: Pennsylvania State University Press, 1997), 12.

41. Blecki and Wulf, eds., *Milcah Martha Moore's Book*, 11–13.

42. "By the Same on reading Eliza. Carters Poems," in *Milcah Martha Moore's Book*, ed. Blecki and Wulf, 263–64.

43. Blecki and Wulf, eds., *Milcah Martha Moore's Book*, 42, 152, 172, 173, 246–47.

3. Daughters of Columbia

1. William Smith, *An Oration, Delivered in St. Philip's Church, Before the Inhabitants of Charleston, South-Carolina, on the Fourth of July, 1796, in Commemoration of American Independence*

(Charleston: W. P. Young, 1796), 9; on the conceptualization of women's rights and duties after the revolution, see Linda K. Kerber, *No Constitutional Right to be Ladies: Women and the Obligations of Citizenship* (New York: Hill and Wang, 1998); and Rosemarie Zagarri, "The Rights of Man and Woman in Post-Revolutionary America," *William and Mary Quarterly* 55 (April 1998): 203–230.

2. Recent works on women and print culture in the aftermath of revolution include Susan Branson, *These Fiery Frenchified Dames: Women and Political Culture in Early National Philadelphia* (Philadelphia: University of Pennsylvania Press, 2001); Mary Kelley, *Learning to Stand and Speak: Women, Education, and Public Life in America's Republic* (Chapel Hill: Published for the Omohundro Institute of Early American History and Culture by the University of North Carolina Press, 2006), chap. 1; Cynthia A. Kierner, *Beyond the Household: Women's Place in the Early South, 1700–1835* (Ithaca: Cornell University Press, 1998).

3. David Ramsay, *Memoirs of the Life of Martha Laurens Ramsay* (Charlestown, MA: Samuel Etheridge, 1812), 34.

4. Ibid., 31, 33, 34.

5. Sharon M. Harris, ed., *Selected Writings of Judith Sargent Murray* (New York: Oxford University Press, 1995), xv, xvi.

6. Harris, *Selected Writings*, xxii, xx; Emily Pendleton and Milton Ellis, *Philenia: The Life and Works of Sarah Wentworth Morton 1759–1846* (Orono, ME: University Press, 1931), 41–43.

7. Samuel B. Fortenbaugh, Jr., *In Order to Form a More Perfect Union: An Inquiry into the Origins of a College* (Schenectady: Union College Press, 1978), 73–89.

8. Howard Peckham, *The Toll of Independence: Engagements and Battle Casualties of the American Revolution* (Chicago: University of Chicago Press, 1974), 130. Peckham includes casualties in some naval skirmishes of 1782 and 1783.

9. J. G. A. Pocock, *The Machiavellian Moment. Florentine Political Thought and the Atlantic Republican Tradition* (Princeton: Princeton University Press, 1975), 89; Harrington, "Political Papers: On the Dissolution of the Federal Union," *Rural Magazine, or Vermont Repository*, May 1796, 236; "The Explanation of the Frontispiece," *Philadelphia Magazine and Review*, Jan. 1799, 4; "Soliloquy on the Death of Washington," *Columbian Phenix and Boston Review*, April 1800, 213; Gary Wills, *Cincinnatus: George Washington and the Enlightenment* (Garden City: Doubleday, 1984).

10. An American Woman, *The Sentiments of an American Woman* (Philadelphia: John Dunlap, 1780).

11. "The Life of Lycurgus," *American Universal Magazine*, 10 July 1797, 46; "Is it Desirable that the State Should Interfere in the Education of Youth?" *American Universal Magazine*, 9 Jan. 1797, 45; Carl J. Richard, *The Founders and the Classics: Greece, Rome, and the American Enlightenment* (Cambridge: Harvard University Press, 1994), 73–74; Elizabeth Rawson, *The Spartan Tradition in European Thought* (Oxford: Clarendon Press, 1969).

12. "Lycurgus," in *Plutarch's Lives, Translated from the Original Greek, with Notes Critical and Historical, and a Life of Plutarch*, trans. John Langhorne and William Langhorne (London: Edward and Charles Dilly, 1770), 1:97–147. On Plutarch in eighteenth-century America, see Meyer Reinhold, *Classica Americana: The Greek and Roman Heritage in the United States* (Detroit: Wayne State University Press, 1984), 250–64, and Reinhold, *The Classick Pages: Classical Reading of Eighteenth-Century Americans* (University Park, PA: American Philological Association, 1975), 39–47; H.E.I., "On the Study of History," *Philadelphia Repository and Weekly Register* 1, 22 (11 April 1801): 173; Hester Chapone, *Letters on the Improvement of the Mind, Addressed to a Young Lady* (London: H. Hughs, 1773), 2:190–91; John Adams, *The Flowers of Ancient History* (Newtown: William Coale, 1804), 139.

13. *The Juvenile Plutarch: Containing Accounts of the Lives of Children and of the Infancy of Illustrious Men, Who Have Been Remarkable for their Early Progress in Knowledge* (London: R. Phillips, 1801); the image of *A Girl in Blue* appears in *The Classical Spirit in American Portraiture. An Exhibition Sponsored by the Department of Art, Brown University* (Providence: Department of Art, Brown University, 1976), 60.

14. "Lycurgus," in *Plutarch's Lives*, trans. Langhorne, 1:119; the story is repeated in Weatherwise's *Father Abraham's Almanack*, 1774, reprinted in Marion Barber Stowell, *Early American Almanacs: The Colonial Weekday Bible* (New York: Burt Franklin, 1976), 202; "General Ideas on the Legislation of Lycurgus," *American Universal Magazine*, 21 Aug. 1797, 244.

15. "Lycurgus," in *Plutarch's Lives*, trans. Langhorne, 1:119.

16. Abigail Franks to Naphtali Franks, 3 June 1742, in *The Lee Max Friedman Collection of American Jewish Colonial Correspondence: Letters of the Franks Family (1733–1748)*, ed. Leo Hershkowitz and Isidore S. Meyer (Waltham, MA: American Jewish Historical Society, 1968), 103; Stockton, "Impromptu On hearing that a print of the Guliteene with our beloved presidents figure under it was executed in Mr Genets family—under his Sanction," in *Only for the Eye of a Friend: The Poems of Annis Boudinot Stockton*, ed. Carla Mulford (Charlottesville: University Press of Virginia, 1995), 178.

17. "Amazons: Women in Control," in Elaine Fantham et al., *Women in the Classical World: Image and Text* (New York: Oxford University Press, 1994), 128–35; "Account of the Amazons," *Massachusetts Magazine*, Feb. 1796, 107–9; "The Modern Amazons," *Weekly Magazine of Original Essays, Fugitive Pieces*, 9 March 1799, 274–76; Thomas Jefferson to Anne Willing Bingham, 11 May 1788, in *The Papers of Thomas Jefferson*, ed. Julian P. Boyd et al. (Princeton: Princeton University Press, 1956), 13:152.

18. "Particulars of the Assassination of Marat," *National Gazette*, 25 Sept. 1793, 379; "Paris, July 18," *National Gazette*, 2 Oct. 1793, 387; Incognita, "On Female Talent," *New-York Weekly Museum*, 2 March 1816, 277; "Charlotte Corday," *New-England Quarterly Magazine*, April–June 1802, 85; "Charlotte Corday," *Saturday Evening Post*, 3 Feb. 1827, 288; "Charlotte Corday," *Casket*, March 1827, 102.

19. Rawson, *Spartan Tradition*, plates 2 and 4, and 286; Charles Rollin, *Ancient History*, 2nd ed. (London, 1738–1740), 2:335–36.

20. David Ramsay, *History of the Revolution of South-Carolina from a British Province to an Independent State* (Trenton: Isaac Collins, 1785), 2:123–24; Andrew Beers, *The Farmer's Calendar* (Bennington: Anthony Haswell, 1811); *Raleigh Register*, 9 Oct. 1812.

21. Judith Sargent Murray, "Observations on Female Abilities," in *The Gleaner: A Miscellaneous Production* (Boston: I. Thomas and E. T. Andrews, 1798), 3:196–97; Sheila Skemp, *Judith Sargent Murray: A Brief Biography with Documents* (Boston: Bedford Books, 1998), 34.

22. Murray, *Gleaner*, 3:192.

23. Ibid.

24. Ibid., 3:198.

25. Mariette de Vos, "La ricenzione della pittura antica fino alla scoperta di Ercolano e Pompei," in *Memoria dell'antico nell'arte italiana*, ed. S. Settis (Torino: Giulio Einaudi, 1985), 2:360–61 and plates 289, 290.

26. Valerius Maximus, *Memorable Doings and Sayings*, ed. and trans. D. R. Shackleton Bailey (Cambridge: Harvard University Press, 2000), Book V.4; W. Martin Bloomer, *Valerius Maximus and the Rhetoric of the New Nobility* (Chapel Hill: University of North Carolina Press, 1992), 226–29; *Conciliation with the Colonies: The Speech by Edmund Burke* (1775), ed. Archibald Freeman and Arthur W. Leonard (Boston: Houghton Mifflin, 1943), 55.

27. *Westminster Magazine* 4 (1778), frontispiece and 4, in *The American Revolution in Drawings and Prints: A Checklist of 1765–1790 Graphics in the Library of Congress*, compiled by Donald Cresswell (Washington, DC: U.S. Government Printing Office, 1975), 303.

28. William Cadogan, *An Essay upon Nursing and the Management of Children, from their Birth to Three Years of Age, by a Physician* (London: J. Roberts, 1748), 6; Marilyn Salmon, "The Cultural Significance of Breast Feeding and Infant Care in Early Modern England and America," *Journal of Social History* 28 (Winter 1994): 247–70; Jean-François Marmontel, *Les Incas, ou La Destruction de l'Empire du Pérou* (Paris: Lacombe, 1777), 165–66; Hugh Honour, *The European Vision of America* (Cleveland: Cleveland Museum of Art, 1976), 269; Robert Rosenblum, "Caritas Romana

after 1760: Some Romantic Lactations," in *Woman as Sex Object: Studies in Erotic Art, 1730–1970* ed. Thomas B. Hess and Linda Nochlin (London: Allen Lane, 1973), 43–63.

29. On John Gregory's popularity in the revolutionary era, see Jay Fliegelman, *Prodigals and Pilgrims: The American Revolution against Patriarchal Authority* (Cambridge: Cambridge University Press, 1982), 39; Mary Willing's portrait appears in Carrie Rebora Barratt and Ellen G. Miles, *Gilbert Stuart* (New Haven: Yale University Press, 2004), 201; M. H. Hoeflich, *Roman and Civil Law and the Development of Anglo-American Jurisprudence in the Nineteenth Century* (Athens: University of Georgia Press, 1997); Herbert A Johnson, *Imported Eighteenth-Century Law Treatises in American Libraries, 1700–1799* (Knoxville: University of Tennessee Press, 1978); Judith Hallett, *Fathers and Daughters in Roman Society* (Princeton: Princeton University Press, 1984), 77, 79.

30. Joanna Bowen Gillespie, *The Life and Times of Martha Laurens Ramsay, 1759–1811* (Columbia: University of South Carolina Press, 2001), 22, 31–33, 100, xix; Henry Laurens to Martha Laurens, 24 Aug. 1782, in *The Papers of Henry Laurens*, ed. David R. Chesnutt and C. James Taylor (Columbia: University of South Carolina Press, 2000), 15: 590.

31. *Worthy Example of a Married Daughter, Who Fed Her Father with Her Own Milk, He Being Commanded by the Emperor to Be Starved to Death, and Afterwards Pardoned* (Boston: T. and J. Fleet, 1776); *A Worthy Example of a Virtuous Wife* (Boston: E. Russell, 1794); *The Grecian Daughter. Or, an Example of a Virtuous Wife, Who Fed Her Father with Her Own Milk—He Being Condemned to Be Starved to Death by Tiberius Caesar, Emperor of Rome; but Was afterwards Pardoned, and the Daughter Highly Rewarded* (Vermont: Alden Spooner, 1798); Arthur Murphy, *The Grecian Daughter: A Tragedy* (Philadelphia: Henry Taylor, 1791), 11, 39, 67; "The Drama," *Repository and Ladies' Weekly Museum*, 4 Jan. 1806, 23; the image of Roman charity also appears in Alfred Mills, *Pictures of Roman History in Miniature* (Philadelphia: Johnson and Warner, 1811).

32. Margaret Law Callcott, ed., *Mistress of Riversdale: The Plantation Letters of Rosalie Stier Calvert, 1795–1821* (Baltimore: Johns Hopkins University Press, 1991), 242 n. 2, 395; Robert C. Alberts, *The Golden Voyage: The Life and Times of William Bingham, 1752–1804* (Boston: Houghton-Mifflin, 1969), 159; *Rembrandt Peale, 1778–1860, A Life in the Arts: An Exhibition at the Historical Society of Pennsylvania, February 22, 1985 to June 28, 1985*, organized by Carol Eaton Hevner (Philadelphia: Historical Society of Pennsylvania, 1985), 14–15.

33. *A Worthy Example*; *Grecian Daughter*.

34. Martha Laurens Ramsay to David Ramsay, 17 Dec. 1792, in Ramsay, *Memoirs*, 208.

35. Murray, *Gleaner*, 3:208–9.

36. Nicholas Biddle, "First Greek Journal," in *Nicholas Biddle in Greece: The Journals and Letters of 1806*, ed. R. A. McNeal (University Park: Pennsylvania State University Press, 1993), 50.

37. John Milton, *Paradise Lost*, in M. H. Abrams, *The Norton Anthology of English Literature* (New York: W. W. Norton, 2000), 1887, 1903, 1949; *Aristotle's Compleate Master Piece: In Three Parts* (1749; New York: Garland, 1986), 80, 97–99, 109, 117. On Milton's Eve in eighteenth-century America, see George F. Sensabaugh, *Milton in Early America* (Princeton: Princeton University Press, 1964), 195–217; Laurel Thatcher Ulrich, *Good Wives: Image and Reality in the Lives of Women in Northern New England 1650–1750* (New York: Knopf, 1982), chap. 6; on Eve's transmutation in the early republic, see Jan Lewis, "The Republican Wife: Virtue and Seduction in the Early Republic," *William and Mary Quarterly* 3rd ser., 44 (Oct. 1987): 689–721; on "martyrdom to Venus" as venereal disease see Richard Godbeer, *Sexual Revolution in Early America* (Baltimore: Johns Hopkins University Press, 2002), chap. 9.

38. Mother of Cupid: "Anacreon: Ode 40—Imitated," *Columbian Phenix* 1 (July 1800): 446; "Venus Outwitted, or the Triumph of Pallas," *Massachusetts Magazine*, April 1794, 147–48; Hive, "Original Song," *American Gleaner and Virginia Magazine*, 1807, 15; among the pictorial representations of the cestus of Venus at this time was Joshua Reynolds, *Cupid Unfastening the Belt of Venus* (1788).

39. Francis Haskell and Nicholas Penny, *Taste and the Antique: The Lure of Classical Sculpture, 1500–1900* (New Haven: Yale University Press, 1981), 325–30; William Vance, *America's Rome*, vol. 1: *Classical Rome* (New Haven: Yale University Press, 1989), 200; Kenneth Clark, *The Nude: A Study of Ideal Art* (New York: Pantheon Books, 1956), 88–89; "Beauty, and Venus de Medicis," *Monthly Anthology*, June 1805, 303; Charles Edwards, *The Antique Statues* (New York: Osborn and Buckingham, 1830), 52.

40. E. McSherry Fowble, "Without a Blush: The Movement toward the Acceptance of the Nude as an Art Form in America," *Winterthur Portfolio* 9 (1974), 105; Wendy A. Cooper, *Classical Taste in America 1800–1840* (New York: Abbeville Press, 1993), 79; *The Eye of Thomas Jefferson*, ed. William Howard Adams (Charlottesville: University Press of Virginia, 1981), 80.

41. *Inventory of the Contents of Mount Vernon 1810*, prefatory note by Worthington Chauncey Ford (Cambridge: Harvard University Press 1909), 3–5; Anna Maria Thornton, diary entry of 14 Oct. 1800, *Diary of Mrs. William Thornton, 1800–1863* (Washington, DC: 1907), 201.

42. Rosalie Stier Calvert to Charles J. Stier, 26 April 1807, in Callcott, ed., *Mistress of Riversdale*, 166.

43. Thomas Slothard, "Voyage of the Sable Venus from Angola to the West Indies," in Bryan Edwards, *List of Maps and Plates for the History, Civil and Commercial, of the British Colonies of the West Indies* (London: John Stockdale, 1794), frontispiece; Isaac Teale, *The Sable Venus: An Ode* (Kingston, Jamaica: Bennett and Woolhead, 1765), Library Company of Philadelphia; Virgil, *Eclogue* 10:38–39, in *Virgil: Eclogues, Georgics, Aeneid I-VI*, trans. H. Rushton Fairclough (Cambridge: Harvard University Press, 1999), 91–93; Hugh Honour, *The Image of the Black in Western Art. IV. From the American Revolution to World War I. 2. Black Models and White Myths* (Cambridge: Harvard University Press, 1989), 52.

44. Franklin Scott, *Wertmüller: Artist and Immigrant Farmer* (Chicago: Swedish Pioneer Historical Society, 1963), 19; Charles Willson Peale to Benjamin Henry Latrobe, 13 May 1805, in *The Papers of Benjamin Henry Latrobe*, Series IV: *The Correspondence and Miscellaneous Papers*, ed. John C. Van Horne and Lee W. Formwalt (New Haven: Yale University Press, 1986), 2:106; Thomas Cooper, "Remarks on Various Objects of the Fine Arts," *Port Folio* 7, 6 (June 1812): 542.

45. *The Diary of Harriet Manigault 1813–1816* (Rockland: Maine Coast Printers, 1976), 61.

46. Entry for 11 Jan. 1797, *The Letter-book of Mary Stead Pinckney, Nov. 14th 1796 to August 29th 1797*, ed. Charles McCombs (New York: Grolier Club, 1946), 57; on Sèvres, see Tamara Préaud et al., *The Sèvres Porcelain Manufactory: Alexandre Brongniart and the Triumph of Art and Industry, 1800–1847*, ed. Derek Ostergard (New Haven: Yale University Press, 1997).

47. Gelles, *Portia*, 86; Abigail Adams (hereafter AA) to Mary Smith Cranch, 20 Feb. 1785, in *Letters of Mrs. Adams, The Wife of John Adams*, ed. Charles Francis Adams (Boston: Little, Brown, 1841), 2:82–83; Thomas Jefferson to AA, 25 Sept. 1785, in *The Adams-Jefferson Letters: The Complete Correspondence between Thomas Jefferson and Abigail and John Adams*, ed. Lester J. Cappon (1959; Chapel Hill: University of North Carolina Press, 1988), 69–70.

48. AA to Lucy Cranch Greenleaf, 3 Oct. 1787, in Adams, ed., *Letters*, 2:154, 191–92.

49. On Abigail Adams as Lucretia, see Philip Hicks, "Portia and Marcia: Female Political Identity and the Historical Imagination, 1770–1800," *William and Mary Quarterly* 62 (April 2005), 25; William Smith Shaw to AA, 25 May 1800, in Andrew Oliver, *Portraits of John and Abigail Adams* (Cambridge: Harvard University Press, 1967), 137.

4. Grecian Luxury, 1800–1830

1. John Wells to Miss Huger, 25 July 1815, in Nancy McClelland, *Duncan Phyfe and the English Regency, 1795–1830* (New York: Dover, 1980), 302.

2. Hugh Honour, *Neo-Classicism* (Harmondsworth: Penguin, 1968); Albert Boime, *Art in the Age of Revolution, 1750–1800* (Chicago: University of Chicago Press, 1987); Albert Boime,

Art in the Age of Bonapartism, 1800–1815 (Chicago: University of Chicago Press, 1990); Adrian Forty, *Objects of Desire: Design and Society, 1750–1980* (London: Thames and Hudson, 1986), 11–28; Barry Bergdoll, *Karl Friedrich Schinkel: An Architecture for Prussia* (New York: Rizzoli, 1994); Fernando Mazzocca, *L'Ideale Classico: Arte in Italia tra Neoclassicisimo e Romanticismo* (Vicenza: Nevi Pozza, 2002); *Il Neoclassicismo in Italia: Da Tiepolo a Canova* (Milano: Skira, 2002); Manos G. Biris, *Neoclassical Architecture in Greece*, trans. David Hardy (Los Angeles: J. Paul Getty Museum, 2004).

3. Wendell Garrett, *Neo-Classicism in America: Inspiration and Innovation, 1810–1840* (New York: Hirschl and Adler Galleries, 1991); Wendy A. Cooper, *Classical Taste in America, 1800–1840* (New York: Abbeville Press, 1993); Stuart Feld, *Boston in the Age of Neo-Classicism, 1810–1840* (New York: Hirschl and Adler, 1999); Ronald L. Hurst and Jonathan Prown, *Southern Furniture, 1680–1830: The Colonial Williamsburg Collection* (New York: Harry Abrams, 1997); Newark Museum Association, *Classical America, 1815–1845* (Newark, NJ: Newark Museum Association, 1963); Peter Thornton, *Authentic Decor: The Domestic Interior, 1620–1920* (New York: Viking, 1984); Edgar de N. Mayhew and Minor Myers, Jr., *A Documentary History of American Interiors: From the Colonial Era to 1915* (New York: Scribner, 1980).

4. Francis Haskell and Nicholas Penny, *Taste and the Antique: The Lure of Classical Sculpture, 1500–1900* (New Haven: Yale University Press, 1981), 108; Patricia Tyson Stroud, *The Man Who Had Been King: The American Exile of Napoleon's Brother Joseph* (Philadelphia: University of Pennsylvania Press, 2005), 68–70; Glenn J. Lamar, *Jérôme Bonaparte: The War Years, 1800–1815* (Westport, CT: Greenwood Press, 2000).

5. James Madison, "Political Reflections," 23 Feb. 1799, in *The Papers of James Madison*, ed. David C. Mattern et al. (Charlottesville: University Press of Virginia, 1991), 17:237.

6. Mary Beard, *The Parthenon* (Cambridge: Harvard University Press, 2003), 67, 68, 77; Deborah Howard, *Venice and the East: The Impact of the Islamic World on Venetian Architecture, 1100–1500* (New Haven: Yale University Press, 2000); John Adams to Benjamin Rush, 13 Oct. 1810, in *The Spur of Fame: Dialogues of John Adams and Benjamin Rush, 1805–1813*, ed. John A. Schutz and Douglass Adair (San Marino: Huntington Library, 1966), 170.

7. Thomas Hope, *Costumes of the Ancients* (1812; New York: Dover, 1962), xxv.

8. *The Arts Under Napoleon. An Exhibition of the Department of European Sculpture and Decorative Arts . . . April 6–July 30, 1978* (New York: Metropolitan Museum of Art, 1978), unpaginated 2; Julia Sarah Symmons, "Flaxman and Europe: The Outline Illustrations and Their Influence," Ph.D. diss., Courtauld Institute, 1984, 60; Forty, *Objects of Desire*, 15–16.

9. Eleanor P. DeLorme, ed., *Joséphine and the Arts of the Empire* (Los Angeles: J. Paul Getty Museum, 2005).

10. Catherine Allgor, *Parlor Politics: In Which the Ladies of Washington Help Build a City and a Government* (Charlottesville: University Press of Virginia, 2002).

11. McClelland, *Duncan Phyfe*, 287.

12. Samuel Smith to Dolley Payne Madison, 10 March 1809; Benjamin Latrobe to Dolley Payne Madison, 22 March 1809, Dolley Madison Digital Edition. http://rotunda.upress.virginia.edu:8080/dmde/

13. Jean-Jacques Barthélemy, *Travels of Anacharsis* (1788; Philadelphia: Jacob Johnson and W. F. M'Laughlin, 1804), iii–iv; 17 Sept. 1814 and 28 July 1814, in *Diary of Harriet Manigault* (Rockland, ME: Colonial Dames of America, 1976), 9, 30; Anna Maria Thornton, diary entry for 21 Sept. 1800, in *Diary of Mrs. William Thornton, 1800–1863* (District of Columbia, 1907), 194.

14. Thomas Sheraton, *The Cabinet-Maker and Upholsterer's Drawing-Book. In Four Parts* (London: T. Bensely, 1802), unpaginated 9, illustration is plate 38; for New York ownership, see Vincent Scully, *New World Visions of Household Gods and Sacred Spaces: American Art and the Metropolitan Museum of Art 1650–1914* (Boston: Little, Brown, 1988), 64–65.

15. Anne Willing Bingham to Thomas Jefferson, 1 June 1787, in *The Papers of Thomas Jefferson*, ed. Julian P. Boyd (Princeton: Princeton University Press, 1955), 11:392–93.

16. John Marshall to Mary W. Marshall, 14 July 1797, in *The Papers of John Marshall*, ed. William C. Stinchcombe and Charles T. Cullen (Chapel Hill: University of North Carolina Press, 1979), 3:102; Robert C. Alberts, *The Golden Voyage: The Life and Times of William Bingham, 1752–1804* (Boston: Houghton-Mifflin, 1969), 306–7; Carrie Rebora Barratt and Elaine Miles, *Gilbert Stuart* (New Haven: Yale University Press, 2004), 196–98.

17. Aaron Burr [hereafter AB] to [Mrs.] Theodosia Burr, 15 Feb. 1793, in Charles Pidgin, *Theodosia, the First Gentlewoman of Her Time* (Boston: C. M. Clark, 1907) 165–66; AB to Theodosia Burr (hereafter TB), 11 June 1803; AB to TB, 24 June 1804, in *A Correspondence of Aaron Burr and His Daughter Theodosia*, ed. Mark Van Doren (New York: Covidi-Friede, 1929), 117, 165.

18. AB to TB, 11 Aug. 1804, in Van Doren, ed., *Correspondence*, 174.

19. AB to TB, 16 Dec. 1793; AB to TB, 13 Jan. 1794; AB to TB, 14 Aug. 1794; AB to TB, 23 Jan. 1797; AB to TB, 21 Dec. 1794, in Van Doren, ed., *Correspondence*, 8, 16, 27, 45, 31.

20. Betty-Bright P. Low, "Of Muslins and Merveilleuses: Excerpts from the Letters of Josephine du Pont and Margaret Manigault," *Winterthur Portfolio* 9 (1974), 29; Aileen Ribeiro, *Fashion in the French Revolution* (London: BT Batsford, 1988), 108–35.

21. Sally McKean d'Yrujo to Anna Payne Cutts, 10 June 1796, in *Memoirs and Letters of Dolly [sic] Madison, Wife of James Madison, President of the United States*, ed. Lucia B. Cutts (Boston: Houghton-Mifflin, 1886), 18–19; Dolley Madison to Anna Payne Cutts, 22 May 1805, in *The Selected Letters of Dolley Payne Madison*, ed. David B. Mattern and Holly C. Shulman (Charlottesville: University Press of Virginia, 2003), 60.

22. "From Ackerman's [*sic*] London Repository. Female Fashions for June," *Repertory*, 5 Aug. 1813, 1.

23. Rhodri Windsor Liscombe, *The Church Architecture of Robert Mills* (Easley, SC: Southern Historical Press, 1985); Gretchen T. Buggeln, *Temples of Grace: The Material Transformation of Connecticut's Churches, 1790–1840* (Hanover: University Press of New England, 2003), 105.

24. Entry for 13 Dec. 1796, *The Letter-book of Mary Stead Pinckney, Nov. 14th 1796 to August 29th 1797*, ed. Charles F. McCombs (New York: Grolier Club, 1946), 31.

25. Paul C. Nagel, *The Adams Women: Abigail and Louisa Adams, Their Sisters and Daughters* (New York: Oxford University Press, 1987), 166; Hope, *Costumes*, plate 125; Sheraton, *Cabinet-Maker*, unpaginated 4.

26. Judith L. Sebesta and Larissa Bonfante, *The World of Roman Costume* (Madison: University of Wisconsin Press, 1994); Norah Waugh, *The Cut of Women's Clothes, 1600–1930* (New York: Theatre Arts Books, 1968), 74, 131–32, 137, 148; Meredith Wright, *Everyday Dress in Rural America 1783–1800: With Instructions and Patterns* (New York: Dover, 1990), 47–49; "Observations on Fashion," *Lady's Weekly Miscellany*, 11 July 1807, 287; George Turnbull, *A Treatise on Ancient Painting, 1740*, ed. Vincent M. Bevilacqua (Munich: Wilhelm Fink Verlag, 1971), 71.

27. Thomas Law quoted in *Mistress of Riversdale: The Plantation Letters of Rosalie Stier Calvert, 1795–1821*, ed. Margaret Law Callcott (Baltimore: Johns Hopkins University Press, 1991), 78; Waugh, *Cut*, 137; C. Willett Cunnington, *The History of Underclothes*, rev. ed. (London: Faver and Faver, 1981), 73–74; Linda Baumgarten, *What Clothes Reveal: The Language of Clothing in Colonial and Federal America* (New Haven: Yale University Press, 2002), 157, 219.

28. Martha Gandy Fales, *Jewelry in America, 1600–1900* (Woodbridge, Suffolk: Antique Collectors' Club, 1995), 80–82, 115; *Poulson's American Daily Advertiser*, 30 Sept. 1807, 3.

29. Sally McKean d'Yrujo to Anna Payne Cutts, 10 June 1796, in Cutts, ed., *Memoirs and Letters*, 2:20; Mary Boardman Crowninshield to Mary Hodges Boardman, 2 Jan. 1816, in *Letters of Mary Boardman Crowninshield 1815–1816*, ed. Francis Boardman Crowninshield (Cambridge: Riverside Press, 1905), 35.

30. On the American parlor and its furnishings, see Katherine Grief, *Culture & Comfort: People, Parlors, and Upholstery, 1850–1930* (Rochester, NY: Strong Museum, 1988); Louise

Stevenson, *The Victorian Homefront: American Thought and Culture, 1860–1880* (New York: Twayne, 1991), 1–29, and Richard Bushman, *The Refinement of America: Persons, Houses, Cities* (New York: Vintage, 1992), 250–52, 272.

31. Diary of Margaret Boyle Harvey, June 1809, in *A Journal of a Voyage from Philadelphia to Cork* (Philadelphia: West Park Publishing, 1915), 47–48.

32. John Crowley, *The Invention of Comfort: Sensibilities & Design in Early Modern Britain & Early America* (Baltimore: Johns Hopkins University Press, 2001); Frances Parkes, *Domestic Duties; Or, Instructions to Young Married Ladies* (New York: J. and J. Harper, 1829), 173–74; Barbara G. Carson, *Ambitious Appetites: Dining, Behavior, and Patterns of Consumption in Federal Washington* (Washington, DC: American Institute of Architects Press, 1990).

33. Diane Kleiner and Susan Matheson, eds., *I Claudia: Women in Ancient Rome* (Austin: University of Texas Press, 1996), 149–50; Kenneth Ames, *Death in the Dining Room and Other Tales of Victorian Culture* (Philadelphia: Temple University Press, 1992), chap. 2. The simultaneous dining and erotic and possibilities of *klinai* were expansively illustrated in Jacques Roergas de Serviez, *The Lives and Amours of the Empresses, Consorts to the First Twelve Caesars of Rome*, trans. George James (London: Abel Roper, 1723). Thomas Hope's interior furniture guides show bacchanalian scenes occurring on sofas: see, for example, Hope, *Costumes of the Ancients*, plate 127.

34. "Who'd Have Thought It," *New-York Weekly Museum* 114 (17 July 1790), unpaginated 1; for Sempronia in Sallust, see Sarah Pomeroy, *Goddesses, Whores, Wives, and Slaves: Women in Classical Antiquity* (New York: Schocken Books, 1975), 171–72; Joanna Brown, "Such Luxuries as Sofas: An Introduction to North Carolina Moravian Upholstered Furniture," *Journal of Early Southern Decorative Arts* (Winter 2001): 1–50; Canning quoted in Beckles Willson, *Friendly Relations: A Narrative of Britain's Ministers and Ambassadors to America (1791–1831)* (Boston: Little, Brown, 1934), 113.

35. *Oxford English Dictionary*, s.v. "sofa" and "ottoman"; Maxine Berg and Elizabeth Eger, eds., *Luxury in the Eighteenth Century: Debates, Desires, and Delectable Goods* (Basingstoke: Palgrave Macmillan, 2003); Thomas Hope, *Household Furniture and Interior Decoration* (1807; New York 1971), 30, 74; Hope, *Costumes*, plates 25 and 127; Rebecca Gratz to Maria Gist Gratz, 7 Nov. 1821, in *Letters of Rebecca Gratz*, ed. David Philipson (Philadelphia: Jewish Publication Society of America, 1929), 48.

36. Jeanne Boydston, *Home and Work: Housework, Wages, and the Ideology of Labor in the Early Republic* (New York: Oxford University Press, 1990), chap. 1–2.

37. A. DuPrat, *Vénus dans le Cloître* (1672; Paris: Actes Sud, 1994), 13. Crébillon-fils, *The Sopha: A Moral Tale. Translated from the French of Monsieur Crébillon* (London: T. Cooper, 1781); Madeleine Dobie, *Foreign Bodies: Gender, Language, and Culture in French Orientalism* (Stanford: Stanford University Press, 2002), chap. 3; Christopher Flint, "Speaking Objects: The Circulation of Stories in Eighteenth-Century Prose Fiction," *PMLA* 113 (March 1998): 212–26; Helen Maitland, "Autobiography of an Old Sofa," *Godey's Magazine and Lady's Book* 28 (June 1844), 278; Marah, "A Leaf from a Sofa's Experience," *Godey's Lady's Book and Magazine*, Sept. 1874, 225–27.

38. Ewa Lajer-Burcharth, *Necklines: The Art of Jacques-Louis David after the Terror* (New Haven: Yale University Press, 1999), 244–68; "Madame Récamier," *Evening Fire-Side*, 7 June 1806, 177; "Amusing," *Monthly Magazine and Literary Journal*, March 1813, 313.

39. "Cornelia," *Lady's Weekly Miscellany*, 3 Jan. 1807, 75. The story is precisely rendered from Valerius Maximus, Book IV.4: "Cornelia, mother of the Gracchi, had a Campanian matron as a guest in her house, who showed her jewelry, the finest in existence at that period. Cornelia kept her in talk until her children came home from school, and then said, 'These are my jewels,' " in *Valerius Maximus: Memorable Doings and Sayings*, ed. and trans. D. R. Shackleton Bailey (Cambridge: Harvard University Press, 2000).

40. The Bartolozzi engraving is reproduced in David Alexander, "Kauffman and the Print Market in Eighteenth-Century England," in *Angelica Kauffman: A Continental Artist in Georgian*

England, ed. Wendy Wassyng Roworth (Brighton: Royal Pavilion Art Gallery and Museum, 1992), 154; the academy girl's embroidery is reproduced in Betty Ring, *Girlhood Embroidery: American Samplers and Pictorial Needlework, 1650–1850* (New York: Knopf, 1993), 1:96; the fan appears in Helmut Von Erffa and Allen Staley, *The Paintings of Benjamin West* (New Haven: Yale University Press, 1986), 173; the Philadelphia artist Xanthus Smith had a glass slide, "Cornelia and her Jewels" in his magic lantern slide collection, displayed in a show in Philadelphia in the 1870s, Library Company of Philadelphia; Thomas Seir Cummings, "A Mother's Pearls," watercolor on ivory (1841), Metropolitan Museum of Art.

41. *Ladies' Magazine*, 13 Feb. 1819, in *Early Georgia Magazines: Literary Periodicals to 1865*, ed. Bertram Holland Flanders (Athens: University of Georgia Press, 1944), 14.

42. Mary T. Boatwright, "Just Window Dressing? Imperial Women as Architectural Sculpture," in *I Claudia II: Women in Roman Art and Society*, ed. Diane E. E. Kleiner and Susan B. Matheson (Austin: University of Texas Press, 2000), 62; Corrado Petrocelli, "Cornelia the Matron," in *Roman Women*, ed. Augusto Fraschetti, trans. Linda Lappin (Chicago: University of Chicago Press, 2001), 34–65.

43. Catharine Maria Sedgwick to Frances Sedgwick Watson, 20 April 1810, in *Life and Letters of Catharine M. Sedgwick*, ed. Mary E. Dewey (New York: Harper and Row, 1871), 87–88; Rosalie Calvert to Charles J. Stier, 23 July 1810, in Callcott, ed., *Mistress of Riversdale*, 222; *Letter book of Mary Stead Pinckney*, 56–57.

44. Petrocelli, "Cornelia the Matron," 45–46; *Oxford English Dictionary*, s.v. "paraphernalia."

45. Petrocelli, "Cornelia the Matron," 45–46.

46. *The Eye of Thomas Jefferson*, ed. William Howard Adams (Washington, DC: National Gallery of Art, 1976), 80; "The Diamond Necklace Affair Revisited (1785–1786): The Case of the Missing Queen," in *Marie-Antoinette: Writings on the Body of a Queen*, ed. Dena Goodman (New York: Routledge, 2003), 73–98; Madame Rigal, "Discours prononcé par Mme. Rigal, Dans une assemblée de femmes artistes et orfèvres, tenue le 20 septembre, pour délibérer sur une Contribution volontaire" (1789?), in *Women in Revolutionary Paris 1789–1798: Selected Documents Translated with Notes and Commentary*, ed. Darline Gay Levy, Harriet Branson Applewhite, and Mary Durham Johnson (Urbana: University of Illinois Press, 1979), 32.

47. Adam Smith, *An Inquiry into the Nature and Causes of the Wealth of Nations* (London: W. Strahan and T. Cadell, 1776), 1:34.

48. Charles de Secondat, Baron de la Brède et de Montesquieu, *The Spirit of Laws*, trans. Thomas Nugent (London: J. Nourse and P. Vaillant, 1750), 2:155; "To the Editor," *Royal American Magazine*, June 1774, 233.

49. Esther DeBerdt Reed, "The Sentiments of an American Woman" (1780), in *American Women Writers to 1800*, ed. Sharon M. Harris (New York: Oxford University Press, 1996), 256–58; *An Ode Written for the Ladies Fair in Aid of the Bunker Hill Monument Fund* (Boston: Dickinson, 1840).

50. *Address of the American Society for the Encouragement of Domestic Manufactures, to the People of the United States* (New York: Van Winkle, Wiley, 1817), 7, 30.

51. James Sterling Young, *The Washington Community, 1800–1828* (New York: Columbia University Press, 1966), 41; the "romance" was probably Fénelon, *Les Aventures de Télémaque* (1699); Margaret Bayard Smith, notebook entry for 1 Aug. 1809, in *The First Forty Years of Washington Society in the Family Letters of Margaret Bayard Smith*, ed. Gaillard Hunt (New York: Charles Scribner's Sons, 1965), 71; James Gilreath and Douglas Wilson, *Thomas Jefferson's Library: A Catalogue with Entries in His Own Order* (Washington, DC: Library of Congress, 1989), 113–114.

52. Smith (1807) quoted in Fredrika J. Teute, "Roman Matron on the Banks of Tiber Creek: Margaret Bayard Smith and the Politicization of Spheres in the Nation's Capital," in *A Republic for the Ages: The United States Capitol and the Political Culture of the Early Republic*, ed.

Donald R. Kennon (Charlottesville: University Press of Virginia, 1999), 94, 105; Margaret Bayard Smith to Mrs. Kirkpatrick, 4 May 1806, in *First Forty Years*, 50.

53. T. E. J. Wiedemann, "Nero," in *The Cambridge Ancient History*, vol. 10: *The Augustan Empire, 43 B.C.–A.D. 69* (Cambridge: Cambridge University Press, 1996), 241–55; Patricia Okker, *Our Sister Editors: Sarah J. Hale and the Tradition of Nineteenth-Century Women Editors* (Athens: University of Georgia Press, 1995), 8; M. B. Smith, "Roman Sketches. *Poetus Thrasea, or the Closing Scene of a Good Man's Life*," *Ladies' Magazine* 5 (1832), 341; M. B. Smith, "Roman Sketches.—Fannia [in four parts]," *Ladies' Magazine* 7 (1835), 134.

54. M. B. Smith, "Arria, Or the Heroism of Affection," *Ladies' Magazine* 5 (1832), 296; Smith, "Poetus Thrasea," 341.

55. M. B. Smith, "Cornelia the Mother," *Ladies' Magazine* 5 (1832), 241–42.

56. Valerius Maximus, *Memorable Doings and Sayings*, IV.4.

5. Climbing Parnassus

1. P. A. M. Taylor, *More Than Common Powers of Perception: The Diary of Elizabeth Rogers Mason Cabot* (Boston: Beacon Press, 1991), 46.

2. Ralph Waldo Emerson, "History," in *Essays: First Series* (1841; Boston: Phillips, Sampson, 1857), 21, 22.

3. On philhellenism in American higher education, see Caroline Winterer, *The Culture of Classicism: Ancient Greece and Rome in American Intellectual Life, 1780–1910* (Baltimore: Johns Hopkins University Press, 2002), chaps. 2–3.

4. Asher Benjamin, *The Architect, or Practical House Carpenter* (1830; Boston: L. Coffin, m 1844), iv, 78; Andrew Jackson Downing, *Cottage Residences* (1842; New York: Library of Victorian Culture, 1967), 22–23.

5. Linda Baumgartner, *What Clothes Reveal: The Language of Clothing in Colonial and Federal America* (New Haven: Yale University Press, 2002), 198–99; Carolyn Kinder Carr and Ellen G. Miles, *A Brush with History: Paintings from the National Portrait Gallery* (Washington, DC: Smithsonian Institution Press, 2001), 106–7.

6. Mary Kelley, *Learning to Stand and Speak: Women, Education, and Public Life in America's Republic* (Chapel Hill: Published for the Omohundro Institute of Early American History and Culture by the University of North Carolina Press, 2006), chaps. 3–4; Margaret A. Nash, *Women's Education in the United States, 1780–1840* (New York: Palgrave Macmillan, 2005), chap. 3; Thomas Woody, *A History of Women's Education in the United States* (New York: Science Press, 1929), 1:413, 418, 563–64; Kim Tolley, "Science for Ladies, Classics for Gentlemen: A Comparative Analysis of Scientific Subjects in the Curricula of Boys' and Girls' Secondary Schools in the United States, 1794–1850," *History of Education Quarterly* 36, 2 (1996), 137; Barbara M. Solomon, *In the Company of Educated Women: A History of Women and Higher Education in America* (New Haven: Yale University Press, 1985), 15; Kathryn Kish Sklar, "The Schooling of Girls and Changing Community Values in Massachusetts Towns, 1750–1820," *History of Education Quarterly* 33 (Winter 1993), 520–21.

7. "On Female Authorship," *Lady's Magazine and Repository of Entertaining Knowledge*, Jan. 1793, 69; George B. Emerson, *A Lecture on the Education of Females* (Boston: Hilliard, Gray, Little, and Wilkins, 1831), 3.

8. "Female Education," *Ladies Repository* 1 (Feb. 1841), 50, 51; "Female Biography," *American Quarterly Review* 5 (June 1829): 473; Thomas H. Gallaudet, *An Address on Female Education, Delivered, Nov. 21st, 1827, at the Opening of the Edifice Erected for the Accommodation of the Hartford Female Seminary* (Hartford: H. and F. J. Huntington, 1828), 12.

9. Lynne Templeton Brickley, "Sarah Pierce's Litchfield Female Academy, 1792–1833," Ed. diss. Harvard University, 1985, 20, 22, 23, 31, 32, 35, 46, 52, 60, 81.

10. Brickley, "Sarah Pierce's Litchfield Academy," 307, 308.

11. Diary of Julia Cowles, 6 July 1797, in *Chronicles of a Pioneer School from 1792 to 1833. Being the History of Miss Sarah Pierce and Her Litchfield School*, ed. Emily Noyes Vanderpoel (Cambridge: Harvard University Press, 1903), 18; Brickley, "Sarah Pierce's Litchfield Academy," 255, 256, 257.

12. Sarah Pierce, *Sketches of Universal History, Compiled from Several Authors* (New Haven: Joseph Barber, 1816), 2:228; Brickley, "Sarah Pierce's Litchfield Academy," 258.

13. Betty Ring, *Girlhood Embroidery: American Samplers and Pictorial Needlework, 1650–1850* (New York: Knopf, 1993), 1:221; Madame de Genlis, *Arabesques Mythologiques* (Paris: Charles Barrois, 1810).

14. "From the Salutatory Oration Delivered by Miss Priscilla Mason, May 15 1793," in *Women of America: A History*, ed. Carol Ruth Berkin and Mary Beth Norton (Boston: Houghton Mifflin, 1979), 89–91; Maria, "To Mr. James A. Neal . . ." *Philadelphia Repository and Weekly Register*, 10 Jan. 1801, 6; Jonathan Barber, *A Practical Treatise on Gesture, Chiefly Abstracted from Austin's Chironomia; Adapted to the Use of Students, and Arranged According to the Method of Instruction in Harvard University* (Cambridge, MA: Hilliard and Brown, 1831), 92, plate 12.

15. Anne Firor Scott, "The Ever Widening Circle: The Diffusion of Feminist Values from the Troy Female Seminary, 1822–1872," *History of Education Quarterly* 19 (1979): 3–25; Almira Phelps, *The Fireside Friend, or Female Student. Being Advice to Young Ladies, on the Important Subject of Education* (Boston: Marsh, Capen, Lyon, and Webb, 1840), 107; on women and botany, see Ann B. Shteir, *Cultivating Women, Cultivating Science: Flora's Daughters and Botany in England, 1760 to 1860* (Baltimore: Johns Hopkins University Press, 1996).

16. Ralph Waldo Emerson, William Channing, and J. F. Clarke, *Memoirs of Margaret Fuller Ossoli* (Boston: Roberts Brothers, 1874), 1:15–16, 21, 28; Caroline W. Healey Dall, *Margaret and Her Friends. Or, Ten Conversations with Margaret Fuller upon the Mythology of the Greeks and Its Expression in Art* (Boston: Roberts Brothers, 1895); Charles Capper, *Margaret Fuller: An American Romantic Life*, vol. 1: *The Private Years* (New York: Oxford University Press, 1992), 45–48.

17. Ellen Tucker Emerson to John Haven Emerson, 1 Aug. 1856; Ellen Tucker Emerson to John Haven Emerson, 15 Dec. 1855; Ellen Tucker Emerson to Ralph Waldo Emerson, 22 Jan. 1857, in *The Letters of Ellen Tucker Emerson*, ed. Edith W. Gregg (Kent, OH: Kent State University Press, 1982), 116, 105, 127.

18. Beverly Wilson Palmer, ed., *A Woman's Wit and Whimsy: The 1833 Diary of Anna Cabot Lowell Quincy* (Boston: Northeastern University Press, 2003), 86, 143.

19. Beatrice B. Garvan, *Federal Philadelphia, 1785–1825: The Athens of the Western World* (Philadelphia: Philadelhia Museum of Art, 1987); diary entry for 12 Sept. 1814, in *Diary of Harriet Manigault* (Rockland, ME: Colonial Dames of America, 1976), 97.

20. Mary Monsigny, *Mythology: or, a History of the Fabulous Deities of the Ancients* (Randolph, VT: Sereno Wright, 1809); Marie Cleary, " 'Vague Irregular Notions': American Women and Classical Mythology, 1780–1855," *New England Classical Journal* 29.4 (2002): 222–35; Phelps, *Fireside Friend*, 151.

21. Samuel Augustus Mitchell, *Mitchell's Ancient Geography, Designed for Academies, Schools, and Families* (Philadelphia: E. H. Butler, 1859), 88, 148; John Ludlow, *An Address Delivered at the Opening of the New Female Academy in Albany, May 12, 1834* (Albany: Packard and van Benthuysen, 1834), 10.

22. *P. Ovidii Nasonis Metamorphoseon Libri X . . . with an English Translation* (Philadelphia: Spotswood, 1790); Meyer Reinhold, *The Classick Pages: Classical Reading of Eighteenth-Century Americans* (University Park, PA: American Philological Association, 1975), 137; John Mustain, *In Folio: Rare Volumes in the Stanford University Libraries: Catalogue of an Exhibition* (Stanford: Stanford University Libraries, 2004), 69; George K. Smart, "Private Libraries in Colonial Virginia," *American Literature* 10 (1938): 37; Walter B. Edgar, "Some Popular Books in Colonial South Carolina," *South Carolina Historical Magazine* 72 (July 1971), 177; Joseph

Towne Wheeler, "Booksellers and Circulating Libraries in Colonial Maryland," *Maryland Historical Magazine* 34 (June 1939), 130.

23. Harriet Beecher Stowe to Charles Edward Stowe, 1886, in *The Limits of Sisterhood: The Beecher Sisters on Women's Rights and Women's Sphere,* ed. Jeanne Boydston, Mary Kelley, and Anne Margolis (Chapel Hill: University of North Carolina Press, 1988), 57; Ellen Tucker Emerson to Ralph Waldo Emerson, 4 March 1854, in *Letters of Ellen Tucker Emerson,* ed. Gregg, 58, 56.

24. Thomas Bulfinch quoted in Marie Cleary, " 'Vague, Irregular Notions,' " 230.

25. A sampling of classicized, mid-century pornography would include: *The Countess; or, Memoirs of Women of Leisure, Being a Series of Intrigues with the Bloods, and a Faithful Delineation of the Private Frailties of our First Men* (Boston: Berry and Wright, 1849); George Thompson, *Venus in Boston. A Romance of City Life* (New York: Printed for the Publisher, 1849); Appollonius of Gotham, "The Loves of Cleopatra or, Mark Anthony and His Concubines," *Venus' Miscellany* (11 July 1857): 1, Department of Rare Books and Special Collections, Princeton University; on the varieties of sexual subcultures in Victorian America, see Helen Lefkowitz Horowitz, *Rereading Sex: Battles over Sexual Knowledge and Suppression in Nineteenth-Century America* (New York: Alfred A. Knopf, 2002).

26. *Memoir of the Boston Athenaeum: With the Act of Incorporation and Organization of the Institution* (Boston: Munroe and Francis, 1807), 11.

27. Ibid., 13.

28. Mabel Muson Swan, *The Athenaeum Gallery 1827–1873: The Boston Athenaeum as an Early Patron of Art* (Boston: Athenaeum, 1940) 18, 20; Pamela Hayle, *A Climate for Art: The History of the Boston Athenaeum Gallery 1827–1873* (Boston: Thomas Todd, 1980), 9.

29. Swan, *Athenaeum Gallery,* 134–39.

30. Mrs. Jameson, "Sacred and Legendary Art," *Anglo-American,* 22 Feb. 1845, 429; *Woman's Wit and Whimsy,* ed. Palmer, 91; Ellen Tucker Emerson to "Emma," 6 Nov. 1854, in *Letters of Ellen Tucker Emerson,* ed. Gregg, 80–81.

31. *Woman's Wit and Whimsy,* ed. Palmer, 101, 133.

32. "Literary Notices," *Ladies' Magazine,* Feb. 1831, 91; Charles Caldwell, *Thoughts on Physical Education* (Boston: Marsh, Capen & Lyon, 1834), 119; "Stays and Busks," *Boston Medical Intelligencer,* 5 July 1825, 84; John Bell, *Health and Beauty* (Philadelphia: E. L. Carey and A. Hart, 1838), 96; Valerie Steele, *The Corset: A Cultural History* (New Haven: Yale University Press, 2001), 69.

33. 1 May 1857, *More Than Common Powers,* 166; William Vance, *America's Rome.* Vol. 1: *Classical Rome* (New Haven: Yale University Press, 1989), 229.

34. Swan, *Athenaeum Gallery,* 35, 109; Robert F. Perkins, Jr., and William J. Gavin III, *The Boston Athenaeum Art Exhibition Index, 1827–1874* (Boston: Library of the Boston Athenaeum, 1980), 41.

35. Quoted in Swan, *Athenaeum Gallery,* 16.

36. Maurie McInnis, *The Politics of Taste in Antebellum Charleston* (Chapel Hill: University of North Carolina Press, 2005), 135–46.

37. McInnis, *Politics of Taste,* 309–10.

6. The Greek Slave

1. Richard P. Wunder, *Hiram Powers, Vermont Sculptor, 1805–1873* (Newark: University of Delaware Press, 1991), 1:207–74; *Frederick Douglass Paper,* 26 June 1851; on the *Greek Slave,* see also Joy Kasson, *Marble Queens and Captives: Women in Nineteenth-Century American Sculpture* (New Haven: Yale University Press, 1990), ch. 3.

2. Edmund Burke, *Reflections on the Revolution in France* (London: J. Dodsley, 1790), 112; Sarah Haight, *Letters from the Old World, by a Lady of New-York* (New York: Harper and Brothers, 1840), 1:112–13. On the parable of the continence of Scipio and its relation to the traffic in

Notes to Pages 168–175 / 229

women, see Caroline Winterer, "From Royal to Republican: The Classical Image in Early America," *Journal of American History* 91 (March 2005): 1264–90; on the traffic in women in early societies, see Gayle Rubin, "The Traffic in Women: Notes on the Political Economy of Sex," in *Feminism and History*, ed. Joan W. Scott (New York: Oxford University Press, 1996), 105–51; Marcel Mauss, *The Gift: The Form and Reason for Exchange in Archaic Societies*, trans. W. D. Halls (1950; New York, 1990), 6.

3. Angelo Repousis, "The Trojan Women: Emma Hart Willard and the Troy Society for the Advancement of Female Education in Greece," *Journal of the Early Republic* 24 (Fall 2004), 463; Emma Willard, *Advancement of Female Education, Or, a Series of Addresses, in Favor of Establishing at Athens, in Greece, a Female Seminary, Especially Designed to Instruct Female Teachers* (Troy: Norman Tuttle, 1833); Stephen A. Larrabee, *Hellas Observed: The American Experience of Greece, 1775–1865* (New York: New York University Press, 1957), 199–200; "Speech of Ernestine Rose to the Seventh National Woman's Rights Convention, New York, November, 1856," in *History of Woman Suffrage*, vol. 1: *1848–1861*, ed. Elizabeth Cady Stanton, Susan B. Anthony, and Matilda Joslyn Gage, 2nd ed. (Rochester: Charles Mann, 1889), 666.

4. George Bancroft, "Slavery in Rome," *North American Review* 39 (1834): 413–37; for a representative Southern proslavery counterargument, see George Frederick Holmes, "Observations on a Passage in the Politics of Aristotle Relative to Slavery," *Southern Literary Messenger* 16 (April 1850): 193–205. For discussions of the Southern appeal to antiquity to defend slavery, see Drew Harrington, "Classical Antiquity and the Proslavery Argument," *Slavery and Abolition* 10 (May 1989): 60–72; and David Wiesen, "Herodotus and the Modern Debate over Race and Slavery," *Ancient World* (1981), 3, 1.

5. Carolyn Karcher, *The First Woman in the Republic: A Cultural Biography of Lydia Maria Child* (Durham: Duke University Press, 1994), 3, 129.

6. Ibid., 3, 12, 15, 48.

7. Books borrowed by Lydia Maria Child 1832–1835, Archives B.A. 17.1 (1827–1872). Volume 1 (1827–1834), 66, Boston Athenaeum, Circulation Department. The edition of William Alexander is not specified, and it is only listed as *The History of Women*. The entry on Scudéry reads "Scudery Women's Tomes," but it is likely to be Madeleine de Scudéry, *The Female Orators* (1714). The edition of Josephus is listed as "Josephus by Whiston," which may refer to William Whiston, *The Genuine Works of Flavius Josephus* (1737). William Alexander, *History of the Condition of Women* (1779; Philadelphia: J. H. Dobelbower, 1796), 1:106; William Cowper, *The Iliad and Odyssey of Homer* (London: 1791), 1:82; John Stedman, *Narrative, of a Five Years' Expedition: Against the Revolted Negroes of Surinam* (London: J. Johnson and J. Edwards, 1796); James Alexander, *Transatlantic Sketches . . . With Notes on Negro Slavery and Canadian Emigration* (London: R. Bentley, 1833), 2:241.

8. Lydia Maria Child, *An Appeal in Favor of that Class of Americans Called Africans*, ed. Carolyn Karcher (1833; Amherst: University of Massachusetts Press, 1996), 5.

9. Ibid., 36–37, 28.

10. Karcher, *First Woman in the Republic*, 192, 221.

11. Lydia Maria Child, *History of the Condition of Women, in Various Ages and Nations* (London: Simpkin, Marshal, 1835), 1:53; 2:29, 30, 212, 220, 265.

12. Lydia Maria Child, *Philothea* (Boston: Otis, Broaders, 1836), 284.

13. Ibid., 24, 35, 37, 283, 109.

14. Ibid., 113, 114, 279.

15. Ibid., 10, 36, 23, 264.

16. Cornelius Conway Felton, "Philothea," *North American Review* (January 1837), 86; Edgar Allan Poe, "Critical Notices," *Southern Literary Messenger* 2 (1836), 662.

17. Juliana Tappan to Anne Weston, 21 July 1837, quoted in Lori D. Ginzberg, *Women and the Work of Benevolence: Morality, Politics, and Class in the Nineteenth-Century United States* (New Haven: Yale University Press, 1990), 24.

18. Sarah Grimké, *Letters on the Equality of the Sexes, and the Condition of Woman* (Boston: Isaac Knapp, 1838), 37, 38, 40, 43.

19. Ibid., 46, 47, 81, 85; Sarah Grimké, "The Education of Women" (1852–1857), in Gerda Lerner, *The Feminist Thought of Sarah Grimké* (New York: Oxford University Press, 1998), 79, 81, 85.

20. Grimké, *Letters*, 16.

21. Sarah Grimké, *An Epistle to the Clergy of the Southern States* (New York: n.p., 1836), 6–7.

22. Leigh Fought, *Southern Womanhood and Slavery: A Biography of Louisa S. McCord, 1810–1879* (Columbia: University of Missouri Press, 2003), 88.

23. *Louisa S. McCord: Poems, Drama, Biography, Letters*, ed. Richard C. Lounsbury (Charlottesville: University Press of Virginia, 1996), 2; Barthold Georg Niebuhr, *The History of Rome*, trans. Julius Hare and Connop Thirlwall, 4th ed. (London: Taylor and Walton, 1847), 1:vii–viii; Louisa McCord to William Porcher Miles, 12 June 1848, in *Louisa S. McCord: Selected Writings*, ed. Richard C. Lounsbury (Charlottesville: University of Virginia Press, 1997), 259–60.

24. L. S. M., "Carey on the Slave Trade," *Southern Quarterly Review* (Jan. 1854), 169, 171.

25. L. S. M., "Diversity of the Races; Its Bearing on Negro Slavery," *Southern Quarterly Review* (April 1851), 411.

26. L. S. M., "Carey on the Slave Trade," 169; L.S.M., "Woman and Her Needs," *De Bow's Review*, (Sept. 1852), 274, 283, 280–81.

27. Louisa McCord to William Porcher Miles, 12 June 1848, in *Louisa S. McCord: Selected Writings*, ed. Lounsbury, 260; Susan Bennett, "The Cheves Family of South Carolina," *South Carolina Historical Magazine* 35 (1934), 91.

28. Louisa McCord to William Porcher Miles, 12 June 1848, in *Louisa S. McCord: Selected Writings*, ed. Lounsbury, 260; Louisa McCord, *Caius Gracchus: A Tragedy in Five Acts* (New York: H. Kernot, 1851), in *Louisa S. McCord: Poems, Drama, Biography, Letters*, ed. Lounsbury, 161–232; on the growing popularity of the historical novel among women, see Nina Baym, *American Women Writers and the Work of History, 1790–1860* (New Brunswick: Rutgers University Press, 1995).

29. McCord, *Caius Gracchus*, 161; *Mary Chesnut's Civil War*, ed. C. Vann Woodward (New Haven: Yale University Press, 1981), 428.

30. Elizabeth McHenry, *Forgotten Readers: Recovering the Lost History of African-American Literary Societies* (Durham: Duke University Press, 2002), 57–63; Letitia W. Brown, *Free Negroes in the District of Columbia, 1790–1846* (New York: Oxford University Press, 1972), 118; Department of Education, *Special Report of the Commissioner of Education on the Condition and Improvement of Public Schools in the District of Columbia* (Washington, DC: GPO, 1871), 257, 380.

31. Joseph Wilson, *Sketches of the Higher Classes of Colored Society in Philadelphia, by a Southerner* (1841; Philadelphia: Historic Publications, 1969), 108; Julie Winch, " 'You Have Talents—Only Cultivate Them': Philadelphia's Black Female Literary Societies and the Abolitionist Crusade," in *The Abolitionist Sisterhood: Women's Political Culture in Antebellum America*, ed. Jean Fagan Yellin and John C. Van Horne (Ithaca: Cornell University Press, 1994), 105–8.

32. A Member, "Address to the Female Literary Association of Philadelphia, on Their First Anniversary," *Liberator*, 13 Oct. 1832, 163.

33. Edwin Wolf, *Philadelphia: Portrait of an American City: A Bicentennial History* (Harrisburg: Stackpole Books, 1975), 141, 173; Josiah Nott and George Gliddon, *Types of Mankind* (1854; Philadelphia: J. B. Lippincott, 1857), 431.

34. Wilson, *Sketches*, 26–27; Martin R. Delany, *The Condition, Elevation, Emigration, and Destiny of the Colored People of the United States* (1852), in *Martin R. Delany, A Documentary Reader*, ed. Robert S. Levine (Chapel Hill: University of North Carolina Press, 2003), 211–12.

35. Sophanisba, "Extract from a Letter," *Liberator*, 14 July 1832; Sophanisba, "Ella: A Sketch," *Liberator*, 4 Aug. 1832; Sophanisba, "Family Worship," *Liberator*, 8 Sept. 1832; Julie Winch, *A Gentleman of Color: The Life of James Forten* (New York: Oxford University Press,

2002), 170; Winch, " 'You Have Talents—Only Cultivate Them,' " in *Abolitionist Sisterhood*, ed. Yellin and Van Horne, 105; McHenry, *Forgotten Readers*, 63. The Carthage debate, which awaits thorough examination from historians, appears in pro- and anticolonization pamphlets and magazines in the 1820s and 1830s, such as *African, African Repository and Colonial Journal, African Repository and Colonial Journal,* and the *Liberator;* David Walker, *Walker's Appeal in Four Articles; Together with a Preamble to the Coloured Citizens of the World* (Boston: D. Walker, 1829); Thomas Hodgkin, *An Inquiry into the Merits of the American Colonization Society: and a Reply to the Charges Brought against It* (London: J. and A. Arch, 1833); James W. C. Pennington, *A Text Book of the Origin and History, &c. &c. of the Colored People* (Hartford: L. Skinner, 1841).

36. "The Runaway," *Anti-Slavery Record* 3 (July 1837), 1–2.

37. David W. Blight, ed., *Passages to Freedom: The Underground Railroad in History and Memory* (Washington, DC: Smithsonian Books, 2004), 134.

38. Blight, ed., *Passages to Freedom,* 60.

39. Joe William Trotter, *River Jordan: African American Urban Life in the Ohio Valley* (Lexington: University Press of Kentucky, 1998).

40. Martin R. Delany to Frederick Douglass, 20 May 1848, *North Star,* 9 June 1848, 2–3; Frederick Douglass, "A Slave Heroine," *Frederick Douglass' Paper,* 16 Nov. 1855.

41. Charles Darwin, 8 Apr. 1832, in *Journal of Researches into the Geology and Natural History of the Various Countries Visited by the HMS Beagle* (1839; New York: D. Appleton, 1871), 20.

42. Edmund Quincy, "Mother Coelia," *North Star,* 25 Feb. 1848.

43. Steven Weisenburger, *Modern Medea: A Family Story of Slavery and Child-Murder from the Old South* (New York: Hill and Wang, 1998), 74–75.

44. James M. Bell, "Liberty or Death," *Provincial Freeman* (8 March 1856); Frances Ella Watkins Harper, "The Slave Mother: A Tale of the Ohio," in *A Brighter Coming Day: A Frances Ellen Watkins Harper Reader,* ed. Frances Smith Foster (New York: Feminist Press, 1990), 85; Weisenburger, *Modern Medea,* 86.

45. Gary Wills, *Lincoln at Gettysburg: The Words that Remade America* (New York: Simon and Schuster, 1992), 213–15.

46. Mary Boykin Miller Chesnut, 10 March 1862, *A Diary from Dixie,* ed. Isabella D. Martin and Myrta L. Avary (New York: D. Appleton, 1905), 137.

47. James D. Birchfield, Albert Boime, and William J. Hennessey, *Thomas Satterwhite Noble, 1835–1907* (Lexington: University of Kentucky Art Museum, 1988), 7. It also appeared in *St. Louis Guardian,* 27 April 1867; *New York Daily Standard,* 9 May 1867; *Round Table,* 18 May 1867; *American Art Journal,* May 1867; *Boston Herald,* 3 Jan. 1869, 330.

7. *Antigone and the Twilight of Female Classicism*

1. Barbara Solomon, *In the Company of Educated Women: A History of Women and Higher Education in America* (New Haven: Yale University Press, 1985), 62.

2. George Steiner, *Antigones* (New York: Oxford University Press, 1984). For a list of some of Antigone's representations in literature, art, and music in Europe and America, see Jane Davidson Reid, *The Oxford Guide to Classical Mythology in the Arts, 1300–1900* (New York: Oxford University Press, 1993), 105–9.

3. "Character of Medea," *Southern Literary Messenger* 5, 6 (June 1839), 392; "The Antigone of Sophocles," *Christian Review* 16 (1851), 64–65; "Beauties of the Grecian Drama," *Southern Literary Messenger* 24, 1 (Jan. 1857), 58; "Antigone," *Methodist Quarterly Review* (Jan. 1852), 103–4.

4. Rebecca Edwards, *Angels in the Machinery: Gender in American Party Politics from the Civil War to the Progressive Era* (New York: Oxford University Press, 1997), 3; Paula Baker, "The Domestication of Politics: Women and American Political Society, 1780–1920," *American Historical Review* 89 (June 1984), 631; Carroll Smith-Rosenberg and Charles Rosenberg, "The Female

Animal: Medical and Biological Views of Woman and Her Role in Nineteenth-Century America," *Journal of American History* 60, 2 (1973): 332–56.

5. "Two Acts of Self-Devotion," *Littell's Living Age*, 5th ser., vol. 2, no. 1514 (14 June 1873), 646; Theodore Dwight Woolsey, *The Antigone of Sophocles* (Boston: James Munroe, 1841), iv.

6. Pamela Helen Goodwin, "Shakespeare's Cordelia," *Ladies Repository* 2, 3 (Sept. 1875), 203; Pamela Helen Goodwin, "Medea," *Ladies Repository* 1, 4 (Apr. 1875), 326–27.

7. On the popularity of classical female subjects in nineteenth-century American sculpture, see Joy Kasson, *Marble Queens and Captives: Women in Nineteenth-Century American Sculpture* (New Haven: Yale University Press, 1990).

8. Goodwin, "Medea," 326–27; Helen W. Besant, "By Celia's Arbor," *Appleton's Journal* 3, 6 (Dec. 1877): 503; Anon., "Character of Medea," 385; Davis, "Fine Arts in the South," 657; Anon, "The Balsam: A Tale, Part II," *Southern and Western Literary Messenger* 12, 11 (Nov. 1846), 675; Grace Thalmon, "The Daughter," *Ladies Repository* 18, 8 (Aug. 1858): 452.

9. "Eugénie de Guérin," *Ladies Repository*, 25, 1 (Jan. 1865), 33; "Eugénie and Maurice de Guérin," *Princeton Review* 37, 4 (Oct. 1865), 555; Margaret Fuller, "Goethe," in *Life Without and Life Within* (New York: Tribune Association, 1869), 60; Friedrich Augustus Rauch, *Psychology: or, A View of the Human Soul, Including Anthropology* (1840; New York: M. W. Dodd, 1853), 351; Marguerite E. Easter, "Antigone's Farewell to Haemon," *Southern Magazine* 16 (1875): 404; see also Alice Mackay "Haemon to Antigone," *Argosy* 66 (1898): 679.

10. "Two Acts of Self-Devotion," 651; Goodwin, "Shakespeare's Cordelia," 203.

11. "alone": Goodwin, "Shakespeare's Cordelia," 203; "anarchic": Shuckburgh, ed., *Antigone*, xxvi; "secluded": Woolsey, *Antigone*, 4; Smith-Rosenberg and Rosenberg, "The Female Animal," 346.

12. "Masculine": Woolsey, *Antigone*, iv; Augustus Taber Murray, *Antigone: An Account of the Presentation of the Antigone of Sophocles at the Leland Stanford Junior University* (San Francisco: Paul Elder, 1903), 14; Shuckburgh, ed., *Antigone*, xxv.

13. "Two Acts of Self-Devotion," 646; Murray, *Antigone*, 14; Woolsey, *Antigone*, v.

14. George Eliot, *Middlemarch* (1871; repr. William Blackwood, 1874), 139; George Eliot, "The Antigone and Its Moral," *Leader* 7 (29 March 1856), in *Essays of George Eliot*, ed. Thomas Pinney (London: Routledge and Kegan Paul, 1963), 261–65. For Antigone in George Eliot, see Masako Hirai, *Sisters in Literature: Female Sexuality in Antigone, Middlemarch, Howard's End, and Women in Love* (London: Macmillan, 1998), 25–27; for Eliot's relationship with Phelps, see Carol Farley Kessler, *Elizabeth Stuart Phelps* (Boston: Twayne, 1982), passim; and Timothy Hands, *A George Eliot Chronology* (Boston: G. K. Hall, 1989).

15. Lori Kelly, *The Life and Works of Elizabeth Stuart Phelps: Victorian Feminist Writer* (Troy, NY: Whitston, 1983), 60; Kessler, *Elizabeth Stuart Phelps*, 35–36; biographical specifics from her youth are in Kessler, *Elizabeth Stuart Phelps*, and Kelly, *Life*, passim.

16. Kelly, *Life*, 53–60; Phelps, "The True Woman," *Independent* (12 Oct. 1871), 1.

17. Elizabeth Stuart Phelps, "The 'Female Education' of Women," *Independent* (13 Nov. 1873), 1409.

18. Elizabeth Stuart Phelps, "The Sacrifice of Antigone," in Phelps, *Fourteen to One* (Boston: Houghton Mifflin, 1891), 242–43, 245.

19. Among the 349 college productions of Greek tragedies and comedies on American campuses between 1881 and 1936, Antigone had a total of 75, more than twice as many as any other. The next most performed were *Iphigenia, Alcestis*, and *Trojan Women* and *Oedipus Tyrannus*. Dommis Pluggé, *History of Greek Play Production in American Colleges and Universities from 1881 to 1936* (New York: Teachers College, Columbia University Press, 1983), 31.

20. Pluggé, *History of Greek Play Production*, 13–32; *Bryn Mawr College Program* (Philadelphia: Sherman, 1885), 7, 20; *Harvard University Catalogue* (Cambridge, MA: The University, 1885), 3, 84.

21. T. Allston Brown, *A History of the New York Stage, from the First Performance in 1732 to 1901* (New York: Dodd, Mead, 1903), 1:341.

22. Murray, *Antigone*, 2; R. H. Chapman, Los Angeles *Herald*, reprinted in Stanford *Alumnus*, 3, 7 (April 1902), 98, Stanford University Libraries.

23. *Treasures from Olana: Landscapes by Frederick Edwin Church*, essay by Kevin J. Avery, introduction by John Wilmerding (Ithaca: Cornell University Press, 2005).

24. Charles W. Eliot, "What Is a Liberal Education?" *Century* 28, n.s. 6 (May–Oct. 1884), 207.

25. Carroll Smith-Rosenberg, "The New Woman as Androgyne: Social Disorder and Gender Crisis, 1870–1936," in *Disorderly Conduct: Visions of Gender in Victorian America* (New York: Oxford University Press, 1985), 245–96; for M. Carey Thomas on Sappho, see Helen Lefkowitz Horowitz, *The Power and Passion of M. Carey Thomas* (New York: Alfred A. Knopf, 1994), 395. Sappho for centuries had been conventionally used to describe women with intellectual and literary gifts. See Peter Tomory, "The Fortunes of Sappho: 1770–1850," in G. W. Clarke, *Rediscovering Hellenism: The Hellenic Inheritance and the English Imagination* (New York: Cambridge University Press, 1989), 121–35; Yopie Prins, *Victorian Sappho* (Princeton: Princeton University Press, 1999); Steiner, *Antigones*, 6.

26. Jean Bethke Elshtain, "Antigone's Daughters," in *Freedom, Feminism, and the State: An Overview of Individualist Feminism*, ed. Wendy McElroy (New York: Holmes and Meier, 1991), 61–75. For other recent interpretations of Antigone that form with Elshtain a contemporary conversation about Antigone's implications for gender and conceptions of public participation, see Linda Zerilli, "Machiavelli's Sisters: Women and 'the Conversation' of Political Theory," *Political Theory* 19, 2 (May 1991): 252–76; Luce Irigaray, "The Eternal Irony of the Community," in *Speculum of the Other Woman* (Ithaca: Cornell University Press, 1985), 214–26; Mary Dietz, "Citizenship with a Feminist Face: The Problem of Maternal Thinking," *Political Theory* 13, 1 (Feb. 1985): 19–37; Warren J. Lane and Ann M. Lane, "The Politics of Antigone," in *Greek Tragedy and Political Theory*, ed. J. Peter Reuben (Berkeley: University of California Press, 1986), 162–82; and Catherine A. Holland, "After Antigone: Women, the Past, and the Future of Feminist Political Thought," *American Journal of Political Science* 42, 4 (Oct. 1998): 1108–32.

INDEX

Numbers in italic refer to pages with illustrations.